NEIGHBOURHOOD PARTICIPATION

Peter Hain

Temple Smith . London

First published in Great Britain in 1980
by Maurice Temple Smith Ltd
37 Great Russell Street, London WC1

ISBN   0 85117 197 4 (Cased)
          0 85117 198 2 (Paper)

Photoset in Times 10/12pt
by Margaret Spooner

Printed in Great Britain by
Billing and Sons Ltd
Guildford, London, Worcestor, Oxford

Contents

ACKNOWLEDGEMENTS

Many different people helped with this study, but it is not possible to name them all. Some of the busiest individuals were the most generous with their time, including those whom I interviewed. I would like to record my special gratitude to Pat Williams who was the GLC's Covent Garden Forum Liaison Officer whilst I was undertaking my research. Nothing was too much trouble for her, although that does not commit her to the contents of this book, still less to its conclusions. The same qualification is true for others who gave particular help to me in Covent Garden: Janet Sutherland, Geraldine Petterson, Derek Blackhurst and Jim Monahan. Nick Deakin was initially instrumental in securing officially approved access to the GLC for me; whilst Bob Dixey was always helpful over the general neighbourhood council movement. The book is based upon research conducted for a Master of Philosophy thesis in politics submitted at Sussex University, where John Dearlove, Bob Benewick and Bruce Graham gave me a great deal of assistance and advice, as did Tim Young, to whom I am especially indebted.

Finally, my family have had to endure what at times appeared to be a never-ending saga to finish first the thesis and then the book. Special thanks to my wife Pat for her constant encouragement and sacrifices and to Sam and Jake; thanks also to my parents for their support over the years. Molly Turpin typed the manuscript for which I am very grateful.

Peter Hain
Putney, April 1980

Preface

> ... the question of how far the local state necessarily comes to reflect in its politics the interests of dominant groups can only be answered by considering the limits which it encounters when it attempts to act in accordance with the interests of opposing groups. The question of discretion and constraint is thus ultimately an empirical rather than a theoretical question. It follows from this that the study of community power and the analysis of urban managers—the problems of where power resides, how it is used, how it is influenced, and how far it is restricted—must remain central to discussions of urban politics, and that empirical work will continue to play a fundamental role in the development of such discussions.
>
> Peter Saunders, *Urban Politics: A sociological interpretation* (Hutchinson, 1979), pp. 196-7.

During the past decade, 'public participation' has become a major concern, both for local activists and for the public authorities. In response, different concepts of participation have been usefully distinguished (Parry, pp 3-38, Pateman, Pranger, Milbrath, Verba & Pie, Lucas) and there have been equally useful case studies (Davies, Ferris, Dennis 1972), especially with regard to the relationship between planning and participation. However, there is a general absence of a systematic evaluation of the practice of public participation and, more specifically, of its potential and limitations in a social system where resources are not equally distributed and where the mode of politics is representative rather than participatory.

The purpose of this book is therefore threefold. First to attempt such an evaluation by contrasting the *aspirations* of the participation advocates with the *experience* of participation through neighbourhood councils. Second, to suggest an alternative approach which might account for the practice of participation by relating it to the distribution of power and resources. And third to draw lessons for future activity. Although reference is made to other localised initiatives neighbourhood councils provide the central focus. This is principally because neighbourhood councils are seen by both activists and government as a means by which community participation can be ordered and placed upon a more permanent institutional footing: they stand at the interface between government and the neighbourhood. Moreover, research into neighbourhood councils has been sparse.

As will be evident, the analysis is not confined within any one of the social science disciplines of sub-disciplines. Many of the obvious areas of study, such as local government, planning and community work, have been considered and drawn upon, but have important limitations, especially in dealing with the question of power and its distribution, with which this book is primarily concerned. The approach adopted, therefore has been deliberately eclectic (Smith 1973, Saunders 1979, p.14), drawing on politics, sociology and, particularly towards the end, adopting a political economy perspective.

One of the central themes of the book is the extent to which those in authority see participation as a means of neutralising dissent or mobilising support for their policies. The organisation of the argument may imply that I approached the empirical research with the mobilisation theme as my basic framework, in which case I could be vulnerable to the methodological criticism that I had merely 'found' what my theoretical perspective had encouraged me to look for. Of course, the force of such criticism is greatly diminished by the argument that 'when a scientist observes a fact, he "sees" it through concepts which are normally defined from a theory' (Wolin, p. 1073). Nevertheless, whilst my own political experience and my awareness of the available literature had fostered an interest in the concept of participation as a method of political mobilisation, it only became a central theme for me as my empirical work in Covent Garden unfolded; to a large extent, it 'grew out' of my research rather than being imposed on it from the outset.

Indeed, my basic approach changed considerably during the research programme and a comment on this change may help to explain the organisation of the book. I started my research in mid-1974 on the assumption that those engaged in participation wished to replace the existing structure of 'representative democracy' with 'participatory democracy'. That indeed had been one of my own objectives as a political activist. The focus of the research was therefore to be on the apparent clash between the concepts of participation advocated, on the one hand by activists and, on the other, by government, to see whether there could be a meeting point between the two, or whether notions of 'representative' and 'participatory' democracy were in reality incompatible as certain writers from quite different standpoints suggested.[1]

But as my work unfolded, it became clear that this approach was misplaced. There were a number of reasons for this. First, both at a theoretical and at a practical level, local activists seemed unable to offer a coherent rationale for their activity other than in such vague terms as 'more power to the people'. Moreover, they differed amongst themselves in their objectives, reflecting different ideological commitments or class interests. So it emerged that, far from there being a cohesive force for participatory democracy coming up against a system of representative democracy, the reality was a great deal more complex. Therefore it appeared that a more fruitful approach would be to examine the relationship between participatory groups and the public authorities, to establish who benefited from participation and to gain a detailed understanding of the process of power involved in that relationship.

[1] There are often references in passing to the contrast between 'representative' and 'participatory' democracy, but where the implications are not pursued: see Pateman, p. 28, and Dilys M. Hill, pp. 37-8, for just two examples. Where, however, the implications are pursued, three major points are emphasised: the historical, the spatial and the question of power. First, where the question is treated in terms of the history of political theory, it is argued that, up until the late eighteenth century, democracy was equivalent to 'direct democracy' in the tradition of the Greek *polis* and of Rousseau; by the mid-nineteenth century, however, the emergence of elected, representative legislatures had provided an attractive alternative to direct democracy: see Dahl and Tufte, p. 8 and Holden, p. 5. Historically, it is possible to distinguish between what Holden refers to as 'direct' and 'indirect (representative)' democracy. Second, the question is approached from the standpoint of size and there is some overlap with the historical treatment. For instance, Dahl and Tufte p. 27 define 'direct' and 'representative' democracy primarily in terms of size, arguing that the former constituted the core of democratic theory in the age of the city-state, with the latter taking over in the age of the nation-state. Third, it seems generally to be assumed that 'the difference between direct and indirect democracy is radical . . . In direct democracy there is continuous participation of the people in the direct exercise of power, whereas indirect democracy amounts to a system of *limitation* and *control* of power.' (Sartori, p. 252)

This necessity to adopt a different approach was reinforced in late 1976, at the end of my fulltime programme of research, when a new series of writings and studies began to appear which interpreted participation in much the same light as my empirical observation and research had by then encouraged me to do. In particular, this material focused on the relationship between the state and participation under modern capitalist conditions, and marked the rise of a new urban sociology. If my original framework became less valid, however, in my situation it would have been methodologically false to have revised the study in such a way that I considered this new literature at the beginning, when in reality it had not been available to guide my research in general, still less my empirical work.[2] Furthermore, participation advocates and activists *themselves* usually begin from standpoints which tend to ignore such wider questions of political economy, and one of my principal objectives has been to examine their own ideas, particularly since it is clear that these ideas underly their approaches to practical participation projects. Accordingly, the book deliberately avoids considering at the outset either state sponsorship of participation or issues of resources, class and other conflicts of interest until, as it were, these suggest themselves as the neighbourhood councils experience is evaluated. One of my major concerns, in short, is to challenge the orthodoxies which have been implicit in the advocacy of public participation and to do that it is necessary initially to describe that advocacy largely in its own terms.

The development of the Covent Garden Forum of Representatives between 1974 and 1977 forms the empirical core of the book and is based almost entirely on primary material. I was aware of the difficulties of attempting to generalise from one case study and I do not pretend that Covent Garden is a 'typical' inner city area. Indeed, I originally sought to study some four neighbourhood councils in depth.

[2]   My personal circumstances prevented further time and resources being spent on fresh empirical work and, indeed, events had by then 'moved on' in Covent Garden, the principal area of my study, so that the value of any 'retrospective' research data would have been somewhat questionable, given that I relied heavily on interviews and attendance at meetings. Similar time and resources constraints—partly determined by being in fulltime employment from 1976, partly because of the priority I personally give to political action and partly because of family responsibilities—prevented the kind of theoretically integrated, extensive re-working of the material I had, as, for example, Saunders did when faced with a similar problem over his study of Croydon (see pp. 207–8).

But, as my research evolved, it quickly became evident that this would be far too ambitious and that a narrower focus was required. Covent Garden provided the richest material and I was granted virtually unlimited access to information, both by the Greater London Council and local community organisations. Moreover, other neighbourhood councils were examined (albeit less intensively) to reduce the dangers of using what may have been seen as a unique exeriment to draw representative conclusions.

I am also conscious that—in the penultimate chapter especially— insufficient attention is given to so much of the important theoretical debate now dominating urban sociology, which is well reviewed and analysed in Saunders' *Urban Politics*. What may be seen as a weakness was in part unavoidable in my case. First, because that debate is relatively new and therefore could not feasibly be accomodated within the scope of my research project. Second, because, as Saunders himself points out (p. 201), there has been a 'division of labour', particularly in the study of urban politics from a sociological standpoint, with some

> . . . devoting most of their time to the development of often highly sophisticated theoretical perspectives with little concern for their empirical applications, while others busy themselves with large-scale research projects which generate interesting case material but which sometimes appear to bear little relation to the dominant theoretical concerns of the day.

Whilst I was anxious to relate my study to more general issues of theory and practice, I found progressively as it unfolded that my empirical work and detailed discussion of neighbourhood councils could offer a sharper contribution, both towards a better understanding of urban political participation and a challenge to the orthodoxies surrounding it, than could any contribution I might have tried to make at a more theoretical level.

It should also be noted that, where no source is cited for either a quote or an argument attributed to one of the participants in the neighbourhood councils' movement, I have drawn it from interview notes formulated as part of my empirical work.

However, the book does not simply confine itself to criticism of the orthodox approaches to public participation. There ought to be some responsibility to leave the comfortable armchair of the academic critic and the final chapter therefore suggests a more fruitful way forward for activists.

Part One

PUBLIC PARTICIPATION – THEORY AND PRACTICE

1

The Promise of Participation

> In a participatory democracy, decision-making is the process whereby people propose, discuss, decide, plan and implement those decisions that affect their lives. This requires that the decision-making process be continuous and significant, direct rather than through representatives . . . It requires that the decision-making process be set up in a functional manner, so that the constituencies significantly affected by decisions are the ones that make them and elected delegates can be recalled instantly . . . Participatory Democracy assumes that in a good society people participate fully, and that a society cannot be good unless that happens. Participation and control must be *one*.
>
> C. George Benello and Dimitrios Roussopolous, *The Case for Participatory Democracy* (New York, Viking, 1972), pp. 5-6.

It is widely asserted that public participation offers the promise of 'more power to the people', of a greater say for the individual citizen in the decision-making process and, even, of a different kind of political system, sometimes called a 'participatory democracy'. This chapter describes the aspirations of the advocates of participation, in order to provide the basis for contrasting these *aspirations* with the *practice* of participation examined in later chapters.

For our purpose, public participation is defined as 'taking part in the formulation, passage or implementation of public policies' (Parry, p. 5), and our interest is in those forms or examples of participation which are both 'important' (Schattschneider, p. 140) and have 'political'[1] consequences. That is to say, our concern is with the

---

[1] That is not to say however that consideration of public participation should be confined to the area which impinges directly upon the framing or implementation of *government* policies, as, for example, Finer argues (pp. 59-60). We shall adopt Pateman's standpoint that effective participation depends upon an extension of the idea of 'the political' beyond the arena of strictly government policy-making to include, for instance, participation in industry and education (see pp. 43-4).

impact of participation on the decision-making process and the degree to which, if at all, it alters the balance of power between citizens and the public authorities. The analysis therefore focuses on the question of political impact, rather than what may well be other consequences of participation, for example, its educational (Thompson, Kariel 1966) or psychological (Dowse & Hughes, p. 291, Barber, Keniston) value for those involved.

Impetus for Modern Participation

That there has been in the 1960s and 1970s a massive growth in participation through various pressure groups is not in question: it is a phenomenon which has occurred throughout the Western capitalist societies (DoE 3, Kalk, pp. 190-4). Part of this has been a 'burgeoning of micro-politics, particularly within the inner city' (Donnison). Such 'micro-politics' has operated largely beneath the official arena of government and has often involved hostility to the statutory authorities as a multitude of local groups have pressed their demands. Since our concern is with examining neighbourhood councils, the focus for the analysis below will be on participation in the micro-political arena, rather than participation through nation-ally-oriented pressure groups (Benewick & Smith, Rivers, Frost, Benewick).

As well as examining what advocates of participation have actually said or written, an understanding of their objectives can be obtained by identifying the factors which *they perceive* as giving rise to or producing a necessity for greater participation.

First, what is described as an 'urban crisis' (Blair, Yates, pp. 19-21) afflicting especially the bigger cities—problems of urban disorder, inadequate housing and transportation, lack of finance and environmental destruction—is seen as being so intransigent that a different political response is required to solve it. That is to say, the 'urban crisis' is not conceptualized as a series of discrete or technical problems but instead as an essentially political crisis (Goodman, R., Katznelson 1973, Kotler) to which participation is a response. By organising citizens into groups to tackle urban problems it is argued that results can be achieved which the established system cannot deliver (Clark, G.).

Second, though this is mainly confined to middle class radical movements such as the 'New Left' in America, participation is conceived as an invigorating, personally fulfilling strategy to pose an alternative to a 'mechanised, bureaucratised, dehumanised society' (Lasch, p. 180).

Linked with this second factor is a *third* one: the rebirth of the óld ideal (Pateman, pp. 22-44, Lucas, Dilys Hill, p. 47, Dearlove 1973, p. 16) of a self-governing community which might give the citizen a sense of place which is lacking in ccntemporary society (Greaves, Dennis 1968). Closely connected, in turn, is the high premium placed on the question of *size*: the small community is seen as the basis for regenerating democracy, and there is typically a desire to have 'maximum feasible power for minimum feasible areas' (Cox, p. 207, Crick, p. xix). One advocate of decentralisation and participation goes so far as to argue: '. . . there seems to be only one cause behind all forms of social misery: *bigness*' (Kohr, p. ix). Although this is a somewhat extreme position, it reflects an important theme in the motivation for participation and is expressed in a desire for 'small face-to-face-groups' to be organised and to act as channels for participation (Fromm, Schumacher, Weil, pp. 99, Goodman, E.).

Fourth, participation was developed as a means of combating the exclusion of the poor from the political system. This factor came against a background of the 'rediscovery' of poverty in the allegedly 'affluent' post-war societies of the West (Harrington, Baine, pp. 13-7, Coates & Silburn, pp. 13-20). If the poor could be organised into participating groups in order to fight for their rights then they might win some recognition (Lees, p. 44). For liberal advocates of participation, this reflected a pluralist analysis of politics in which the problem was how to organise the poor into groups which could successfully compete with other groups in society for a fair share of the national cake (for criticisms of this, see Gitlin 1967, Lowi 1969, Ono, Green, P. 1968, 1970). For radical advocates however there was also the notion of the poor and minorities constituting an 'underclass' or an 'extruded class' which was deprived of the rewards of the capitalist system—even those rewards won by the organised working class—and was therefore potentially a source of radical change (Kotler, p. 97, Gitlin 1970, Jordan, Moody, Aronson, Wilson, D., Piven & Cloward 1977).

Fifth, participation sprang out of either an estrangement from the conventional structure of representative democracy, or an awareness of its shortcomings (Kotler, pp. 97-8, Yates, pp. 4-5, Green, G., p. 11, Blondel, J.). The former position is typically adopted by radical activists, one of whom argued: 'Democracy conceived as a system of electoral politics has shown itself to be a farce for a substantial portion of the population' (Megill, p. 17). The latter position is typically expressed by the liberal concern for participation which grew up in Britain in the reformist climate of the 1960s. Voter apathy and disenchantment with the major political parties encouraged a view that the political system was too 'closed', 'elitist' and 'unresponsive' to public opinion, and that more 'open government' and a greater involvement by individuals in the decision-making process was required (Lucas, Lapping & Radice). Whereas the radical position amounted to a rejection of the structure of representative democracy, the liberal one expressed a disenchantment not so much with the principles underlying the system as with the 'political parties' temporary inability to make it work' (Green, G., p. 7).

Flowing from the above factor was a *sixth* one peculiar to the British context, namely, disillusionment with the Labour Party on the part of those who believed it had ceased in the 1960s to represent the interests of the working class and had therefore abandoned the very heritage which many modern community activists sought to re-assert (Cockburn, O'Malley, Radford, Hindess). One former Labour member turned community organiser described his disillusionment: 'For me . . . the Labour Party was dead as a possible organisational form. The same was true of hundreds of other young, and not so young, people who turned to the ideas of community action as a basis for their political life' (Baine, p. 10).

Seventh, and partly in response to the very disillusionment identified above, came a revival in the early 1970s of support for participation and workers' control within the Labour Movement (Benn, Barratt Brown, Holland). This reflected a strong strand in the British socialist tradition, including Robert Owen's early 19th century ideas on communal life and the workers' control of 20th century guild socialism (Cole, 1917, 1920). The more radical community activists have aligned themselves with a socialist analysis of capitalism and envisage participation in terms of a strategy to confront it (Buckman). That too was the broad objective of many involved in the uprising in Paris in May 1968 and in the student movements which led to scattered unrest and demands for participation throughout the Western world in the late 1960s (Cockburn & Blackburn, Cohn-Bendit, Bourges).

Aims of Participation

Having identified the factors contributing to the rise of participation as seen by those who have advocated it, and so established what the participation phenomenon was reacting *against*, what precisely has it been *for*? Before discussing this, however, it should be noted that the analysis above has pinpointed two broad perspectives of participation (see also Holden, pp. 223-5, Kay 1974, p. 210). The first is what we shall call the 'liberal' perspective which is predominantly concerned with *modifying* the structure of representative democracy and the capitalist relations underpinning it, so as to make that structure more responsive to the individual citizen, thereby improving the quality of democracy. The second is the 'radical' perspective, a generic term used to denote those theorists and activists who seek to confront and *replace* representative democracy, usually with something called 'participatory democracy'.

In effect, the liberal interpretation amounts to the removal of bureaucratic obstacles to participation; the encouragement of less secrecy in government; and more information to people so that they can express their preferences before decisions are taken. Thus, although a certain amount of reform is proposed in the system of representative democracy—at the micro-political level, for example, this might be through formally granting legitimacy to pressure groups by conceding access to council committees (Rees, A.)—the desire to promote participation expresses itself practically in proposals which would do little more than open up channels of influence and persuasion: no fundamental change in the structure of power is envisaged.

(It is true that a more analytical advocacy of participation has come from Pateman who is not easily placed into either one of the liberal or radical categories. Her important book, *Participation and Democratic Theory,* was concerned to refute the mainstream political science orthodoxy of the 1950s and 1960s which argued that notions of popular participation were the romantic offspring of classical democratic theory and had little if any relevance in modern mass society. She argues instead that we can still have 'a modern , viable theory of democracy which retains the notion of participation at its heart' (p. 111). However, apart from her discussion of industrial democracy— which is both detailed and illuminating in its focus on the extent to which the power relations within industry can neutralise the impact of workers' participation—her discussion of governmental decision-making is confined to the level of democratic theory and is elusive on the question of meshing participation into the structure of representative democracy.)

The radical interpretation of participation stresses the concept of 'community control' which would involve a complete re-distribution of power and its location at the neighbourhood level (Green, P., 1970, Kotler, Yates, Altshuler). Although these radicals differ amongst themselves in their approaches—one describes the neighbourhood 'as the source of revolutionary power', another stresses extensive decentralisation—it is clear that their brand of participation starkly challenges the existing structures of government. It has affinities with the advocacy of 'participatory democracy' by the American 'New Left' movement which began in the early 1960s, developing from the civil rights movement (Newfield, Jabobs & Landau, Bottomore, Aronson & Cowley, Stolz, Mairowitz, Teodori). The New Left's aim was to 'reintroduce the concept of democracy from the ground up' (Benello & Roussopolous, p. 4), through a strategy of radical protest and community action.

However, an examination of New Left writings and programmes for action reveals that, whilst they pursue to its conclusion the logic of participation in their advocacy of 'participatory democracy', it tends to be rhetorical. Moreover, it '. . . has no analysis of society to explain *why* poverty, disenfranchisement, concentration of power in elites occur. Nor does it offer an analysis of the historical tendencies that may make social changes possible. It provides no long term strategy for change' (Aronson). But, whilst the New Left advocacy expresses sharply many of the problems associated with the radical position, its importance is twofold: first, it expresses clearly the demand for participation which would require different political structures to the present ones and, second, it provides a link between theory and practice (Teodori, p. 86). Many of the notions which have pervaded the drive for participation at the neighbourhood level in Britain express the New Left's position on participatory democracy, whether this is acknowledged or not, and whether it is conscious or not (Baldock). To give just one example, the New Left's insistence on the notion of 'instant recall' of delegates is echoed in the claimants union movement in Britain (East London Claimants Union). No other writings provide such a rich insight into the assumptions and ideas guiding radical activists involved in promoting participation.

Part of the significance of the participatory democracy school is that it predominantly constitutes what I shall call *activist theory*, as opposed to what may be called the *reflective theory* of writers on participation, many of whom fall into the liberal category. The distinction is made because when it comes to consider the extent to which the aspirations of the participation advocates match up with the practice, a different order of comparison is involved. For the activists—who do not purport to advance a coherent theory—the issue is: how far is it or has it been feasible to realise their prescriptions? For the reflective theorists, the issue is how the theoretical assumptions upon which they base their advocacy of participation stand scrutiny.

Strategy for Participation

Having reviewed the aims of those who advocate participation, it is necessary to refer to the strategies they envisage, in order to establish a more comprehensive picture of, not merely their long term ideals, but their short term aims as well. Here again the distinction drawn above between the liberal position which seeks to modify representative democracy, and the radical position which seeks to confront and replace that system, is clearly evident. While liberals speak of neighbourhood organisations as 'complementing' the structure of local government and providing a useful link between the elected councillor and the electorate (Hampton & Chapman, p. 253, Rowe 1975b), the radicals propose 'counter-institutions' and 'parallel structures' from which it is envisaged their alternative society would begin to emerge alongside the existing system, and would eventually replace that system (Lynd, Cowley). Similarly, whilst liberals emphasise a 'consensus' model of change at the community level, radicals adopt a 'conflict' model (Smith & Anderson, Bryant 1972). The former stresses constructive integration within the processes of law and government, and individual participation is seen as having the advantage of educating the citizen, creating an informed and involved electorate (Thompson, Pateman, J.S. Mill). The latter promotes 'direct action' (Kay 1974, pp. 207-8, Carter) and aims to involve deprived groups, initially through tackling the problems which beset them, and then broadening this out into a wider struggle for community control and against the capitalist system (Gitlin, 1970, Fruchter and Kramer, O'Malley, Barr).

Levels of Participation

In distinguishing between the liberal and radical advocates of participation, it is not pretended that these are rigorously defined, nor that every writer or activist concerned with participation would necessarily fit neatly into either one of these categories: it would be conceivable to straddle the two, as Pateman does to an extent. Nevertheless, it is a helpful way in which to examine the case for participation as it is variously advanced, and the question arises as to whether there is any systematic relationship between the two categories, and also what can be said about the circumstances in which a liberal as opposed to a radical strategy might be pursued by, for instance, a community group.

A useful approach is suggested by Pateman who distinguishes three types of participatory situation: 'pseudo', 'partial' and 'full' participation. Although her typology sprang directly from analysis of *industrial* participation, it can have a wider application. 'Pseudo-participation' is described as a situation where those in authority go through the motions of consultation to give the impression of being reasonable and responsive—but in fact the decision has already been taken (see also Verba, pp. 219-21, 224). Pateman describes 'partial participation' as a situation where two or more parties influence each other in a participatory decision-making process, but where the final power to decide rests with one party alone. Firstly, 'full participation' implies a situation where each individual or group in a decision-making process has equal influence over the final decision.

It is clear that, while the rhetoric of participation has suggested situations of 'full participation', in practice situations involving Pateman's other two types have been more frequent. Recognition of this led Sherry Arnstein to suggest (1971, 1972, Kalk, pp. 190-4) her 'ladder of citizen participation', with its eight rungs from 'manipulation' and 'therapy' at the base to 'delegated power' and 'citizen control' at the top (see table 1, p. 22).

If we now apply our liberal and radical categories to this typology it would on the face of it, appear that the liberal advocacy tends to fall into the 'lower rung' levels of Arnstein or the 'partial' concept of Pateman. Equally, the radical advocacy conforms more to higher rung levels or to full participation. But neither Arnstein nor Pateman suggest any systematic relationship between higher and lower levels. Is there some power process linking them which would ensure that even the aspiration towards a higher level is in practice inevitably thwarted and forced downwards to lower levels? Equally, in what circumstances would it become viable for a neighbourhood council to pursue a radical strategy, or will it in practice automatically be relegated to pursuing liberal goals, despite an attachment to radical ideology?

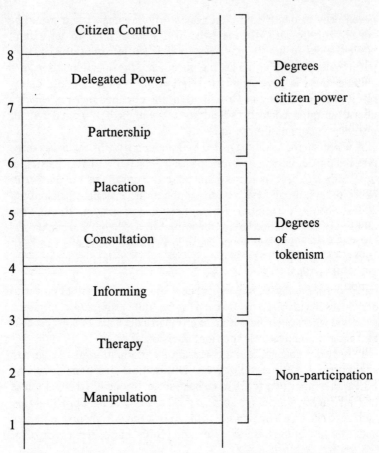

What needs to be established, therefore, before the analysis can be taken much further is, first, whether it is *necessarily* the case that attempts by liberals to mesh participation into the structure of representative politics results in lower rung levels or even the 'pseudo' concept of Pateman. For if this turns out to be the case then the liberal advocacy will be seen as somewhat shallow, hardly altering at all the existing balance of political power: their expressed aspirations to a greater say for citizens may be found wanting when the practice is examined. Second, it needs to be established whether the somewhat romantic advocacy of the radicals has been practised to any serious extent and, if not, why not. Third, the impact of the distribution of resources and the class structure on the role of citizen participation is neglected by both liberal and radical advocates and this, too, needs to be examined: for example the higher level categories of Pateman and Arnstein may only be valid when considering very limited forms of decisions; it seems reasonable to suggest that external constraints imposed by central government and the private sector could severely restrict the range of decisions amenable to 'full' participation. Indeed, it will become apparent that public participation should be viewed within a 'political economy' perspective and that conflicts of interest play a far more critical role than is assumed in the general advocacy of participation.

It should also be noted that no consideration has so far been given to *government* sponsorship of participation. This is because the intention has been to begin from the assumptions of those who advocate participation from a non-governmental standpoint, and then critically to evaluate their assumptions. We should however be aware that government too has encouraged participation which, as will be shown in chapter three, can be understood in terms of a process of 'mobilisation' of support upwards from the populace rather than a redistribution of power or influence downwards to the citizen.

Meanwhile the promise of participation is at least for a much greater say for citizens in the process of government and at most for a quite different kind of democracy. In the following chapter the experience of neighbourhood councils will be described to establish to what extent that promise has been fulfilled, and also how far it is possible to answer the questions posed immediately above.

2
Neighbourhood Councils

As the organisations of the oppressed win their battles, however, they are gradually integrated into the system of welfare administration. Their purposes are not given up, or not wholly given up, but rather give rise, under new circumstances, to new organisational forms: the struggle groups become pressure groups. Public life ceases to engage the minds and emotions of their members; local activity drops off; popular participation declines sharply. The tenacious sense of detail peculiar to highly qualified bureaucrats replaces the enthusiasm of members: it is more useful, even to the members themselves.
Michael Walzer, 'Politics in the Welfare State', *Dissent*, vol. 15 (January-February 1968), p. 29.

A series of neighbourhood councils have been established in England in the past decade, in working class areas and in middle class areas, in the big conurbations and in small towns. Geographical variety has been complemented by a range of different types of neighbourhood council, with the term being officially endorsed by the Government on the one hand, and, on the other, used to describe the Bogside Community Association in Derry, Northern Ireland. There is also a national pressure group, the Association for Neighbourhood Councils.

Origins

In keeping with the rhetoric of advocates of participation, the neighbourhood council movement persistently characterises itself as a 'grass roots' phenomenon. But an examination of its origins suggests that this is only one of its dimensions: although local initiative and activity remains its principal feature, there has been, from its inception, an important national and governmental input which has shaped the style of the movement.

By the end of the 1960s, the community action movement in Britain was well established and some of its spokesmen were considering ways of obtaining additional resources and also more representative structural forms, so that the movement could be placed on a permanent footing which its heavy reliance on spontaneity and voluntary campaigning did not allow. Conscious of the American experience—reflected in both the New Left community projects, and the Federal Government sponsored 'community action programmes'—several key British community organisers began to promote neighbourhood councils in this country.

The Director of the Institute of Community Studies, Michael Young, widely known for his research in deprived areas of the East End of London, and with good connections with senior politicians and public officials, decided that an organisation was needed to promote the concept of neighbourhood councils.

The Association for Neighbourhood Councils (ANC) was set up in January 1970 and the Institute of Community Studies seconded one of its workers to the Association. Amongst its founder members were leading figures from all three major political parties.

The dominant thinking within the ANC was for the setting up in cities of bodies such as the parish councils which existed in rural areas. (The organisation even gave itself the subtitle: 'The Campaign for Urban Parish Councils'.) As is described in chapter three, parish councils enjoyed something of a revival after the Second World War, and the idea of introducing them into urban areas had been suggested by the National Association of Parish Councils as far back as 1958: in a memorandum to the Government, the Association urged the formation of what it termed 'urban village councils'. Later, in 1967, the Association urged the Royal Commission on Local Government to incorporate such councils in a reformed local authority structure. This impetus was strengthened by the view that the 1963 reform of London's local government—which created the Greater London Council and a second tier of 32 Boroughs, but made no provision for a third or lower tier structure—had made local government too remote from Londoners. On 18th June 1973, the 'London Parish Councils Bill', sponsored by the Liberal Peer, Lord Avebury, was given its first reading in the House of Lords. It provided for the establishing of urban parish councils in London, and was later taken up by the Liberal MP, Graham Tope, and introduced as a Private Members Bill, only to fall when the General Election was called in February, 1974. The Bill had the enthusiastic backing of the ANC.

From its inception, the ANC was committed to statutory neighbourhood councils and has since worked primarily as a 'parliamentary pressure group'. In 1970, the ANC commissioned the Gallup Poll organisation to mount a nationwide survey of public attitudes to councils at the neighbourhood level. It found that the majority of people were favourable to the idea, with most of the rest being uncertain rather than opposed, and with support being greater in the conurbations than in other urban areas, and greatest of all in London. These findings were reported and analysed in the ANC's first major publication, *The Hornsey Plan*, and used to lobby for statutory neighbourhood councils during the period of parliamentary debate on the reorganisation of local government in 1970-72.

During the Committee stage of the 1972 Local Government Act a founder member of the ANC, the Labour MP, Arthur Blenkinsop, pressed amendments to the Conservative Bill urging neighbourhood councils in the form of parish councils in urban areas. He was supported by the Labour front bench spokesman on Planning and Local Government, John Silkin, in whose constituency, Lewisham Deptford, there was a thriving body, the Telegraph Hill Neighbourhood Council. Although they failed to secure the Conservative Government's support, it was at this time that neighbourhood councils were perceived as a 'live issue' by the Department of the Environment. Some two years later, after Labour returned to power in 1974, the DoE issued a consultative document backing neighbourhood councils, which is discussed fully in chapter three.

Meanwhile activity had been continuing apace at the local level. Institutions called 'community councils' had been set up in Liverpool as early as 1963, on the initiative of the local Council of Social Service and with the blessing of the local authority (Philo, Ridley & Banks). The Telegraph Hill Neighbourhood Council in the Borough of Lewisham was set up independently in 1968, and by 1971 Lambeth Council had launched a scheme of funded neighbourhood councils (both these latter initiatives will be referred to later).

The best known neighbourhood council was in Notting Hill, scene of widely publicised community action projects. The Golborne Neighbourhood Council (GNC) was established in 1971 after a locality-wide ballot costing £2500. It was the first neighbourhood council to have a direct election. Although the intention is not to explore in any detail its thorny and controversial history, the interest at this stage is how it came to be launched. To summarise: it originated from a combination of local community workers and outside bodies including the ANC. The ANC saw the opportunity in Notting Hill in terms of a 'prototype urban parish council', and assisted local groups to obtain finance and support. Local workers needed external support and, as George Clark, a key figure in the project, put it: 'Golborne was to everyone involved in the ANC a heaven sent opportunity for a living example on the ground. For our part, we wanted to land money, legitimacy and respectability for the body we had set up.' By 1973, however, the GNC had effectively collapsed amidst considerable acrimony, and attention was directed at another neighbourhood council pilot scheme, this time in the nearby London Borough of Hammersmith. The latter, together with the issues raised by the experience of Golborne, will be discussed later in the chapter.

In these early years of the neighbourhood council movement, therefore, two major ingredients can be discerned: first an element of local interest and initiative and, second, a strong external interest, usually expressed through the ANC and coming as part of a broader lobby for what amounted to statutory parish councils in urban areas.

Definition

Having sketched in the origins of neighbourhood councils, it is important to define what they are. This is by no means easy, since the term is used with a conspicuous lack of precision to denote a wide variety of community bodies—and is sometimes used interchangeably with the terms 'community council' or 'urban parish council'.

Although descriptions of neighbourhood councils are offered in various publications of the ANC, the most rigorous definition has been suggested by Humble and Talbot in their 'Investigation into Neighbourhood Councils' carried out between late 1975 and early 1977 under the auspices of the Institute for Local Government Studies; their investigation was funded by the Department of the Environment. They analysed 224 'approximate' neighbourhood councils located in a 1974 census of neighbourhood organisations in England which was organised by the ANC and financed by the DoE. From a combination of the ANC's concept of neighbourhood councils and an examination of the attributes of the 22 groups out of the full sample calling themselves 'neighbourhood councils', they were able to suggest a working definition:

Both 1. aims to make representation on behalf of the local community to public bodies,

and 2. actually *does* make representation on behalf of the local community (i.e. is 'politically active')

3. Covers a defined area

4. Considers all residents (or at least those on the electoral roll) within the area to be *members with full voting rights,* whether these members are also enrolled or not

5. Has a council committee the majority of whose members are directly elected by residents

6. Covers an area of not less than 3,000 and not more than 15,000 population

After having selected those organisations possessing *all* of these attributes, they were left with only 15 (7%) out of the 224, and, of those 15, only 7 were from the 22-strong group of so-called neighbourhood councils. Although the ANC's preferred method of election is through a direct ballot on conventional election lines, the above definition allows for election by a general meeting so long as each registered elector is entitled to attend the vote. The investigation shows that the principal characteristic distinguishing 'neighbourhood councils proper' from the remaining 209 groups surveyed was 'the abandonment of an enrolment requirement for membership and eligibility to vote.' In other respects they were found to be remarkably similar to the rest. Their definition will be adopted principally because it distinguishes so clearly between neighbourhood councils and other community groups (e.g. tenants' associations).

The aims of neighbourhood councils have been listed in the constitution of Lymington Neighbourhood Council which is put forward by the ANC as a model for others:

The aims and objects of the Neighbourhood Council shall be as follows:

a.   to represent local opinion on any matter which concerns the wards;

b.   to press governmental and other public or local authorities, charitable organisations and other interests in the wards to take action on such matters as may in the opinion of the Neighbourhood Council be necessary or desirable;

c.   to promote widespread and well informed interest in local governmental and local affairs;

d.   to consider such matters as the District Council may refer to the Neighbourhood Council for consultation and to represent opinions thereon;

e. to undertake lawful activities on their own behalf or in consort or association with other Neighbourhood Councils or individuals, bodies, organisations, societies or associations to the benefit of the people of the wards conducive to these objects.

Notwithstanding the limitations of its somewhat formal and legalistic tone in giving an accurate picture of the general aims of neighbourhood councils, this would appear fairly to represent these aims. To them, however, should be added several others which are more or less explicitly endorsed by the neighbourhood councils movement (that is to say the 'proper' neighbourhood councils and the ANC), and which may be of greater significance. For instance, they see their role as being to act as a link between the people of an area and its local district council; indeed, much of the fervour for neighbourhood councils has been generated by a feeling that the local government structure was too remote from the citizen. There is also a strong 'self-help' ideology in neighbourhood councils, encouraging people to join together to improve their neighbourhood themselves, and specifically encouraging the apathetic or inarticulate individual to become active.

The Role of Neighbourhood Councils

Having established a working definition and touched on the aims of neighbourhood councils, what role do they play?

First, there is general acceptance of the view that they represent a 'resurgence of the idea of community' (Ridley & Banks, p. 3), and a response to an unrepresentative and insensitive political party system (Rowe, 1975b, pp. 15-6). Second, they are distinct from many community groups in being based on a 'geographical understanding of the community', as opposed to the alternative of a 'functional community of interest' where organisation is based around specific issues or needs (Hampton & Chapman). Much of what Donnison referred to as 'micro-politics' involves action and campaigning on a particular issue, for example, homelessness, planning, amenities, the environment or welfare. Neighbourhood councils, by contrast, are conceived as bodies which can serve as a 'focal point' for single-issue community groups, attempting to fashion a general view and acting as a forum in which specific issues can be brought to the attention of the wider community (Rowe, 1975, p. 6, Hampton & Chapman, p. 252).

The role of such a forum is also seen in terms of a bridge between 'the growth of spontaneous grass-roots activity and traditional representative institutions', as Hampton and Chapman put it (p. 414), or as providing 'informal and local access to government', as Humble put it (p. 87). Here the neighbourhood council is seen as a medium through which local participation can be linked to the local government structure (Hampton & Chapman, p. 253):

> . . . a neighbourhood council would be an institution of participatory, not representative democracy. Neighbourhood councils would be only on the periphery of the real political decisions concerning the allocation of resources; the main resources available to them would be their own energy and the effort they could inspire in others.

This appears to confirm the suggestion (identified in the Preface) that participatory and representative democracy are distinct concepts. But Hampton and Chapman clearly believe that a reconciliation between the two is feasible and that neighbourhood councils can help to facilitate it. They also assume that public participation essentially relies for its influence on activity and publicity, and is therefore of necessity on the 'periphery' of political decision-making (corresponding to Arnstein's 'lower rungs'). This liberal perspective is echoed elsewhere. Rowe (1975b, pp. 15-6), for example, rules out 'full participation' and argues that neighbourhood councils must necessarily be limited to 'partial participation'. He believes that full participation would require a revolutionary change in the structure of power which is both unrealistic and undesirable. And—save for isolated analyses (Boddington) by radical community activists and socialists who see neighbourhood councils as precursors to the 'self-managed community'—this view is widely adopted by reflective theorists and, indeed, amongst the main protagonists of neighbourhood councils.

The broadest investigation of neighbourhood councils to date is by Humble and Talbot. They expose what they term 'the myth of spontaneous neighbourhood councils'. Contrary to the rhetoric of some community activists who stress the importance of 'the community' itself establishing its own groups and initiating methods of action appropriate to what it defines as its own needs, Humble and Talbot found that the initiative in every case they studied came from a community worker together with bodies external to the community. This is not just the case for neighbourhood councils however, but for community groups in general (Mitton & Morrison, Thomas). The main bodies concerned were the ANC and the relevant local authority.

They further show that neighbourhood councils depended for their formation upon 'key personalities' rather than upon a sense of alienation from existing institutions or on the condition of the neighbourhood. In support of this argument they point to the existence of neighbourhood councils in 'all kinds of urban areas, from affluent South Coast small towns to deprived, inner city locations'. They also found that neighbourhood councils did not seem in general to be a product of a major threat to the community, neither a product of a 'big' or 'visible' issue (which contrasts starkly with the Covent Garden experience, as will be seen in later chapters). Moreover, 'The concern of the neighbourhood councils was essentially parochial. They did not take on board large issues such as unemployment probably because issues such as this are not neighbourhood-based. . .' Linked with this is a preoccupation with a 'social role' (i.e. a concern with fundraising and voluntary social activities) rather than a 'political role'; they are explicitly non-party political, though they may share a common political identity within themselves or with the local authority. Again this reflects a liberal perspective.

Humble and Talbot found that the crucial factor was the relationship with the local authority:

> A major theme in the argument for neighbourhood councils is that they provide a countervailing force to the remoteness of post-reorganisation local government. It would be wrong to conclude from this that neighbourhood councils operate in isolation from local government. They are enmeshed with it. The livelihood of all the sample neighbourhood councils depended to some degree or other on their local authorities, financially and otherwise. They could not afford to ignore local government.

But notwithstanding this close dependency, the exact relationship differed between semi-institutionalised and informal contact. When the local authority took the initiative in establishing the neighbourhood councils, they were given official consultative rights in decision-making. This did not, however, mean that there was a general acceptance of neighbourhood councils as a 'third tier' of local government. Indeed, the investigation found that both sides were at pains to stress the autonomy of the neighbourhood council.

The study shows, however, that it would be mistaken to conceive of a single, unitary relationship between the neighbourhood council and the local authority. For example, while senior officers of the authorities generally treated neighbourhood councils either with indifference or with suspicion, this was not the case for those community workers who were paid officers of the authority. The latter usually identified with the neighbourhood council and were highly supportive of it, even to the point of pressing its aspirations against the wishes of the local authority.

In the case of ward councillors, as others have also noted (Williams, p. 167, Hampton 1973), the relationship was found to be a 'delicate' one:

> No ward councillors have given an unequivocal welcome to neighbourhood councils. Their opinion is variously manifested, from open hostility and suspicion that the neighbourhood council will undermine their position (though this opinion is expressed infrequently), through a mixture of faint suspicion and welcome of the possible assistance they might bring, even to a feeling, though a rare one, that the neighbourhood council might not be independent enough of themselves, the ward councillors.
>
> The relationship between neighbourhood councils and ward councillors is far from systematic, even where they are on good terms with one another. Where they are on good terms, few ward councillors attend neighbourhood council meetings regularly and no neighbourhood council has a regular and systematic means of communication with ward councillors. Both ward councillors and neighbourhood councils do bring matters to each other's attention, but on an *ad hoc* basis. Neighbourhood councils do engage in what is said to be detailed business that ward councillors have no time for (e.g. a housebound pensioner needing a house repair, carrying out a survey of residents of a local council estate) but there is no clear chain of communication from neighbourhood councils upwards.

In addition, although neighbourhood council supporters see their role as a 'focal point' for community groups, the study tends to dispute that this is the case in practice. The authors found that, whilst neighbourhood councils worked alongside other voluntary groups, they did not act as federal organisations for voluntary groups. In some areas the relationship with other local groups was uneasy, and in fact other evidence suggests that neighbourhood councils can be viewed with considerable suspicion by community groups and community workers.

On the other hand the argument of the advocates of neighbourhood councils that they can be genuinely representative of their locality does appear to be confirmed by the study. It was found that neighbourhood councils were not dominated by the articulate and the middle class, but reflected the social composition of the neighbourhood. (Although, elsewhere, Humble (p. 88) has pointed out that even in areas with a high proportion of Black people, there is little involvement by them in neighbourhood councils.) Significantly, it was found that, for the working class people involved, 'the neighbourhood councils seemed to be their first major opportunity to participate in local organisation'.

But although Humble and Talbot provide useful data, by its terms of reference their study drew back from examining the structure of power of which neighbourhood councils may be part, their role in that structure and how they might alter the balance of forces in society.

Neighbourhood Councils: the Debate

A better understanding of neighbourhood councils emerges from the debate amongst those actively involved. This debate has been especially wide-ranging due to what a senior civil servant described as a 'staggering' response from local groups to the Government's 1974 Consultative Document on neighbourhood councils. Submissions on the Document to the Department of the Environment (DoE) varied from enthusiastic support to suspicious antagonism. The Association for Neighbourhood Councils (ANC) warmly welcomed the concept of statutory neighbourhood councils suggested by the Government: 'Legislation ... would represent a major step forward for urban communities. At last it would be possible to give a formal statutory voice to the most deprived neighbourhoods who would be able to raise small sums for themselves ...' But, echoing the majority of submissions to the DoE, the ANC also argued that legislation should be 'permissive rather than mandatory'. In other words, the ANC did not want legislation which imposed on localities an obligation to establish neighbourhood councils: there had to be evidence of a clear desire by local people for such a body, expressed initially through a petition signed by 250 electors.

Similarly, the National Association of Local Councils (previously called the National Association for Parish Councils, the body which acts as the voice of parish councils) welcomed the Government's proposals. But it argued 'that the right way to proceed in establishing statutory neighbourhood bodies in un-parished areas is to extend the parish council system to them.' This could be done, the NALC stated, by implementing the provisions of the 1972 Local Government Act for 'parish reviews', backed up by Government legislation to enable statutory bodies to be established.

However, the Government's proposals provoked opposition which, broadly speaking, divided into two areas: local authorities and radical community activists.

Typical of such local authority reaction was the London Borough of Sutton's view that there were sufficient opportunities already available for participation and communication with electors, to make neighbourhood councils an unwarranted intrusion. This reflected the standpoint of the London Boroughs Association which questioned 'what alternative neighbourhood councils would present to the allegedly "large and remote organisations" of local authorities. With statutory status, statutory powers and limitations, with elections run by the local town hall, with probable involvement by the political parties, they could well appear no closer and no more personal to the man in the street than his local authority.' (Ironically, this view echoed criticisms by radical activists that neighbourhood councils would become indistinguishable from the structure of local government.) The LBA went on to argue that neighbourhood councils would be even less able to represent and express local opinion because they lacked the powers and resources possessed by local authorities:

> The consultation paper refers to choice of the individual as lying at the centre of democracy, and neighbourhood councils of such powerlessness are quite unfitted for the expression of such choice. Their functioning is likely to be within a vicious circle—with limited powers they will attract a small following and a low poll at elections, and with a low poll the authority they do have—that of being a representative body—will be suspect from the start.

This criticism, whilst no doubt reflecting an unease of bodies that might rival and challenge the role of local authorities, is telling to the extent that it questions the very assumptions upon which neighbourhood councils are usually advocated—as representative bodies but without resources.

From a markedly different standpoint, radical community action practitioners also criticised the Consultative Document. Expressing a more general suspicion of the Government's motives, the Telegraph Hill Neighbourhood Council stated:

The Government may be interested in doing something to revive local democracy. Alternatively, this proposal may be a deliberate attempt to undermine the growth of neighbourhood organisations. The working party (of the THNC) was not sure whether the government was being deliberately destructive, or was attempting to be creative . . . The document appears to have originated from the manipulations of a small number of professional academics, central government politicians and administrators of national organisations. It has not originated from the demands of existing neighbourhood organisations in inner-city areas.

More analytically, the *Community Action* magazine (No. 15, p. 10) interpreted the Government's concept of neighbourhood councils as one in which they would perform 'a *management function* as opposed to being a *political organisation*' and argued that they would undermine independent political action by neighbourhood bodies.

As was suggested earlier in the chapter, many activists see neighbourhood councils as an alternative to party politics which they believe to be too remote from citizens. In particular, they feel that the Labour Party has ceased to represent working class interests in the locality. For example, a woman from a South London working class and staunch Labour background who, in middle age, became a fulltime worker for a neighbourhood council, explained:

Although I never got involved, I had actually joined the Labour Party in the early 1960s. I got my socialist instincts from my Dad. But the Party never came and asked me to get involved. It seemed a very remote kind of organisation.

But members and active supporters of the Neighbourhood Council did not get involved because of such abstract ideas as a rejection of the party set-up—at least not explicitly or consciously. They are all suspicious of parties but their involvement was more in terms of 'there are no facilities on my estate'.

This is fairly typical of the more 'political' of the neighbourhood council activists and, although it may appear to contradict the finding of Humble and Talbot that the role of neighbourhood councils was perceived by those involved as being 'non-political', closer consideration reveals that not to be the case. The attraction for some of those who left Labour Party politics was for a method of consensus politics they believed should be expressed by neighbourhood councils. In the sense that it denies both *conflict* and *ideology*, it can be regarded as a form of 'anti-politics' (Smith, T., 1972).

On the other hand, the aim of neighbourhood councils is in part to give practical expression to political and community initiatives which it is perceived by those involved cannot be achieved through the political parties. Linked with this is a desire to 'improve community life' and somehow to combat what is seen as the insensitive face of modern urban society. Such an aim is very much a part of the Association for Neighbourhood Council's *raison d'être*. One of the clearest local examples illustrating this aspect is the Southern Neighbourhood Council (SNC) in a deprived area of Liverpool. Amongst those who have been most active are mothers in the local authority housing estates and for them a major aim of the neighbourhood council was to reduce the youth vandalism which disfigured the estates and threatened its inhabitants. Through the SNC it was hoped to create a sense of community spirit and interaction in specific projects which would combat vandalism by ameliorating many of the factors which encouraged it. And vandalism reputedly reduced by 43% once the SNC had established itself. This particular neighbourhood council appeared to spend most of its time performing a 'community care' role, by, for instance, pressing the council to provide early warning systems in elderly residents' flats; by regular contact with all residents; and by an advice centre staffed by local women. This 'preventative role' in pinpointing problems before they reached crisis level was regarded as being so important by one of the local women who became a fulltime worker for the SNC that she could insist: 'Southern Neighbourhood Council is the only thing holding the area together. I would move out if it collapsed.'

However, there is considerable disagreement amongst liberal advocates of neighbourhood councils on the specific political role which they should perform. What may be termed the 'mainstream' liberal view argues that neighbourhood councils 'should have no administrative *duties*, no service-running functions which they are obliged to perform; but they certainly should have powers to provide, for the benefit of the people in their areas, facilities and amenities which no other statutory bodies have a mandatory duty to provide; and their financial resources must not be so limited that they cannot effectively use such powers' (Derek Senior). Yet, others within the liberal perspective argue that neighbourhood councils should possess neither statutory powers nor have duties imposed upon them, but should nevertheless have *rights* of consultation in the local authority decision-making process.

Behind these differing standpoints is the question as to whether neighbourhood councils should or should not be statutory bodies. Broadly speaking, the case for statutory status rests on the belief that it will bring with it official recognition and therefore greater influence, as well as financial support. For example, the Town and Country Planning Association argued in its response to the DoE Consultative Document: 'Only by making statutory status available to such bodies can one be sure ... that they are established where they are most needed, that they represent the whole of a neighbourhood and have the necessary resources.' The TCPA also argued for statutory consulta- tion rights on local authority proposals such as planning schemes.

The case against rests essentially on the belief that statutory status will result in the incorporation of neighbourhood action and will thereby blunt the effectiveness of neighbourhood councils. As South Lambeth Neighbourhood Council argued in its DoE submission: 'The idea of neighbourhood councils featuring in statute has the big disadvantage of tending to become too official, in people's eyes even if not in reality. Local groups function best when they are most spontaneous and feel free from establishment restraints.'

For radical community activists, however, the issue is less one of statutory status (to which they are opposed) than the relationship with the local authority which Humble and Talbot found to be a critical factor. While there is a desire amongst liberal advocates to see neighbourhood councils as 'counter-weights' to local government, this is frequently coupled with the belief that there should be a close working relationship with local authorities and even a suggestion that the latter can play a role in initiating neighbourhood councils. The implications of such a close yet ostensibly independent relationship with local authorities are rarely explored and the debate tends to polarise between liberals who believe in the value of a 'constructive' working relationship and radicals who see almost any formal link with local authorities in terms of subverting community action. Even where a reconciliation is attempted between these two positions, it is less than convincing. For instance, the City Poverty Committee, in arguing for statutory status, insisted that neighbourhood councils 'should *not* be part of a local government machinery established by central government'; yet the Committee also urged formal rights of consultation in the local authority decision-making process and

financial aid from local authorities, whilst simultaneously warning of
the danger that the neighbourhood council could become 'a buffer
between legitimate minority concerns and the elected local government.' At the end of its evidence, the Committee suggested that
neighbourhood councils could be linked directly to the local authority's
area management system—something which occurred in for example
the Southern Neighbourhood Council in Liverpool.

It is left to others to analyse in any depth the implications for
neighbourhood councils of a close relationship with local government.
Commenting on the Golborne Neighbourhood Council (GNC), the
magazine *Community Action* (No. 7, p. 32) argued: 'Neighbourhood
councils of the GNC type are purpose-designed to dovetail into the
bottom of the local government pyramid—a pyramid in which
freedom of political action is practically impossible.' This leads to
local action being 'diffused and outflanked', the magazine asserted.
Such a view is widely held amongst the more radical community
activists, although (prior to this study) no detailed empirical investigation had been made to test its validity. The broadest investigation to
date—that by Humble and Talbot, described earlier—found that the
relationship with the local authority was crucial and that it varied
according to local circumstances. They also give some credence to the
Community Action view in several of their case studies. In one case,
for instance, they suggested: '. . . the message that seems to be
emerging is that from the local authority point of view neighbourhood
councils were a device partly to reconcile the constituent parts of the
authority and partly to bridge the gap between local authority
councillor and his ward which had increased in size as a result of
reorganisation.' However, that view expressed by *Community Action*
is not shared by those within the liberal mainstream of the neighbourhood council movement, where a typical view might be 'Neighbourhood Councils are not about substituting local government, but about
supplementing it.' From its inception, the movement has encouraged
close ties with local authorities—as was underlined in a guide
produced by a Department of the Environment advisory group which
included several leading individuals from neighbourhood councils
across the country (DoE 9).

But a common worry of community workers and local activists is
that neighbourhood councils might become in the eyes of local
government 'preferred organisations' with 'a privileged status and
funds and access denied to other community groups'. This point was

developed by the Telegraph Hill Neighbourhood Council in their submission on the Government's Consultative Document:

> Elected NC's might act as barriers between community groups and the decision-making power groups of the Town Hall. The chief-officers and councils may recognise only the elected NC as the spokesman of local opinion, and listen to only the views and demands put through the NC. The elected NC will sap the power and the authority of community groups.

However, behind this worry lies a more fundamental question: the political and ideological perspective within which neighbourhood councils are viewed both by their reflective advocates and by community activists. In suggesting below that these perspectives divide broadly into two principal camps we shall rely on the liberal and radical concepts elucidated in chapter 1. First, there are those who seek to promote a consensus view which can straddle class differences and obtain legitimacy and resources from the existing structure of representative government. Second, there are those who assume a class analysis of neighbourhood politics and with it a desire to promote what they variously term 'participatory' or 'direct' democracy. (Of course such a division is inevitably oversimplified and in the process also attributes to those engaged in the debate rather more coherent analyses than their expressed views perhaps justify.)

A good example of the liberal or consensus view was given in a submission to the DoE by Saltdean Residents & Property Owners Association:

> One of the principal aims of the Redcliffe-Maude Commission was to introduce a system of local government which would do away with the 'them' and 'us' mentality of the electorate towards the Town Hall. This, sadly, has failed, perhaps largely because the recommendations of the Commission for some form of 'community' or parish council in towns were ignored.
>
> The establishment of statutory neighbourhood councils could do much to overcome this since they would enable urban communities to communicate more effectively, not only with their own Ward Councillors and the Town Hall, but with other communities within their town, especially if there were a local association of neighbourhood councils. They would be able better to understand and sympathise with the problems of other communities and could also offer advice and help from their own experience. The fact that they

would be non party-political would no doubt encourage responsible citizens to involve themselves in their own local affairs which
they might not otherwise be prepared to do if party politics were
involved.

More community pride would no doubt be engendered, producing a greater feeling of purpose, which is now so lacking in many
quarters. It could help to overcome the anonymity of housing
estates, and could well result in less juvenile delinquency as the
community would be seen to care more for its inhabitants through
its own community council.

Even though the Association for Neighbourhood Councils might
quarrel with the somewhat timid tone suggested by the Saltdean
submission, it would be in broad agreement with it. This expresses
itself, for instance, in the view that direct elections 'give the
Neighbourhood Council some real authority,' principally by impress-
ing on the local authority that it is a representative and therefore a
legitimate group. As one leading member of the ANC put it:

> One rationale of an elected neighbourhood council is legitimacy in
> ordinary people's terms of an elected body. You have got to be seen
> to be part of an ongoing system: therefore it has to be explained in
> terms of another tier to people. The contradiction is that most
> advocates of neighbourhood councils do not see it as another tier.
> But without the legitimacy of an elected body you will never get
> resources. Also, you get to a stage after a period of community
> action when the activism engenders its own alliances, interests,
> passions and jealousies—and where an elected body becomes the
> only way of resolving it.

By contrast, radicals who associate themselves with a class
analysis of politics see the role of neighbourhood councils in quite
different terms. They see the aim as being to advance the interests of
working class people, to the extent of advocating an approach to
public participation which will include 'positive discrimination in
favour of the disadvantaged and inarticulate'. Their objection to the
consensus model assumed by those who advocate statutory bodies is
therefore political and ideological—and is acknowledged as such.
They strongly dispute that directly elected bodies are more representative than more loosely structured community organisations, partly
on the grounds that the former encourage an absorption into the local
government system and partly that they of necessity mean more

formal structures and procedures which will discriminate in favour of articulate middle class residents and undermine independent action. For example, in its submission on the Consultative Document, the Association of London Housing Estates argued:

> Our members are concerned that Legislation promoting 'Neighbourhood Councils' would cause 'community action' to be contained within a recognisable 'institutional' framework. This would condition the scope of the Council, limit its powers and mould it into the 'poor relation' of the local authority, becoming its 'watchdog', whose bark is muted and whose teeth are blunted. It is clear from the 'consultation' document that the role of a statutory organisation would be restricted to a management function. This would allow only a 'consultative', rather than a 'participatory', base for members' involvement. Furthermore, the tenants were worried that such Councils would form yet another obstacle between 'existing' groups and the 'Local Authority'. Such a development is neither necessary nor desirable.

It is apparent here that the issue of what is meant by participation is a controversial one within the neighbourhood council movement. Whereas the mainstream of the movement adopts a liberal concept of participation which sees it in the 'lower rung' terms of Arnstein, radical activists associated with a class analysis see the aim in far more ambitious terms: 'There is a fundamental difference of approach between our work, which is designed to build a participatory democracy, and the proposals in the Consultative Document, which seek to add another tier to a representative democracy,' the full-time worker for Telegraph Hill Neighbourhood Council asserted, 'Our business is one of participation, not representation.' Although such statements are somewhat polemical and contain terms such as 'participatory democracy' whose precise meaning remains elusive, it is possible to establish their general aim. First, a 'delegate system rather than a representative system' is favoured, and with it a priority given to mobilising around specific issue groups which will express the interests of the powerless and the deprived. One body which tried to put these principles into practice was the Angell Ward Neighbourhood Council in the London Borough of Lambeth. It set out to form 'street groups' to oppose the 1972 Conservative Housing Finance Act and to link these up with the Neighbourhood Council: 'The Neighbourhood Council should be seen as the body of collective action of the street and estate groups in the neighbourhood. These will be the democratic base . . .' (Angell, p. 12) The aim was to (p. 63):

> . . . produce a body entirely made up of delegates from effective and developing base groups, both tenants associations and street groups. In the long term there is no need for a set group of people to consider themselves members of the Neighbourhood Council. At each meeting some of the delegates can be different so that the focus of the work and policy of the Neighbourhood Council is not on individuals within it but on the body as a collective group of base groups in Angell Ward. This would cut down the amount of expertise gained by a limited number of people and be a flexible form of direct democracy.

This represents one of the clearest political statements associated with radical community activists, although the objectives expressed here and the rhetoric they contain should not necessarily be confused with the reality of what in practice occurred in Angell Ward. Whilst it generated considerable activity and impact, the neighbourhood council existed for only two years and depended heavily upon a small number of young radicals.

The distinction identified above has been between 'consensus' and 'class-based' views of neighbourhood councils, rather than the more usual 'consensus' and 'conflict'. This is because there is little if any evidence of neighbourhood councils pursuing a 'conflict' strategy, whereas there is a clear division within the movement between those liberals who argue for a consensus approach and those radicals who in the main see merit in neighbourhood councils as instruments of working class politics (see also Bell & Newby). Associated with this division is the issue of the style of action and of structure employed. Discussion of this issue of style is somewhat limited, but it surfaces periodically. For instance, the *Community Action* magazine (No. 7, p. 31) attributed the failure of the Golborne Neighbourhood Council in part to the problem posed by 'formal, essentially middle class structures of the neighbourhood council which have been imposed upon the predominantly working class community of Golborne.' The magazine suggested that these procedures discouraged involvement of indigenous working class residents and meant that they tended to associate the Neighbourhood Council with the local authority rather than the community. This view is echoed elsewhere amongst radical critics of neighbourhood councils. They stress the importance of *action, informality* and *loose* or *flexible* structures in order to involve working class residents who may lack the social confidence and articulateness of middle class individuals and who may resent the formal style of political organisation associated with them. That is not to suggest however that working class participants necessarily align themselves with the ideology of the radicals who claim to represent their interests. For example, in North Lambeth Neighbourhood Council, some of the radicals and the full-time community workers would have liked discussion at meetings to be more overtly ideological and political, whereas working class residents were more concerned with specifics such as demanding more resources for their estates or stopping vandalism. Similarly, in South Lambeth Neighbourhood Council, a typical working class sentiment would be: 'What is the use of talking about vandalism. That is a middle class occupation. Let's *do* something. We turn up at neighbourhood council meetings and our cars get vandalised outside!' In the latter neighbourhood council, it was significant that the most effective activity was mounted over a traffic scheme in a conservation area where many of the middle class activists lived; by contrast activity on problems affecting council tenants was less successful (see Cowley, pp. 178–83 and Ferris 1972 for a similar conflict in Barnsbury).

This ties in with the argument that neighbourhood councils could undermine community development processes which are aimed at enabling the deprived and inarticulate to gain the confidence to fight for their interests in the community. The London Borough of Islington, in its submission to the DoE drawn up by its 'Participation Officer', argued:

> If substantial ground work is not done first, Neighbourhood Councils could well become the preserve of the politically organised and/or the educated and articulate, at the continued expense of those without the experience or self-confidence to organise them-selves ... The existing inadequate resources being put into community development could be diverted into administrating Neighbourhood Councils which would be a talking shop, rather than a basis for stimulating action.

Those who argue in this way express a concept of 'participation as a style, not an entity or structure', and assert that 'neighbourhood consciousness will only come through issue-orientated action, leading to self-confidence and then to federating upwards into groups.' In other words any body that professes to be an umbrella body for different community groups must emerge out of local struggles coming naturally together and not set up 'artificially' without the necessary preparation and base support.

Under challenge here is the notion of an overall representative body, which was identified early in the chapter as being at the heart of the neighbourhood council concept. Instead, those associated with a radical or class view of community politics look towards campaigning based on interest groups. By contrast, the consensus or liberal view would see the essential value of neighbourhood councils as being to provide a forum that can bring together the different interests and establish a common view on behalf of the community as a whole. In its evidence to the DoE, the Civic Trust argues that neighbourhood councils are 'representative' bodies, distinct from special interest groups which are 'pressure groups' (that, as will be shown in chapter 5, was also the local Council's view over Covent Garden). Flowing from this is the principle 'that a neighbourhood council should represent individuals rather than *organisations*.' Hence the basic case for election by direct ballot, which is seen as providing a more representative body—a view disputed by those who adopt the community development approach; they argue that neighbourhood councils composed of representatives of local groups elected at annual general meetings can be just as representative and possibly even more so.

Conclusions

Although the material and evidence examined in this chapter is not sufficient to enable any firm conclusions to be drawn about neighbourhood councils or the nature of public participation, certain key issues have become clearer as the argument has unfolded. Certainly, a far more complex picture has emerged than could have been predicted from the writings surveyed in chapter one, and a number of serious question marks have been raised over both activist theories (whether of a liberal or a radical variety) and reflective theories. Whilst the experience of neighbourhood councils tends to confirm that they are partially a product of the factors identified in chapter one—for example: disenchantment with party politics—it is less clear what their function is. Indeed, there is little agreement about their purpose amongst activists, and there is a notable absence of any deep consideration of their role by reflective theorists.

So far as radical activists are concerned, they appear to have made only a fleeting impact upon the neighbourhood council movement. In the Angell Ward example, their ideas on participatory democracy were not put into practice for a sufficiently long period to enable them to be assessed; indeed, the very brevity of the radicals' attempts to introduce notions of direct democracy and the drama which dogged the experiment tends to underline the scepticism of those who question whether such a strategy is feasible in a social system where resources are not evenly distributed (Dearlove 1974). Nor was there evidence of a practical attempt of any consequence to challenge representative institutions: that is to say, a challenge which might either fundamentally threaten those institutions or become a viable alternative to them. Moreover, rhetoric about 'the people' erupting 'spontaneously' at the 'grass roots' had no validity. Whilst there is irrefutable evidence that those involved in neighbourhood councils were dissatisfied with conventional political methods, their dissatisfaction tended to express itself in the low-key politics of building a community consensus which is inimical to the radical view and which produced an emphasis upon social as opposed to political activity, and upon parochialism.

In addition, although it may be suggested that those liberal activists and liberal reflective theorists who see no conflict between participation and representative institutions can find support in the example of neighbourhood councils, their concepts, too, are flawed. So far as liberal activists are concerned, there is little evidence to suggest that neighbourhood councils do in fact open up the decision-making process to any significant degree when they follow the role advocated by the liberals. Nor is the level of participation which occurs higher than the lower rungs of Arnstein's ladder. The function envisaged for neighbourhood councils of being a focal point for community groups and different interests, does not in reality appear to be carried out and to that extent, their consensus fashioning objective is not successful. Moreover, there is a fairly important debate, not merely between liberals and radicals on the issue of statutory status, but within the liberal camp itself, suggesting that when it actually comes to the practicality of 'supplementing' representative democracy with participation, then severe tensions arise within the liberal perspective.

Of the reflective theorists, perhaps Rowe is found to be the most consistent in not avoiding the problem of power when he rules out anything more than 'partial' participation. He is also quite clear

(1975a, p. 922) about the wider purpose of participation in buttressing the representative system and hints at a link with the analysis in the next chapter:

> It is for the public authorities to accept that modern government needs to be actively supported by a participant population; that the problems are too complex, the professional and economic resources too scarce and the diversity of experience required too wide for any group of councillors and officials to be able to cope without tapping the skills and energies of the local population.

Generally, however, reflective theorists offer somewhat vague and rhetorical evaluations of neighbourhood councils which do not conform to the experience such as it has been touched upon in this chapter. In particular, a neglect of the problem of class and power by both liberal activists and reflective theorists is a fundamental short-coming; and it may be that the whole liberal conception of neighbour-hood councils negates the possibility of working class involvement.

Where radical and liberal activists and reflective theorists are jointly deficient is in their neglect of the role of government. As Humble and Talbot found, and as the general experience confirms, the relationship between the local authority and the neighbourhood council appeared to be the critical one. On the other hand, the material in the chapter poses more questions about this relationship than it answers. First, there does not seem to be any direct correspondence between the consensus view of the liberal activists, and the approval of the local authority. Second, there does not appear to be a single local authority conception of neighbourhood councils, their role in general or their relationship to government; this is clear from the different submissions to the Department of the Environment, for example. It is also the case that even when a local authority embarks on a programme of fostering neighbourhood councils, as in the Lambeth experience (Cockburn, Jackson), it may not be terribly sure itself about what exactly it has in mind. Lambeth's senior officers were generally hostile to their sponsored neighbourhood councils, yet its neighbourhood workers were actively sympathetic. Its Labour councillors were ambivalent, initiating the project and supporting the neighbourhood councils when the council's officers decided that they needed to be more directly controlled, yet also displaying some unease about the role of neighbourhood councils in their own wards. It is therefore necessary to clarify government thinking on neighbourhood councils to establish whether it displays a more coherent conception of the role than the activist and reflective theories which to varying degrees favour 'grass roots' participation, but which have serious shortcomings.

3

The Official Response: Sponsored Participation and Local-level Councils

... the significant feature of Western ideology is the outraged denial that mobilization is in fact the most important, the central, function of many political collectivities i.e. parties, interest groups, etc.... the idea of increasing pluralistic participation—which in most common usage is merely the active political principle of increasing differentiation—also becomes in part an ideological device to scatter and confine any desire or effort for radical social action. This is one way in which 'modern' society can be viewed. The differentiation of political functions, the increasing alienation of one function from another ... and finally the prescriptive grading of one function against another—these are the bastions of stability, of resistance to social change.

J.P. Nettl, *Political Mobilization* (Faber & Faber, 1967), p. 111, p. 114.

Through the previous two chapters ran the 'conventional wisdom' (Galbraith) that public participation is a process thrusting from the citizen below toward the decision-making system above and that, typically, neighbourhood councils depend 'on a bubbling-up of action from the bottom' (Richards, p. 180). And, although the analysis in these chapters has shown that in practice the participation process is more complex and that there are critical shortcomings in the conventional wisdom, we have not so far examined participation from the perspective of government. This omission has been deliberate, since the initial intention was critically to examine the perspective of both activist and reflective advocates of participation. Nevertheless it is clear from chapter two that the local authority in particular and government in general performs a crucial role in relation to neighbourhood councils. A rounded explanation of their role clearly requires the government dimension to be considered, not least because of the 'dialectical pattern' of the politics which, as we saw from the last chapter, neighbourhood councils epitomise—a politics where 'pressure from below for more protection or benefits meets pressure from above for better (more disciplined, or orderly, or sociable) behaviour.' (Walzer, p. 31).

How therefore does government conceive public participation, if indeed there is a uniform conception? What insights are offered into the practice as opposed to the theory of participation, and does the government perspective suggest a more useful basis for understanding and explaining its practice and outcome than has so far been suggested from the non-governmental arena? From the standpoint of the latter, participation benefits the citizen, at least through much greater consultation and at most through a fundamental redistribution of power. But participation may also benefit both government and dominant interests, and the purpose of this chapter is to begin to establish in what way it can do so.

The Mobilisation of Consent

In the first chapter the factors encouraging advocacy of participation from within the non-governmental arena were identified, at least insofar as they were expressed by participation advocates, assisting with an understanding of the latter's objectives. Similarly, an understanding of Government sponsorship of public participation is assisted by attempting to identify the main factors which have encouraged it.

First, like the participation advocates, the 'urban crisis' and dislocation caused by the rapid growth of industrial society, has been perhaps the most immediate factor behind Government promotion of participation (Calouste 1968, p. 9). If however the immediate cause was similar, the reaction to it and the resulting prescription for participation was markedly different. Typically for instance, there is evidence of its use to placate dissent and control unrest cited by the former Mayor of New York City, John Lindsay, in *The City*. Describing participation programmes during his period of office in the 1960s, he states (pp. 115–37) that they were proposed as a cure for the ungovernability of what he calls the 'top-down' system, and for the difficulties faced by the administration in securing the efficient delivery of services to those in need. He describes the events which led to this conclusion (pp. 92, 100): 'what we saw in early 1966 was that within the ghetto, discontent and alienation were at breaking point . . . Thus, throughout the fall of 1966 and into the spring of 1967 we made plans for a structured, formal link between neighbourhoods and the city.'

One of the ways in which this was done was to set up a community forum, which Lindsay points out (pp. 127–9) helped to end bickering and delay caused by remoteness of the administration from the populace, and was a good source of 'honest information about problems within communities.' Similarly, as the then leader of Wandsworth Council in South West London argued (Tilley, p. 90), local councillors in Britain have seen the advantages in community participation of creating better communication, whilst 'Community action is often seen as a way of saving the council money by getting residents to do for themselves what previously the council has done.'

A *second* factor was the problem of poverty in general and the position of black people in particular. For instance, an analysis of the American 'War on Poverty' programme, launched in 1964, highlighted (Rose, pp. 115–6) its overriding concern to:

> tackle the problem of the socially dangerous exclusion of the urban blacks. Excluded from both the economic and the political structure, their lack of social affiliation made them a continuous risk to the stability of the cities . . . The poverty programme was to be a means of incorporating the urban poor, and thereby take the heat out of the dangerous protest of ethnic and minority groups.

This was attempted, not merely through the traditional method of expanding welfare provision when the poor threatened social instability and unrest (Cloward & Piven 1971), but through publicly sponsored participation in the form of community action projects (Marris & Rein). One of the immediate results was indeed the 'co-option' of black leaders and pressure groups, which helped to neutralise dissent (Cloward & Piven 1969b, p. 169).

The first two factors were consequently a product of the political disorder rooted in protest over urban decay and poverty, especially amongst Blacks, although not simply in the USA. Participation was sponsored as a strategy to try to solve that problem of disorder by integrating dissident groups which, at least in the case of Blacks, had never been integrated. But the general dislocation afflicting advanced capitalist nations in the 1960s spread much wider and encouraged the breakdown of established patterns of political integration and social control of the working class in general and not simply of minority groups. This led to a *third* factor behind government sponsorship of public participation, manifested specifically in a British context: a concern at the decline in traditional working class politics (Hindess), and a desire to use participation as a method of providing a link to working class communities (Rose & Hanmer, p. 41). One Labour Party Committee Chairman of the Greater London Council went so far as to say at a GLC meeting on 28th May 1974, 'We will have military government in Britain in ten years time unless there is more participation.'

All three of the above factors are of course inter-linked, as is the *fourth*: a crisis of Western representative democracy. There are various interpretations of this crisis, and in referring to these I am concerned simply to arrive at a better understanding of the thinking they express, rather than to mount a critique of their validity. One of them views the crisis primarily in terms of a problem of 'ungovernability' evidenced by an inability to control inflation, widespread urban unrest and the 'U-turns' performed by successive post-War British governments elected upon programmes they then find they cannot implement (Open Group, King, Wright). Part of the solution to that crisis is seen as being to nurture pressure group participation to enable government to rally support for itself (Open Group, p. 7). A parallel analysis suggests that the whole tendency on the part of modern representative democracies is for them to adopt a system of politics based upon 'concertation', with the express purpose of countering what are termed 'centrifugal' forces which pull power away from governments. This politics of 'concertation' is defined as a process by which various socio-economic interests are systematically absorbed into the decision-making system (Ionescu). Indeed, the post-War evolution of what is variously described as a 'social services state' (Mannheim, p. 336) or an 'organisational state' (Myrdal, pp. 36–40) is said to have transformed the traditional liberal concept of government playing a long-stop role, into one where it is required to adopt an activist role in order to cultivate a consensus and mould the whole of society. Such direct Government intervention has in turn increased the influence of quasi-private organisations and interest groups, so increasing the necessity for organising participation through these groups. This is particularly evident in the rise of economic planning and the expansion of welfare services, both of which have been accompanied by the growth of producer and consumer groups which participate directly with Government in both policy-making and policy-implementation (Beer, Field). Viewed from the position of Government this participation has been interpreted as an exercise in the 'mobilisation of consent' (Beer, p. 421) which has indeed also been one of the principal functions historically of the system of representative government (Birch, pp. 119–20, Rokkan, p. 43).

Here we can distinguish a notion of participation at odds with those adopted by the participation advocates referred to in chapter one. Instead of emphasising re-distribution of power or influence to the citizen, this notion is concerned with mobilising support and legitimacy for Government. The concept of political mobilisation has indeed been described as 'a controlled form of participation' (Almond & Powell, p. 113, Nettl, Etzioni 1968, p. 389, Breed, pp. 140–1). Associated with this, we have Government sponsored participation analysed as a mechanism for 'social control' (Dearlove 1974, Cloward & Piven 1969a, Walzer, p. 27), as was implicit in the responses to the three key factors referred to above. An immediate motive for Government is that 'Participatory leadership reduces the visibility of control. It is a way to exercise such control . . . and at the same time to deny that such control exists' (Verba, p. 225). Participation can also provide the medium for the 'social training' seen as being necessary to achieve a stable consensus (Dahl, pp. 76–7). Hence, participation can be a method of 'co-opting' individuals (Haug & Sussman) or of 'encapsulating' organisations and social movements (Etzioni), by absorbing them into the prevailing social system. All of which suggests that Government may be encouraging participation 'as a substitute for a real distribution of resources. It may be that participation is the one limitless resource contemporary society is prepared to offer the "lower participant"' (Rose & Hanmer, p. 40).

Thus, we have begun to conceptualise different facets of Government participation initiatives—whether in terms of 'mobilisation', 'co-option', 'encapsulation', 'concertation' or 'social control'—and to suggest particular factors which have produced a requirement on the part of government to promote participation. What has not yet been touched upon, however, is *why* liberal democratic institutions have failed to generate sufficient consent and *why* such state intervention has been increasing so rapidly in the post-War era.

One historical explanation for these questions is suggested by Marxist writers (different explanations would of course be given by non-Marxists). First, they suggest that liberal democracy has historically failed to generate social consent during particular periods of economic crisis and that following the collapse of the relative 'boom' of the 1950s in Britain and the subsequent growth of inflation and unemployment, the British state has been faced with a particularly acute problem, requiring new methods for securing consent. Second, Marxists have always seen the capitalist state in terms of furthering dominant class interests and in maintaining ruling ideas in order to legitimate the social relations reinforcing capitalism. But the modern state is no longer confined to establishing general conditions for production as in the classical liberal model, and is instead actively engaged in production. This has occurred because the market economy has—especially over the last two decades—proved unable to sustain itself and has required the state to intervene and ensure that capital continues to accumulate on a profitable basis. The state thus has to secure political and social 'legitimacy' for that direct intervention (Habermas), so that the state's function becomes the dual (and often contradictory) one of creating and maintaining conditions favourable to the profitable accumulation of capital whilst simultaneously creating and maintaining conditions for social harmony (O'Connor). The result is to encourage a process of 'legitimation' in which the state's overriding objective is to secure the acquiescence of the 'subordinate' or 'intermediary' class for the existing order (Miliband, p. 178).

The latter function is well illustrated in the role of the welfare state which as Gough argues 'increasingly controls the level, distribution and pattern of consumption in contemporary capitalist society' (p. 46). Historically, rather than diluting capitalism, it has served its interests, especially in terms of a mechanism for incorporating the working class (pp. 55–74). Its decisive role is reflected in the massive growth of the cost of social services in Britain expressed as a share of Gross National Product: from 4% in 1910 to 29% in 1975, with a particularly large jump after 1961 (p. 76). Moreover, to the extent that welfare expansionism can be interpreted as part of the *quid pro quo* offered by the state in return for cooperation from the trade unions, the welfare state becomes part of 'a mechanism for co-opting the more powerful labour movements in advanced capitalism within the state structure' (pp. 146–7).

The evolution of modern capitalism has consequently required the system of representative democracy to be supplemented. One result has been the promotion of a form of 'dependent participation' (Touraine, pp. 9–14)—a specific example of which was President de

Gaulle's offer of a 'participation proposal' in response to the French governmental crisis following the Paris 'revolt' of May 1968; no redistribution of power or resources was offered by de Gaulle, but rather what was described as 'essentially corporatist participation' (Cohen, S., pp. 253–5).

In the first section of this chapter, the intention has been threefold. First, to suggest that government encouragement of participation posits quite different notions of participation to the ones generally assumed to be advocated in the first two chapters. Second, to emphasise that these notions correspond clearly to the lower rungs of Arnstein's ladder; thereby implying also a more accurate characterisation of the practical *experience* of neighbourhood councils (as opposed to what may have been *idealised objectives*) than was supplied by the participation advocates. And third, to suggest the benefits to government and dominant interests of sponsored participation. The result has been to raise some important themes to bear in mind when examining the official promotion of local level councils.

Government Sponsored Participation in Britain

However, before analysing the question of local-level councils, it is necessary to underline that they must be seen against the background of a more general support for greater participation on the part of the authorities in Britain. In this section, therefore, the major government initiatives will be surveyed and it will be seen that they broadly reflect the themes identified in the previous section of this chapter as being at the heart of the government's sponsorship of public participation. It should be emphasised however that it is not contended that one of these themes—government's desire to control and regulate groups and citizens—is anything new, for it has of course been a major function of the state historically (Hill, M., pp. 16–44, Donajgrodzki). Welfare provision, especially, has been a means of exerting social control since the Poor Law of 1598 (Katznelson & Kesselman, pp. 429–57). The specifically *new* dimension is the sheer scale and depth of these initiatives.

The first major area of post-War Government intervention came in the field of social welfare. Prompted by evidence that the welfare state had not succeeded in eradicating poverty and that many of its services were not reaching the poor, the Government sought to improve monitoring of conditions at the local level. This was reflected in the Seebohm Committee on the social services which reported in 1968.

Its support for increased public participation sprang from a specific desire to improve the delivery of services to deprived groups in particular (paras. 491–5, Rein 1972). This would be achieved in part by the involvement of what the Report called 'consumers' of social services, in local council committees (para. 628). The desirability of advisory bodies to area offices of social services departments was also stressed (para. 506), 'Such bodies would function as a forum for the discussion of local community needs and services and would include in their membership local councillors and other people from the areas, including direct consumers of the services and the volunteers.' The concept of participation offered by Seebohm was in terms of an extension of the arm of government, and the closest the Report came to suggesting that the interests of social services departments and the community may well conflict was when it conceded (para. 494), '. . . the participants may wish to pursue policies directly at variance with the ideas of the local authorities and there is certainly a difficult link to be forged between the concepts of popular participation and traditional representative democracy.'

Such a link was attempted through the twelve 'Community Development Projects' launched by the Home Office in 1969 as part of its Urban Aid Programme. The CDPs, the Government announced, would be '. . . a neighbourhood-based experiment aimed at finding new ways of meeting the needs of people living in areas of high social deprivation: by bringing together the work of all the Social Services under the leadership of a special project team, and also by tapping resources of self-help and mutual help which may exist among the people in the neighbourhood.'

Each project would last 5 years, and contained an action team in the field and a research team based at a nearby university or polytechnic. The action team's major objective was to 'seek to involve people living in the area in community schemes flowing from their own perceptions of need, and translated into action with their participation'. Moreover the action team would attempt to improve the accessibility of local authority services to local people. Control of the projects was exercised through the local authority and they were initiated upon the assumption that they could assist government with the task of finding policies more responsive to the needs of the poor, especially in deprived inner city areas (Young, T. 1974). Another assumption was poverty could be tackled by improving the delivery of services and increasing the ability of the poor to take full advantage of those services—an assumption later rejected by the project workers in their joint progress report published in 1974, when they argued that poverty could only be effectively combated by a national re-distribution of wealth and income (National CDP). As the CDPs neared the end of their five year periods, a major division opened up between the objectives of the Home Office and the project workers. The latter argued that the CDPs represented a token attempt by Government to respond to the urban crisis and to placate dissent. Similar criticisms were of course made about the American Government's 'War on Poverty', launched in 1964, and its emphasis on local citizen involvement has been characterised as a 'sociotherapeutic view of participation' (Miller & Rein, p. 8).

Of particular note is the CDP workers' critique of the project's use of the concept of community as a 'focus for mobilising informal social control mechanisms' (*Gilding the Ghetto*, p. 46). They were an attempt at 'more aggressive problem solving' without vastly increased expenditure or diversion of resources (p. 42). In general, the CDP workers argue that 'the "deprivation initiatives" were not about eradicating poverty at all, but about managing poor people' (p. 63, Heraud, p. 94).

If poverty was a major factor in the central initiatives of this period, so too was race. The Urban Aid Programme was launched in Britain in 1968, principally in response to the deteriorating climate of race relations, and made provision for funds to be channelled through local government to community projects (Demuth, Read, Edwards & Batley, McKay & Cox, pp. 234–48). In 1965 the Home Office (Cmnd. 2739, para. 62) had emphasised the positive role that 'voluntary liaison committees' could play in assimilating immigrants, and the Race Relations Act 1968 established a national community relations council and enabled it to fund local bodies concerned to improve race relations (see Barker). Once more, local citizen involvement was stressed, and local community associations were seen as means of regulating conflict and providing access to the government structure (Hill & Issacharoff, pp. 280–1, 284, Rex, Rex & Moore, p. 284).

Meanwhile the Ministry of Housing and Local Government introduced a scheme in 1968 for renovating housing in deprived areas by designating them 'General Improvement Areas' and enabling local residents to obtain grants for re-habilitation purposes. It was stressed that the co-operation and agreement of local residents was essential, and local authorities were urged to 'be tireless in explaining their proposals, and in gaining the confidence and approval of those whom they affect' (1968, para. 54). This was further developed in a Government circular which urged the formation of residents' associations (1969, para. 23).

The Government was clearly anxious to secure local legitimacy for these housing initatives, as was also the case for town and country planning which will however be considered in the next section.

But if poverty, race, housing and planning saw perhaps the major focus of Government concern to foster citizen participation, the range of initiatives has been even wider. In 1974 provision was made for establishing Community Health Councils to increase the responsiveness of the health services (Klein & Lewis, Leighton). In addition the Housing Rents and Subsidies Act 1975 enabled town halls to delegate management powers and cash subsidies to tenant cooperatives. This support for tenant participation was explained by one commentator: 'Apart from any missionary zeal about participation, pressure for cooperatives may grow if, as seems likely, town halls find it increasingly difficult to provide adequate maintenance at sufficient speed' (Hillman). Another critic questioned the very basis of the participation on offer: 'Tenants "consultation" and tenant "participation" are so obviously designed as a means of manipulating tenants in the interests of housing management . . . They are the shadow, rather than the substance, of tenant control, and the tenants themselves, knowing that real power lies elsewhere, are not fooled' (Colin Ward, p. 75).

As the mood tor participation spread in the early 1970s, the Government saw an increasing need to respond to it. In 1972 a committee convened by the Department of the Environment suggested in its report that there had 'been a massive upsurge in pressure group activity across the whole front of Government' and urged the Government to support pressure groups by means of finance and access to information (DoE (3), pp. 54–5). A similar argument was advanced by an independent report on voluntary organisations under the chairmanship of Lord Wolfenden.

This was taken a step further by backing groups set up to perform a 'watchdog' role. The National Consumer Council was established in 1975 to represent the interests of consumers, rather in the way it was perceived the TUC and CBI represented the interests of workers and employers (Dept. of Prices, Christmas, Toynbee). In short, Government initiated and funded an organisation intended to put pressure upon Government. The same kind of principle applied in the public service industries; for instance, when the Post Office was granted public corporation status in 1969, the Act facilitating this also initiated the Post Office Users National Council. And, on 20th November 1975, the Prime Minister, Harold Wilson, advocated local 'rates-watching' committees, comprising representatives of the community, to scrutinise council spending programmes: 'They could be the start of a new partnership between electors and elected. If successful, they could give added force to unpopular decisions and, perhaps, lead to less violent changes in policy when political control of an authority changes hands.' Athough nothing tangible came from it, the importance of this speech was that it underlined official thinking at a time when the extensive reorganisation of local government had encouraged public controversy over alleged local authority waste and inefficiency.

The examples referred to so far have for the most part been in the field of Government social policy. In 1977, however, official encouragement for participation was extended into industry with the publication of the Report of the Bullock Committee. In the years preceding this there had been a growing consensus on the desirability of workers' participation, accentuated by British membership of the European Economic Community which brought with it an obligation to establish industrial democracy. The key proposal of the Bullock Report was for the election by the workforce of 'worker directors' to the boards of companies. For our purposes the main interest of the Report lies in the arguments it advanced to justify workers' participation, since they throw further light on official attitudes. Echoing a sentiment which figures in Government encouragement of neighbourhood councils, Bullock argued (p. 20): 'As companies have grown in size and complexity, they have also tended to become remote from the communities in which they operate and from the people whom they employ.' The Report pointed to the post-War end of 'the deferential society' and the resulting demand for a greater say in the decision-making process. It suggested (p. 22) that participation would make for greater efficiency because workers would be more directly involved in the company and would thereby have a greater stake in and commitment to it (see also Pateman, pp. 107–8). This view was reinforced by the argument of the Commission of the European Communities that in the long term a failure to involve employees was likely to be more damaging than delays or inconvenience caused by the time-consuming process of participation (p. 9). Thus a strong argument in the Report was that industrial democracy would help to create greater legitimacy for management decisions (pp. 48–51). So far as worker directors are concerned, this view has been supported by a study of conventional company boards which showed that, while the ability of the board to influence policy was limited by management, it was important as a legitimating institution (Pahl & Winkler, p. 110):

> To be sure, the final Yea or Nay, at a board meeting may be seen as the decision point, and may so appear in corporate histories . . . But the board actions we observed are better interpreted, we feel, merely as ratifications of decisions made earlier and elsewhere, sometimes by much more junior men, about which the board had no practical alternative. The distinction between 'making' and 'taking' decisions is relevant. Boards of directors are, we feel, best conceived as decision-taking institutions, rather than as decision-making ones.

It is clear then that government sponsorship of participation has been undertaken not only to mobilise consent but has had other functions as well. These include the necessity for better information; for more efficient implementation of policies and delivery of services; and for improving the system of public administration so that it is technically more sensitive and efficient. In addition it would appear that the concept of mobilising *consent* needs to be broken down into two parts in order to define it more carefully: first, securing acquiescence and support for particular policies or programmes (e.g. improving the housing stock) and, second, securing acceptance for the overall *system* of legitimacy and authority relations.

The Concept of the 'Forum'

One particular feature of the more generalised government sponsorship of participation reviewed above has been repeated references to setting up local 'forums' which could represent neighbourhood feelings and provide a mechanism through which government could relate to those feelings. In the concept of the forum one can clearly distinguish the genesis of the idea of a local representative body along the lines of the neighbourhood council first given official endorsement by the government in 1974.

In 1967, a Ministry of Housing and Local Government report suggested the setting up, with local authority approval and support, of a 'Council of Social Service' in each locality, to bring together different voluntary groups and to act as 'a forum for discussion and a basis for common action' (para. 200). Similarly, as we saw, the Seebohm Report in 1968 advocated the setting up of advisory bodies to the area offices of social service departments which could act as a 'forum' for discussion.

Inherent in both these proposals is the notion of obtaining a *coherent* view of the overall needs of the community from the various 'single-issue' groups operating in the voluntary field, each seeking to bring about more effective social services. Underlying the forum notion were two assumptions: that their function would be essentially *advisory* and that a quasi-*formal* arena was desirable to promote what would otherwise be a series of disconnected contacts with individual welfare groups.

These assumptions were evident in the Skeffington Report on *People and Planning*, published in 1969. One of its key proposals was for a 'community forum'. The forum would bring together different sectional interests 'for corporate discussions so that there might be a cross-fertilisation of ideas and a wider realisation of the problems of an area as a whole, and of the differing needs for which an authority must cater' (para. 60). Although the forum was proposed in the spirit of promoting a more comprehensive form of participation than can be generated by single-issue groups, it was also seen in terms of *educating* the community on the difficulties faced by local authorities. This is a recurring theme in central attitudes to neighbourhood institutions. Significantly, Skeffington saw it as more administratively efficient to operate through the forum, rather than to seek the views of scattered community groups or individuals (para. 66). Exhibited in the Report are the twin desires apparent in all the central initiatives in this area: on the one hand, the desire to promote greater involvement by the general public for almost altruistic reasons: on the other, the recognition that it is far easier to deal with a concrete institution such as a community forum or neighbourhood council than a disparate and often aggressive series of pressure groups.

It is however important to acknowledge that Skeffington's proposals did not arise 'spontaneously' but were a product of the particular problems faced in implementing plans during the previous decade, and the solution to which was partly seen in proposals for local participatory institutions. By the mid-1960s it had become clear that the administrative process created under the 1947 Town and Country Planning Act was grinding to a halt. Various factors were involved, including tension between the cities and the counties; and the lengthy process of registering objections to development plans, of holding inquiries and then unburdening a mass of detail onto the central administration for approval. The Planning Advisory Group, officially set up to examine these problems reported in 1965 and argued that there was a need for the planning authorities to promote public participation expressly in order to secure greater legitimacy for planning—'public acceptance and support' had actively to be rallied (pp. 53–4). The 1968 Town and Country Planning Act therefore proposed a two-tier system: 'structure plans' allowing for wholesale redevelopment which would have to be approved by the Minister; and 'local plans' within these structure plans. The 1968 Act also included proposals for public participation, stressing the need to publicise plans, and the Skeffington Committee was set up to consider in more detail schemes for communicating with and involving the public.

By the time Skeffington reported there were already signs of what Eversley describes as the 'revolt' against comprehensive redevelopment (pp. 165–9). The radical transformation of communities caused by such redevelopment, coupled with lack of consultation of local people, helped to put planners on the defensive for possibly the first time in the post-War era. There thus began what Rein (1969) describes as the planners' 'search for legitimacy'. Means had to be found to counter the 'revolt' and facilitate the orderly progress of plans. Skeffington's proposal seemed to provide a good basis on which to proceed, although it was far from enthusiastically received. Criticisms ranged from the view that it would cause inefficiency, to the radical view that it ignored the maldistribution of resources in society which orthodox planning would simply accentuate (Guthrie, Participation Swindle, Damer & Hague). Especially significant is the point that Skeffington in no way undermined the responsibility of local government, it being stipulated that councils still had 'the final decision about the content of the plan' (para. 25). This notion of participation was underlined by the Department of the Environment in 1972, in a Circular which stressed public involvement as a means of explaining and therefore ratifying plans.

Nevertheless, even such 'pseudo participation' created problems for the authorities. Extensive soundings amongst local people and pressure groups tended to lead to what Eversley describes (p. 202) as 'maximum feasible inaction', where the planner is caught in the middle of a crossfire of conflicting views and interests. Some means had to be found of involving the public in a way that would enable a coherent view to be distilled from a particular community. Hence—as we shall see in later chapters on Covent Garden—the notion of a formally constituted forum. In it community representatives could be encouraged to hammer out a *common* reaction to planning proposals, to substitute, in Rousseauesque fashion, a 'community interest' for their narrow interests.

Local Government Development and Reform

Although the wider sponsorship of participation formed the background against which neighbourhood-level councils were proposed in the 1960s and 1970s, there was a confluence at that time with developments from the local government arena.

Historically, the ideal of local self-government has been a recurring theme in the writings on local government and, moreover, there are historical parallels to the current proposals for neighbourhood councils. In fact, the ideal of the self-governing community 'stretches back to antiquity' in the English tradition (Dilys Hill, p. 47). The concern to establish institutions that would involve local people in the government of their communities surfaces continually in the literature on local government and also in official government statements and legislation. Recent initiatives are consequently seated within a well-defined strand of liberal-democratic thought and practice.

However, this does not mean that local self-government was traditionally promoted for altruistic or democratic reasons. In practice, it was established because it was structurally necessary both for the dispensing of public services and for the private sector. The establishment of a coherent structure of local government in the nineteenth century was thus encouraged primarily on the grounds that it would be administratively *convenient* for the central authorities (Dilys Hill, pp. 15–9). This is the first characteristic which can be identified in central government attitudes to local councils. A second characteristic is the notion that local authorities could be useful agents for *political education*, a notion at the heart of John Stuart Mill's advocacy of democratic local government.

Broadly speaking, Mill's ideas on political education were interpreted in two ways by local government advocates. Ioan Bowen Rees provides a useful division of these advocates into the 'romantic' and the 'classical' schools (pp. 2–3). The romantic school sees the state as a federation of localities, each of which, as it were, surrender part of their authority to the centre but retain some authority of their own. Furthermore the romantics see local authorities as 'nurseries of democratic citizenship' in a framework that stresses power and influence as springing from the local community upwards (p. 2). Thus, the 'romantics' have clear affinities with modern radicals and even many liberals who advocate public participation, as we saw in the first two chapters. By contrast, the 'classical school' views local authorities as appendages to central administration, with citizens as consumers of services rather than participants. The classical school has been generally co-existent with the standpoint of the central authorities who have viewed the notion of political education as a method for helping to ensure democratic stability and order: the more people were educated to appreciate the issues of the day, the better they would be able to appreciate the reasons behind local government policy. Thus, local authorities can be viewed as convenient means by which local people are *mobilised* by the state. As Bulpitt puts it (p. 300), 'local government can be regarded as a method by which the state overcomes the inherent divisions in society. It can bind the individual to the state by involving him in the process of administration at local level, so fostering a sense of national community and duty to the state.'

Furthermore, Dearlove (1979, pp. 233–4) emphasises the importance of situating analysis of local government's evolution within a political economy perspective:

> When local government was democratised it was clearly designed to provide a vehicle for popular participation in government, but at a level where the then range of functions was neither particularly extensive nor such as to touch on issues of redistribution which might adversely affect the propertied classes who provided the finance. Local self-government was to socialise and mobilise the population at large into broad acceptance of the emerging political economy that was to lie beyond popular control.

It can be seen, then, that while the idea of the self-governing community has been important in the history of local government, it has been used to strengthen the standpoint of central government, in much the same way as has public participation in recent times.

Such a conclusion is reinforced by noting the way in which local government has evolved since the last century. The twin themes of nineteenth century reforms were participation and efficiency. On the one hand, there was a desire to promote bodies which would be responsive to local wishes, on the other the overriding concern for the efficient administration of services. Because local government was originally set up for administrative convenience, the efficiency thrust always did have the upper hand, and this became even more so with the evolution of modern mass society in the twentieth century. Such a trend is reflected in the changing pattern of democratic thought in local government in the twentieth century, in its concern with administration rather than ideas of self-government; indeed, when efficiency is deemed incompatible with participation, then the state has been quite prepared to jettison participation, especially if it appeared to be strengthening unduly working class influence (Dilys Hill, pp. 46–75, Dearlove 1979, pp. 250–1).

However some reformers remained concerned to retain local participation as an integral element of local government, for example G.D.H. Cole (1921). And the manner in which they sought to reconcile this with the centralising pulls of efficiency in the modern industrial state helped to provide the setting for contemporary debate and legislation. Cole proposed both larger *and* smaller authorities, at what he called the 'regional' and 'neighbourhood' levels (1947). The regional level would facilitate the Fabians' emphasis on technical efficiency in such spheres as public health, education and generation of electricity. Locally, Cole proposed 'neighbourhood local author- ities' which bear some similarity to contemporary proposals for neighbourhood councils, except that they would have rather more *duties* in terms of providing services. This thinking is echoed today by liberal and reflective advocates of more local participation, such as Hampton (1970, p. 301), who argues: '. . . no local authority area large enough to be efficacious can be small enough to encourage citizen participation . . . There must be two sets of institutions: one concerned with devising and controlling policy; and the other involving people in local community affairs . . . the system . . . would consist not of two tiers sharing the functions of local government but of a single tier supported by a network of community organisation.' Neighbourhood councils, he argued, would be included in these organisations.

The 1972–74 reorganisation of local government into bigger units, coupled with proposals for neighbourhood-level councils, is consequently consistent with the evolution of the local self-government ideal and the simultaneous attempt to secure efficiency. That in turn, as Dearlove (1979) shows, was an attempt to lessen working class control and influence over local government—as well as providing a mechanism for integrating local participation into the official structure (see also Markusen).

Throughout the period 1958–1974 local government was continually reviewed. The period culminated in a reorganisation of the whole machinery of local government that was more fundamental than anything since the creation of county councils in 1888 and parish and district councils in 1894. Redcliffe-Maud and Wood reflect the orthodox view of the reforms in suggesting five broad reasons behind this reorganisation:

1. smallness—causing inability to provide services at the required standard
2. geography—boundaries were out of date causing confusion
3. complexity—there were no fewer than nine different types of elected local authority
4. apathy—there was little sign of public enthusiasm for local government
5. subordination—central government exercised too much control through directives and funding

These explanations reflected the state's rationale for the reforms as well, but they conceal anxieties about working class pressure to which local government as traditionally constituted had become particularly vulnerable. Thus, as Dearlove (1979, p. 245) shows, 'the essential object of reorganisation has been to make local government more functional for dominant interests, by restructuring it so as to facilitate their direct control of its expenditure and interventions.' That is to say, the overriding purpose was to bind it more closely to the national state and dominant class interests, cutting its scale and expenditure and re-directing its scope towards supporting the private sector. We may note that the evolving system of structure planning required local authorities big enough to perform the strategic role necessary for large-scale infrastructure provision (Hall, pp. 172–85). An additional factor arose from the 'imperatives of modern business and investment decisions which encourage centralisation of power' (Dilys Hill, p. 199). The debate over local government reform during this period culminated in the 1972 Local Government Act which established a 'two-tier' system of county and district councils.

The 1972 Act, and the general thrust of the reformist literature which preceded it, was a product of the orthodoxy that bigger authorities were necessary for technical efficiency in the administration of services and in planning. But it was also conceded that these larger authorities would increase the gap between the governors and the governed which was a source of concern to the state. Consequently, local institutions beneath the two-tier system were to be fostered to act as voices of community opinion and as counter-weights to the tendency to centralisation under the reformed structure. This dual thinking was of course identified earlier as a principal characteristic of the tradition of democratic thought on local government. It was however up-dated by several newer trends in local government giving cause for concern about its ability to generate local involvement and commitment.

First there are echoes of the old worry about the remoteness of large authorities, albeit more urgent in temper. The Committee on the Management of Local Government (the Maud Report) reported in 1967 on 'an indefinable gulf between local authorities and the communities which they serve' and on widespread 'alienation' of citizens from the local authority (pp. 94, 92), an issue also referred to later by other official reports (see Dearlove 1979, pp. 236–7). As an analysis (Scottish Council of Social Service, para. 6) of the establishing of statutory 'community councils' in Scotland argues: 'The community council has been created, in part, to offset the remoteness of the new local government system. It is seen as a means of preserving and developing the community's voice and a way of enabling meaningful participation in local affairs in the face of an increasingly distant and complex administrative structure.' As this view implies, the problem of remoteness is concerned not simply with *distance* but with *complexity*. Thus it is further argued that the complexity created by greater centralisation requires local units of expertise, advice and influence that individuals can turn to in their bewilderment (Rees, I. B., pp. 85–6). The tension between complexity and participation has been further sharpened by recent reforms in the internal structures of local authorities—reforms which proposed the introduction of new managerial techniques and systems of 'corporate planning'. Both the Maud Report on the management of local government in 1967 and the Bains Report on the internal structure of local authorities in 1972 have encouraged a tendency to pose problems in terms of managerial efficiency rather than in terms of mobilising democratic consent. As will be seen later, neighbourhood councils have been advocated by central government, partly on the grounds that they could help to maintain contact between the public and local councillors increasingly sucked into a managerial role within the new local authorities. Meanwhile it is important to stress the potential conflict between methods of management efficiency and participation.

We can see then how the drive towards bigger authorities is entirely compatible with the encouragement of neighbourhood-level councils. Before moving on to examine in detail the contemporary attitudes of the central authorities on this question, it is worth underlining the argument with two further points. First, as Dilys Hill argues (p. 199), localised units are necessary in the reformed system for what amounts to technocratic reasons: 'Centralisation does not mean, however, the end of local government. On the contrary, local units become more important, since they must carry out the services which governments determine. As government departments become more overburdened, then pressure to decentralise to field agencies, or devolve more functions to local authorities, increases.' It should be clear, however, that this inbuilt need for a measure of complementary decentralisation does not involve a transfer of *power*; indeed, to the extent that reorganisation reinforced dominant class interests so it reinforced the existing distribution of power. Second, in sponsoring local institutions, central government (as we saw earlier) can create 'all over the country potential allies for itself who were, even if only parochially, championing more general community interests against all the more narrowly drawn sectional ones' (Open Group, p. 7).

In short, local participation was officially encouraged to try to counteract what Dearlove (1979, p. 237) describes as 'the crisis of local representative democracy itself.'

Local Councils

Thus it was that the Royal Commission on Local Government in England (the Redcliffe-Maud Report) proposed in 1969 a system based on unitary authorities, except in three 'metropolitan areas' which, much like London, would have a two-tier structure. But the

Commission also stated (para. 282): 'We always recognised that units of the size appropriate for the operation of services must be underpinned and complemented by other representative bodies to express the interests and sense of identity of the more local communities.' To fulfil this, it proposed a series of what it called 'local councils'. These would be based to some extent on the rural parish councils originally established in 1894. The Commission argued that they would be unnecessary in the two-tier system of the metropolitan areas, although did not preclude them from being set up should this be desired by the local community. The principal functions of the local councils would be in the form of a *duty* to represent the wishes of its constituents. But they would be set up on a statutory basis and would have 'concurrent powers' alongside those possessed by the local authorities. The main authority would also be obliged to consult the local council before taking a decision which would particularly affect its area. Essentially, then, the Redcliffe-Maud Report saw local councils as *complementing* the main authorities, to bridge the gap to the larger, more remote authorities.

Redcliffe-Maud's general attitude towards neighbourhood-level councils was adopted by the Government White Paper which preceded the 1972 Act and the subsequent re-organisation of local government. The White Paper conceded that there was a clear conflict between the drive for greater efficiency inherent in its proposals for a two-tier system of larger authorities throughout the country, and the desire for local control. But this nod in the direction of localised democracy amounted to very little in concrete terms: 'The Government obviously must seek efficiency, but where the arguments are evenly balanced their judgement will be given in favour of responsibility being exercised at the more local level' (DoE (2), para 13). Towards this rather nebulous end, the White Paper gave encouragement to existing parish councils outside the metropolitan counties it envisaged: 'The general character of parishes should remain unchanged; they should remain bodies with powers rather than duties and as much part of the social as the governmental scene' (para. 39). In short, proposals for a 'third tier' of local government were modelled very much on the traditional function of rural parish councils which have tended to act as organs of local feeling, seeking consultation on decisions affecting their constituents but not involved in the dispensing of services.

In the metropolitan districts or town areas outside the metropolitan counties, the White Paper, like the Redcliffe-Maud Report, discouraged an extension of the parish council concept. It assumed that the district level of local authorities in metropolitan or town areas could cope quite adequately with the desire to reflect local feelings; therefore, there was no need for statutory bodies constituting a third-tier in urban areas. The only concession to an additional body at the very local level of urban areas came in the form of an encouragement of non-statutory bodies: '. . . the views and wishes of neighbourhoods, or small communities within larger built-up areas, might preferably be represented by non-statutory bodies; district authorities should have powers to assist such bodies financially and in other ways' (para. 40). It was not specified what these 'other ways' would be and the impression given in the White Paper is that this statement was simply tacked onto the end of a justification for not extending parish councils into city areas; its implications were not systematically considered.

The thinking behind the White Paper was carried through virtually un-amended into the 1972 Local Government Act. The Act effectively came into force on 1st April 1974. Its effect as regards local-level councils in England can be summarised as follows:

a. parish councils existing on 1st April 1974 continued to exist
b. rural borough councils existing on 31st March 1974 became parish councils on 1st April and
c. Borough and Urban Districts existing before 1st April became parishes with councils if before that date the Secretary of State on the recommendation of the English Local Government Commission had so ordered.

Although such councils continue to be discouraged in metropolitan areas, the Act does give the Boundary Commission the right to propose the creation of new parishes and new parish councils. This could in theory be applied to metropolitan or town areas, although to do so on any extensive scale would take many decades—which is why such bodies as the Association for Neighbourhood Councils wish to see a separate Act setting up neighbourhood councils in urban areas. Under the 1972 Act, the functions of the third-tier councils are much the same as for traditional parish councils. They would have responsibility for public clocks, footpaths, bus shelters, allotments, cemeteries, etc., and they would also have the right to be consulted over all planning matters directly affecting their areas.

Welsh Community Councils

A similar concept has been instituted in Wales, except that the term 'community councils' has been employed. Besides flowing from the thinking applied to England under the 1972 Act, the community councils concept arose from a stream of thought apparent in the 1967 White Paper on Local Government in Wales. It argued that rural parish councils 'provide the highest degree of local representativeness' and recognised the need for what it termed 'common councils' in areas other than those where rural parish councils have traditionally existed. In urban areas, such councils could be set up if local opinion favoured this, with the same powers as a council for a rural parish (Welsh Office 1967, paras. 23–4). The scene was consequently set for the later Welsh legislation which gave far more scope for neighbourhood-level councils in *urban* areas than did the English legislation.

During the 1971-72 reorganisation, a consultative document was issued expressing the desire to create 'community councils' in rural parishes and, if local residents wish it, in urban areas (Welsh Office 1971). The document called for a special review to set up these community councils only after the new system of counties and districts had been established. This was done and, in December 1973, a circular was issued detailing proposals for community councils in Wales (Welsh Office 1973). Following the pattern of the English proposals, they were based on revamped and reorganised parishes and had almost identical functions. Elections for these community councils were held in 1974 and it is clear that they are a direct extension of the old local government idea of parish institutions.

Scottish Community Councils

With parish councils having ceased to be a unit of local government under the 1929 Local Government (Scotland) Act, special consideration was needed to meet requirements for more local forms of democracy under the general reorganisation of local government. 'Community councils' was the term chosen (see Prophet) and it evolved from the (Wheatley) Royal Commission on Local Government in Scotland which reported in late 1969. Wheatley, in turn, appears to have derived the term from evidence given to the Commission by the Border Burghs Convention and the Ninth District Council of Lanark who both argued that a two-tier system would be too distant for Scottish electors used to being represented by small burghs.

Wheatley wished to create bodies which were neither merely voluntary nor too rigid and official, aspiring to 'a broadly-based unit, with an official standing, to which the local community as a whole can give allegiance and through which it can speak and act' (para. 848). The Commission emphasised the importance of community councils being organs of the community rather than officialdom, showing more concern over this than can be distinguished in the various White Papers and reports already referred to covering England and Wales. Such an emphasis led it to argue against any statutory functions being given to community councils: 'their purpose would be to complement local government, not to compete with it' (para. 585). However, Wheatley also stated that community councils 'would in no sense be a tier of local government' (para. 718). Obviously, the desire to 'complement' local government can contradict the desire not to act merely as an extra tier of the conventional structure. Yet this key dilemma is not satisfactorily resolved in the Wheatley Report—nor in the other official initiatives examined above.

The basic principles enunciated by Wheatley were adopted in the 1971 Scottish Office White Paper on local government. Community councils would not have any statutory functions, nor would they act as agencies to administer regional or district services. The thinking behind the White Paper was implemented in the 1973 Scottish Local Government Act, and each local authority required to submit schemes for establishing community councils by 1976. Community councils would therefore be initiated by the district and island councils and would be financed by them. The Act defined the purpose of community councils as being: 'to ascertain, co-ordinate and express to the local authorities for its area, and to public authorities, the views of the community which it represents, in relation to matters for which these authorities are responsible, and to take such action in the interests of that community as appears to be expedient and practicable.' This applies to urban areas as well, so there is full scope under the Scottish Act for the kind of neighbourhood councils proposed by the Association for Neighbourhood Councils, except that finance would be dependent on a local authority grant rather than an automatic precept on the rates.

The grant system has led to the criticism (Clarke, Pinkerton) that it will be used as a means of 'controlling' community councils, and the potential certainly exists for local authorities to regulate the style and level of activity of community councils, if only because the *size* of the grant will help to determine the scope and character of their role. Then there are the important issues raised by the district and island councils taking the initiative in setting up community councils. Although the 1974 Scottish Development Department guide to community councils emphasises that they should not be a 'third-tier' and also stresses that the legislation is flexible so as to meet local requirements, analysts of the Scottish scheme have pointed to the danger 'that district councils may favour organisational structures in their own image. Such an approach would smother grass-roots participation . . .' (Clarke, p. 2, Pinkerton, White & Clarke). Implicit in this criticism is an issue which goes to the heart of the problem surrounding central government encouragement of participatory institutions: the problem of reconciling initiatives from above with a desire to promote participation from below—a problem illustrated by the subsequent experience of Scottish community councils.

Precursors to Neighbourhood Councils

Before considering the official promotion of neighbourhood councils and comparing this with the initiatives from the non-governmental arena discussed in chapter two, it is instructive to review historical examples of councils at the neighbourhood level, since there are numerous parallels with the modern concept. The most obvious precursor—and, indeed, the one frequently cited in support of establishing neighbourhood councils in urban areas of England—is the parish council. Parish councils originally developed from the 'parish assembly' which served as a means of regulating local affairs largely in rural areas. In their classic history of the parish, Sidney and Beatrice Webb show how it developed into an organ of local self-government with limited influence and a certain amount of duties. Significantly, they show that, by the early nineteenth century, 'whatever may have been its origin, the parish was . . . in no sense an autonomous and independent entity, but merely the base of a more or less elaborate hierarchy of government' (pp. 5–6). This was especially true in terms of the duties it undertook and indicates how an independent institution can gradually become absorbed into an evolving national structure of government. Moreover, although the vestries were in theory open to all, they were usually occupied by men of status or wealth. It would be very wrong to romanticise about the extent of 'direct democracy' in the parish.

During the nineteenth century, the parish appears to have gone into retreat as reformers concentrated on strengthening the role of local authorities legally and administratively. However, in the last quarter of the century there was renewed interest in reviving the old parish assembly and this led to the passing of the Parish Councils Act of 1894. It provided for elected parish councils in rural areas of England and Wales. Much of the Parliamentary debate over the Act has affinities with modern concerns about the desirability of allowing for the expression of local opinion against a background of higher-level councils geared to administrative efficiency. Introducing the first reading of the Parish Councils Bill in 1893, the Government's spokesman stated: 'The parish is an ancient institution influenced by local sentiment and invested with local interest . . . It is the oldest aggregation in this country of men for the purpose of self-government and local administration . . .'

However the 1894 Act recognised that an elected council is not necessarily appropriate for very small hamlets and the 1933 Local Government Act stipulated that a parish with over 300 people must have a parish council, one of between 200 and 300 may establish one if it so desired, and one of below 200 only if the county council agreed. Parish councils do not *have* to perform particular duties or take specific action, but if they decide to do so then, like local authorities, they must act *intra vires*. They can assume powers over such matters as allotments, footpaths, shelters, clocks, war memorials and open spaces. In 1963 parish councils were enabled for the first time to spend a limited amount of money (they were entitled to the produce of a fifth of a penny rate) on any matter in the interests of the community.

For the most part parish councils behave as what amounts to 'institutionalised pressure groups' (Rose, p. 7), adopting a consensus model of change that does not seek to confront local authorities but rather to lobby and negotiate within the recognised procedures and channels. After the Second World War, parish councils experienced a new lease of life (Arnold-Baker, pp. 217–8, Morton, Cox, pp. 209–13), although the Redcliffe-Maud Report found that there were great differences in the levels of activity across the country (Vol. III, pp. 165–96).

It should also be noted that, during the mid-to-late nineteenth century, there were other attempts to establish movements for self-governing communities. The 'settlement movement' in Victorian times has some affinities with modern community action (Davis, Leat), and support for the concept of 'neighbourhood guilds' derived from ideas remarkably similar to those behind the neighbourhood council movement today (S. Coit). From the standpoint of modern neighbourhood councils, it is significant that the settlements 'lost their way' partly because of their *consensus* approach to social welfare (Richies), so disappointing those involved who held high hopes for their impact, just as modern day activists have been optimistic about the potential of community action. It is equally of interest to note the role played by pressure groups in early Victorian England, between the two Reform Acts of 1832 and 1867. They became 'a mechanism for co-opting working men into the main stream of mid-Victorian liberal politics; and for softening what could have been sharp and severe tension left behind by both Chartism and the League' (Hollis, p. 22).

In Glasgow a series of 'Ward Committees' were set up in the 1870s; at the time of the reorganisation of Scottish local government in 1973–4, 33 of the 37 wards in Glasgow still had such committees. They were elected annually by a public meeting which each elector in the ward was entitled to attend, and they were partly financed by a grant from the Glasgow Council. The role of these Ward Committees, as described in 1896 (Bell & Paton, p. 67), is analogous to the role today envisaged for neighbourhood or community councils: 'The ward committees consist of men who take a lively interest in their own district, discharge also, for the present, the useful function of drawing the attention of the council to the wants and aspirations of their locality, to the sights and neglects under which it suffers patiently, and its demands for a fair share of such good things as it is in the power of the Council to distribute.' In 1912 a Ward Committee secretary wrote: 'I believe . . . that the inhabitants of each locality should be able to express their wants and impress them upon the central governing body' (Pinkerton, p. 40). With some judicious updating of the style of language, much the same sentiments are found behind contemporary moves setting up community councils in Glasgow and other parts of Scotland. The similarity of thought is underlined by the fact that a Glasgow citizen in 1887 submitted to Glasgow's Town Clerk a draft bill for 'legalising' Ward Committees; although it proved unsuccessful it was aimed at providing for similar forums throughout Scotland. Significantly, these Ward Committees did not appear to have made any contribution in altering the distribution of power and resources in Glasgow. They did not achieve high rates of participation and, like parish councils, it is hard to see what substantive influence they have had beyond perhaps a marginal improvement of local amenities.

Government Backing for Neighbourhood Councils

In summary, then, the reorganisation of local government in the 1970s gave sustenance to the idea of neighbourhood-level councils which in any case had close affinities with parish councils and other historical examples of local representative bodies. With party attitudes ranging from enthusiasm on the part of Labour and Liberals to only mild opposition on the part of the Tories, a political climate began to emerge favourable to statutory neighbourhood councils being set up in urban areas. When Labour took office in March 1974, the Government soon expressed the intention of encouraging neighbourhood councils. The Minister of Planning and Local Government, John Silkin, sent a message to the annual conference of the Association for Neighbourhood Councils: 'With the re-organisation of Local Government into larger units it is becoming more important than ever to find the best way of enabling the people of individual areas of our large towns and cities to express a community point of view and influence more effectively the decisions made on their behalf by the main operational local authorities.'

Two months later, Mr. Silkin said in a speech that the Government was considering the best way to support the cause of neighbourhood councils (DoE (7)). He was at pains to state that the neighbourhood council should be 'an organisation of co-operative help, not an organ of government'. This would distinguish them from the existing levels of elected government: they would be 'grass roots' bodies. However, he also stressed that they should have a good relationship with the local authorities so that the two could work together constructively and complement each other. Part of this constructive relationship would involve the neighbourhood council playing a 'watchdog' role, alerting the local authority to the need for action or vociferously warning it when it started to go wrong. But Mr. Silkin's speech displayed an ambivalence that runs to a greater or lesser extent throughout all central initiatives on neighbourhood councils: on the one hand, a genuine desire to encourage local participation; on the other, an anxiety that it should 'constructively' complement the work of existing local authorities. Whether it can fulfil both these functions simultaneously is questionable.

In July 1974 the thinking behind Mr. Silkin's speech was presented more systematically when the Department of the Environment issued a Consultative Document, *Neighbourhood Councils in England*, in which the intention was stated to introduce legislation allowing for neighbourhood councils to be set up in urban areas denied a third tier of local government under the 1972 Act.

It is clear from the Consultative Document that part of the impetus toward neighbourhood councils springs from the administrative and technical load placed on councillors after the recent streamlining of local government along managerial lines referred to above. Neighbourhood councils are seen as mechanisms by which the councillor can be better kept in touch with the wishes of the community (pp. 1–2). Rather in the way that 'local councils' were seen as compensating for the remoteness of the large authorities established by the 1972 Act, so the Document sees neighbourhood councils as compensating for the gap likely to open up between the councillor and his constituents due to his absorption into the general management of the council. This aspect of the Document's argument has been emphasised because it is indicative of the general attitude of government towards neighbourhood councils; but it should also be pointed out that there is good reason to believe that part of the reason for including it was to placate the likely hostility of many local authorities to the basic proposals of the Document.

According to the Document, the Government is 'favourably inclined' towards statutory recognition of Neighbourhood Councils. But it would not wish to 'impose' them on urban areas regardless of need and local wishes. It suggests a series of basic characteristics of such statutory bodies, including that they should be: formally elected and 'responsive' to their electorate; have consultation rights; some limited finance; and be on good terms with local councillors.

The 1974–79 Labour Government did not in fact introduce any legislation implementing the proposals of the Consultative Document, contenting itself with an extensive consultation exercise on the issue. But its 1977 white paper on the future of the inner cities referred to the role of neighbourhood councils in 'representing the community's views and mobilising voluntary effort' (DoE (6), para. 35), and a Department of the Environment Circular suggested them as an option for local authorities to encourage (DoE (1), para. 24).

Official Attitudes

It is clear then that official thinking on local-level councils (whether these be community councils, neighbourhood councils, parish councils or simply the local councils of Redcliffe-Maud) contains the following elements:

1. the *tradition* of local government—recent initiatives are clearly seated within a long tradition, part of which emphasised the ideal of the self-governing community, even though this ideal tended always to take a back seat to the obective of efficient administration which, it was believed, required larger local authorities

2. the *convenience* of local institutions serving as a focus for community involvement—within the local government tradition, it was seen as politically convenient to offset more remote authorities with bodies closer to the public

3. such councils or forums are seen as means of *regulating* conflicting interests—this is highlighted by the experience of planning, but in a broader context community forums provide a quasi-formal setting in which large demands by activist groups can be set against demands from other sections of the community and also placed within the restricted financial framework within which local government works

4. the *mobilisation* of interest groups in the community to take part in the decision-making process, thereby gaining:

5. *legitimacy* for policies which, though marginally modified by public involvement, nevertheless remain substantially as originally proposed by the authorities (see Bulpitt, pp. 290–1)

6. *consultation*—the concept of participation propagated amounts to an extensive process of consultation that can fit easily into the system of representative democracy; it stresses an *advisory* role for local forums and also sees them as means of *communicating* with the public

7. the *education* of the public to appreciate better technicalities of policy decisions and financial and other constraints within which they have to be made—the educative effect of localised involvement has been a continuing thread in the tradition of democratic thought in local government and is especially evident today in the participation programmes of planners. This was well illustrated by an advertisement by the London

Borough of Hammersmith for a 'Public Participation Officer', the job description for which emphasised a requirement to 'work closely with the Council's Press Relations and Information Officer' and emphasised the advantages of a background, not in community action, but 'in education, public relations or, possibly, advertising' (*New Society*, 16th January 1975, p. 156)

8.   linked with the educational aspect is the desire that community involvement should be *constructive*—that it should look constantly to how the council's policies might be improved or made more sensitive, rather than challenging the basic assumptions that generate these policies

9.   thus neighbourhood forums should *complement* the existing system of local government, filling in the gap between the bureaucracy and the public so that government does not lose touch with opinion in the community—even though the central attitudes examined emphasise that neighbourhood forums should be independent, it is difficult to see how the situation can be avoided where, rightly or wrongly, they will be perceived by the public to be a 'third tier' of local government. Moreover, it is apparent that official sponsorship of local-level councils has most emphatically not been in order to create an alternative to representative democracy. As has been shown of analogous groups called 'social planning councils' in the USA, their role 'is to reinforce representative processes in political decision-making . . . they have considerable appeal, if properly organised, for plugging people and groups into this representative process.' (Cohen, A., pp. 31, 32)

This chapter has also endorsed the finding in the previous chapter that neighbourhood councils cannot be considered in isolation from the official structure of local government, and the elements identified in official thinking clearly point to concepts of participation described in the first section of the chapter but which differ sharply from those radical and even liberal aspirations for participation considered to be at the heart of neighbourhood councils. Indeed, the official concepts, to the extent that they correspond to the lower-rung levels of Arnstein's ladder, might apply rather better to non-governmental initiatives as well, in terms of the consequences of these intitiatives as opposed to their *intentions*. It is partly with this in mind, that the experience of Covent Garden will now be analysed.

Part Two

THE CASE OF COVENT GARDEN

4

The Origins of the Covent Garden Forum

When public officials speak of decentralisation, they usually have in mind administrative delegation, or the internal allocation of authority to lower echelons within the governmental system. When neighbourhood activists, on the other hand, employ the term they invariably refer to the transfer of power to locality residents.
Henry J. Schmandt, 'Municipal Decentralization: An Overview', *Public Administration Review*, vol. 32, special issue (October 1972), p. 573.

Covent Garden is commonly regarded as a unique oasis in the middle of an encroaching concrete desert, an area of immense diversity which escaped the massive tide of redevelopment of the 1960s and early 1970s. It is at the heart of London's centre, about 100 acres bounded on the north by Shaftesbury Avenue and High Holborn, to the south by the Strand, to the east and west by Kingsway and Charing Cross Road.

Although popularly known as London's theatreland and the home of the Royal Opera House, it has also been an important focus for publishing and printing. There are a large number of traditional crafts and shops in the area, several hospitals and, of course, there was until 1974 the Market. This flower, fruit and vegetable market had been the main focus for the life of the area since the 18th century, and it was the decision to move the market out of Covent Garden that opened up the possibility of large-scale redevelopment of the area. That decision was finally made in 1964 after various official committees had deliberated on the matter for some 50 years.

A less well-known feature of Covent Garden is its relatively large residential community of about 3000 people jumbled together in tenement blocks, rooftop flats, apartments and a sprinkling of terraced houses. The core of the residents is a tightly-knit, indigenous working class community. An estimate by Anson in 1972 of these 'true Covent Garden people' put their number at 1500. This traditional community, dominated by a number of large families going back generations in the area, was most vulnerable to the wholesale redevelopment envisaged after the market had moved. And it was their fight for survival that played a key role in the community politics of Covent Garden in the 1970s.

Although the GLC only has *strategic* planning powers for the whole of London over such matters as employment, transportation and communications, the London Government Act of 1963 made the GLC the *local* planning authority for the Covent Garden area. When the Covent Garden Market Authority decided that the market should move, the GLC saw the 15 acres of land released by the market as an opportunity to reconstruct, not just these 15 acres, but the whole of Covent Garden. In the middle of 1965 the GLC formed a 'Consortium' together with the City of Westminster and the London Borough of Camden (the two Boroughs which had Covent Garden straddling a common boundary), to secure the comprehensive development of the area.

A planning team was set up in 1966 with a local office on the borders of the area and in November 1968 a draft plan was published in a glossy booklet entitled *Covent Garden's Moving*. The plan was very much a product of the times—the high noon of large scale development planning which, only a few years later, had lost credibility and become unfashionable. The scope of the plan was breathtaking: it plucked out the heart of Covent Garden and bounded it by 3-lane sunken motorways to the north and south. Its financial base was a series of office blocks, hotels and an international conference centre. There was also provision for new housing (more in fact than was subsequently included in the plan drawn up in consultation with the community) and the planning team's leader later claimed that the early impetus of the GLC was to 'control' private capital 'whose lips were drooling' at the scope for redevelopment. But, although the GLC maintained that care had been taken to 'integrate new development, including large-scale projects, while still retaining and extending the small-scale intimacy and local variety which are important and valued elements in the existing local character' (p. 7) critics argued that the plan effectively destroyed that very character. A *Sunday Times* reporter likened it to 'the most concentrated onslaught of change which has been inflicted on any area of London since the Great Fire.'

Despite this, the GLC could claim with justification that the plan had been favourably received. Adulatory press reports appeared and at an exhibition of the plan organised by the GLC in November 1968, about 1500 individual comments and suggestions submitted by members of the public were overwhelmingly in support of the scheme. However it emerged three years later that only 18 of these visitors' comments had come from people who had given a local address. Of their comments, most were completely opposed to the plan, one of them stating: 'I am happy to see that even the present plans will only mature at such a distant date that I shall likely be dead' (Pembroke, p. 92). Inherent here are the seeds of what was in the next few years to become the basic conflict in Covent Garden: between local residents determined to defend their traditional way of life and the GLC equally determined to commercially revitalise the area. This conflict sprang initially from three sources: the failure of the GLC to effectively consult the public; the grand, messiah-like vision which spurred on the GLC planners; and the influence of private developers. A re-considered version of the plan (*Covent Garden: the next step*) was published in May 1971, several months before the Public Inquiry statutorily required for a Comprehensive Development Area.

The Plan and the Public

Although the draft plan had announced the intention of holding 'exploratory meetings with potential developers and existing owners', there was no mention of consulting local residents or the public in general. And, in the three years between the publication of the draft plan and the Public Inquiry no real attempt was made to allow the public to participate in drawing up the final plan. Indeed, the then Chairman of the GLC Committee on Covent Garden wrote confidentially in August 1970 to one of his Team Officers warning about the dangers of consulting local pressure groups: 'I find that these pressure groups lead to a lot more trouble than they are worth. By this I don't mean that one does not want to have as full as possible consultation. I think, therefore, we should back-pedal on this idea.' The letter came into the hands of local residents and reinforced local feeling which saw the GLC as having an intractable stance towards the local community.

It should however be appreciated that the GLC plan was conceived at a time when widespread public participation and agitation on planning issues had not yet really begun. This environmental consciousness only reached a crescendo in the early 1970s (Kimber & Richardson) and the GLC's approach to planning merely reflected the prevailing climate. The *Skeffington Report* advocating greater participation in planning had not yet been published and it would be fair to say that the Planning Team acted less out of a desire to wilfully ignore local feelings than from a standpoint of the planning consensus at the time. It was their misfortune to be caught at a time when the public's reaction to planning was in the middle of an abrupt change: the Covent Garden planners were in their own words trapped as 'the meat in the sandwich', and the Team Leader at the time maintains that the question of public consultation did not receive any priority because 'the local community didn't have a community group we could talk to' at that stage.

Nevertheless, their own conception of their role as planners was one which remained aloof from public consultation. The presentation and character of the plan suggested connotations of Davies' *Evangelistic Bureaucrat* (p. 120): 'The sense of embattlement, of being executors of great power and the carriers of fearful responsibilities: the invocation of the future and the elaboration of the need to off-hand the critics by *knowing* that the planners are right even (especially?) when everyone else says that they are wrong.' *Architectural Design* in July 1971 stated of the Covent Garden planners: 'All were men of goodwill: all were fired with enthusiasm of the most starry-eyed kind ... To read their report today is to be shocked by its naivety. It is the architect's dream of a totally planned environment.'

The third element in the conflict equation was the crucial fact that the scope of the plan required extensive co-operation from private developers if such objectives as were contained in the plan to halt the declining residential population were to be met. The whole financial base of the plan rested on private developers and, as has been a feature of such joint local authority–private developer schemes, it was the developers who set the pace and determined the essential thrust of the plan. Whatever the personal intentions of the Planning Team, their plan became a developers' plan. Aside from the fact that a developers' plan was inevitably going to be one geared to profit rather than to the interests of the indigenous community, the need to rely so heavily on private development determined from the outset a *style* of planning that was antithetical to public participation. A dissident planner on the GLC Team made this clear when he stated (Counter Information Services, p. 60–1. See also Monahan, p. 177 and Elkin, p. 158): 'All our time was being spent on working out implementable procedures for a scheme that had not even been discussed at a single public meeting. No resident groups were formed, no small business associations, no artistic groups. Our files were overflowing with records of meetings with the largest developers around, none of whom had any direct interest in the area except for the smell of profit.'

The influence which the GLC was required to concede to developers is also evident in the dissolution of the Consortium of the three local authorities in 1970 when the GLC assumed primary responsibility for Covent Garden under the aegis of a new Covent Garden Development Committee (later renamed Covent Garden Committee). Grounds for this move were given by the GLC at a meeting on 24th February 1970: 'It is essential to give the private sector the assurance that it will be dealing with one authoritative body capable of a consistent line of policy and able to take speedy decisions, normally without reference to or ratification by, other bodies.'

The Covent Garden Community

Most community studies dwell on the problems of defining that elusive concept, 'the community', and there is the often quoted reference (Hillery) to sociologists finding ninety-four different definitions of 'community'. In Covent Garden this is not merely a matter of academic tidiness for the area consists of not one community, but a whole series of what may be termed 'mini-communities'. These can be regarded as a series of sectional or interest groups which comprise the wider Covent Garden community, where community is used here primarily in a political sense to denote the manner in which such groups relate to each other and come to common arrangements to regulate the life of the area (see Kotler, pp. 8–9, Bell & Held, p. 167, Wolfe).

The two principal groups, which are then sub-divided, are the 3000 people who live in the area and the 33000 workers who commute daily in and out of the area. The local residents are divided in two ways. First by length of residence: in the early 1970s the area was still predominantly populated by those who had been in the neighbourhood for over 25 years, although a quarter had been resident for under two years, showing a combination of a traditional immobile (and largely working class) sector and a new highly mobile (largely young middle class) sector. Second, residents are almost wholly divided into local authority tenants (28%) and private landlord or Peabody Trust tenants (70%).

The distinctive flavour of the area is also provided by a tremendous variety of shops, businesses and offices. There is a strong link between residents and workers through the fact that one third of those residents in paid employment work locally. Although it would be a mistake to romanticise on the extent of community self-identification held by those who work and live in the area, it is undeniable that it does generate an unusually high sense of commitment. Thus a member of the Forum who had come to work in the area from America could remark: 'The exciting thing about Covent Garden is that it is not just a residents' community. It is the only place I have ever been where the working population identifies with the community. There is a sense of community involvement here that I have never seen anywhere else.'

The rather special characteristics of the community were well described by a member of the GLC Covent Garden Team:

> There is not one community—there are many: different residential ones, different working ones. There are even some people who are indifferent here, mostly old private tenants who never talk to anyone.
>
> But the important thing is that this multiplicity of different strands has been moulded into one rope. The rope is what people call 'the community'. The appealing aspect of Covent Garden is that people could accept quite happily that they lived on the same earth—they conceded sufficient to those around them to ease themselves into the cramped space available. There is nothing of the aggressive tension in the area that one finds clouding day-to-day personal relationships in other city centre areas.
>
> It is a coherent place, but one based on *friction* rather than what is popularly understood by *conflict*. The essence of the community springs from an excitement of constant uncertainty where the uncertainty is not threatening in the way, for example, that it is in Soho. It had a great deal of stability as a sub-system.

It should be clear, then, that one can speak in a real sense of Covent Garden being a cohesive community, albeit a cohesiveness founded on constant friction and great complexity. Both this cohesiveness and its complexity were important factors in the struggle against the GLC plan. Before describing this struggle, however, one further ingredient in the attempt to understand the neighbourhood is important. There appears to be a strong self-help tradition within the indigenous community of the area, illustrated by Sam Driscoll, an important figure in the community protest, who lived all his life in Covent Garden and whose family roots in the area went back generations:

In the old days there was a real sense of community in Covent
Garden. The spirit of the people in these poor areas was tremendous.
Everyone looked after each other. Things were done for you by
friends and relatives which the social services do today! We have
gone backwards by breaking up communities. Ordinary people
around here have always stood on their own two feet. They loathe
to use the social services because it is charity. And, even though it
was an upright sort of living community, it was never 'copper-
bound', you would never run to the police.

Although many of the old residents were too scared, tired or
disinterested to join the community protest, this tradition of self-
reliance encouraged local people like Sam Driscoll to involve
themselves in the community politics of the area in a way they had not
ever done before.

Covent Garden Community Association

It may seem surprising that there was no real mobilisation of local
opposition to the plan until early 1971—over two years after the draft
plan had been widely publicised. But there were three reasons for this.
First, the environmental consciousness and community action that
appeared in the 1970s was only in its infancy. Second, as has been
shown, the GLC made no real effort to inform or involve the local
community. Third it is evident that the sheer scope of the plan simply
was not comprehended by local people. As one resident put it: 'I had
actually been aware of the plan after it was published but, like so many
others, I did not think at the time that it could be so monstrous. I didn't
look at it all that carefully.' Another resident said: 'There was a lot of
talk about things happening. But there was nothing definite: just
rumours flying about. Only late in 1970 did we realise it was for real.'
This local public ignorance of the plan was compounded by the fact
that, in a sense, the market had always been going to move. Way back
in 1886, one of Queen Victoria's Ministers apparently stated: 'It is
quite evident that the time cannot be far distant when some fresh
arrangements will have to be made to enable the people of London to
buy their fruit and vegetables without the loss of time, the inconvenience and the danger which at present exists.' The planned removal of
the market in the 1970s was just not believed: after all, its removal had
been talked about for decades.

However, in the summer of 1970, a number of different strands
began to come together to constitute the origins of the formation of the

Covent Garden Community Association (CGCA).

Brian Anson, then a planner on the GLC Covent Garden Team, was becoming uneasy about the implications of the same plan he had himself helped to draw up in some four years of work on the Team. Gradually he began to sound out feeling in the area. It was a letter to a local priest which he wrote expressing 'grave misgivings' about the plan that in turn caused the Chairman of the GLC Covent Garden Committee to write his letter instructing the Team to 'back pedal' on public participation. Anson pressed ahead despite this and arranged a get-together with several local residents in a local pub in October 1970. His defiance of official GLC policy led to an increasing estrangement from his employers until he was finally forced to leave the planning team in February 1971. The publicity this received produced the first major sign that all was not well in Covent Garden, that there was indeed strong antagonism to the GLC plan. Anson became a martyr for the cause at the right time: hungry as always for a 'personality' angle, the media seized on his position and from that time onwards the community movement opposed to the plan enjoyed widespread press coverage.

Anson's departure, then, provided that crucial element of human interest and sympathy that is so often required to launch a campaign in a public way. His was the first 'external' input into the local situation which galvanised the community to rise up against the plan. The second external input came from a group of young architectural students who were working on a nearby project as part of their course at the Architectural Association. One of these students, Jim Monahan, was to play a leading role in the agitation against the plan. Monahan met Anson in January 1971 at a meeting of the Greater London Arts Association where members of the GLC Team had been asked to explain the plan. He was 'furious at the way the planners so arrogantly and ignorantly pontificated about the area.' And from this straight-forward reaction of emotional outrage, Monahan developed a strong commitment to an area he did not live in and knew little about. Anson acted as the intermediary to put Monahan in touch with the local people he had himself already contacted and it was decided to call a public meeting to inform local people about the gravity of the situation.

It is important at this stage of the analysis to emphasise two characteristics of these early times in the battle for Covent Garden. First, as was a characteristic of the neighbourhood councils described

in chapter two, the initiative did *not* come from local people. It came
from a professional and a trainee professional: Anson who provided
most of the information and expertise about the plan and Monahan
who provided most of the activism and dynamism. Second, the early
organisers themselves lacked experience of community action: 'Nobody had a clue what was going to happen. We were all feeling our
way,' said one. 'I got caught up in it all. This is true of many people,'
said another.

Practical tasks rather than theoretical speculation dominated time
and energy as the necessary flyposting and leafletting took place to
publicise the first meeting called for 1st April. To their surprise, the
meeting was packed out with 500 people. The vicar of St. Martins in
the Fields, Austen Williams, a well-respected local figure (who was
also chaplain to the Queen) had been recruited to chair the meeting. It
was a rousing success and a group was convened under the title the
'Covent Garden Community' (later to become the 'Covent Garden
Community Association' when it was formally established with a
constitution in the autumn of 1971). A working group was proposed to
report to a further public meeting and volunteers were called for.

In the aftermath of the meeting there was still no considered
analysis of the CGCA's strategy beyond an urgent need to alert the
whole community to the dangers it faced and to confront the GLC
with the weight of local and environmental opinion. The absence of
deep reflection on the principles of community organising was
probably unavoidable. The activists were simply buried underneath
their sudden new workload: 'There was so much to do—leafletting,
flyposting, fundraising, dealing with enquiries—that things just became
chaotic,' recalled one of the organisers.

The group set up by the public meeting was loose and decentralised,
with the minimum of formality ('A better description for it might be
"mad",' said one activist). Each member of the group 'picked up' the
ability to organise community action as they went along. Jim
Monahan, for example, found himself 'becoming press spokesman
because I was on the end of the phone in the group's office.' It was the
ability of Monahan in particular and the CGCA in general to generate
publicity and thereby keep public attention on their cause that had
much to do with the early momentum of the campaign. Monahan had
intuitively the rare knack of being able to express provocatively and
concisely the demands of the CGCA in language which journalists
could use.

Meanwhile, a solid relationship had been established between the external activists and a small group from the indigenous community, with the expertise of each complementing the other. One working class resident involved at the time says: 'Jim Monahan and his fellow "intellectuals" were very important. He worked very hard and he would push you through the sound barrier too! We couldn't have done it in the early stages without them. They had contacts we never had and they knew how to use the media.' At the same time of course, these (working class) 'locals' provided the (radical) 'externals' with their much-needed point of access into the community they were seeking to save. Working collectively they tried to set up a network of 'street representatives' to form the roots of the community organisation and to involve the maximum possible number of people. This street network did help to activate the area although residents involved at the time warn that its viability and influence should not be exaggerated.

Although the CGCA suffered two central weaknesses at this stage in its failure either to organise effective tenants' associations in the large tenement blocks inhabited by the indigenous community, or to actively involve local trade unionists, it must however be stressed that the pressure of events and the sheer weight of work discouraged attempts to look beyond the next meeting or the next protest. By early June—two months after the action had begun in earnest—there was a considerable awareness of the plan in the area. A measure of the CGCA's success was in forcing the GLC to hurriedly bring out its own information sheets. These had 'every appearance of a reluctant and last-minute response to the widely reported anxieties voiced at the (April 1st) meeting' (Pembroke, p. 92). The CGCA had also been extremely effective in focusing national public attention on the threat to Covent Garden. If the plan were to be stopped it would mean winning over the formal political powers that lay outside the vicinity of Covent Garden. Through presenting a picture of a beleaguered community to a national audience which identified with the area for cultural reasons, the CGCA was able to mobilise national forces that rarely intervene so explicitly on behalf of community struggles. There is no doubt that the imaginative and somewhat irreverent campaigning style of the CGCA achieved a greater impact than could have been achieved by more conventional means of lobbying which could easily have been ignored.

With the opposition to the plan well off the ground attention now turned to consolidating the movement and, in particular, to the Public

Inquiry looming over the horizon. The CGCA's early campaigning had helped to create a snowball effect whereby all manner of objections were being registered for the Inquiry. Local businesses due to be demolished under the plan raised their own objections and so did conservationists. A more 'respectable' lobby with a liberal perspective began to line up alongside the CGCA, with John Wood, Managing Director of Rules Restaurant (the oldest restaurant in London) leading a concerted attempt to influence 'top' people. Rules was due for demolition and a petition was organised to save it. Many people in public life eat at Rules and Wood was able to exploit these contacts and obtain support in what might be regarded as 'establishment' circles: 'The GLC really underestimated us,' he maintains. The controversy over Rules and, therefore, over the plan even reached America as Wood did press interviews with foreign journalists.

For the purposes of this analysis it is not necessary to examine in any depth the proceedings of the Inquiry which took place from 7th July to 16th September 1971. There were 114 objections to the plan, the CGCA briefing its own barrister and solicitor who offered their services for considerably reduced fees, and presenting its case over a period of ten days.

The Inquiry became unwittingly a focus for opposition to the plan. First, it demonstrated the seriousness and strength of the opposition and it is clear that the GLC were somewhat taken aback by this. Second, it left a legacy of bitterness that was to poison relationships between the community and the planning Team. Although the Team's claim that they gave a leeway to the objections that would not normally be tolerated under public inquiry procedure is factually correct, it can be argued that they had little alternative given the strength of feeling locally. Moreover, the GLC's counsel did mount the kind of cross-examination that is usually humiliating to lay people. 'Those lawyers can talk the hindlegs off a donkey,' said one local resident (see also Davies, p. 159). The GLC's counsel also sought to undermine the credibility of the CGCA through questioning its 'representativeness'. Much play was made of the fact that the organisation had no formal constitution, illustrating the classic clash between the bureaucracy and a loosely constituted semi-spontaneous community group: 'Jesus Christ never had a bloody constitution—he just had his disciples,' said one resident. In short, the Inquiry strengthened the atmosphere of conflict between the GLC and the community.

It also brought home to the activists a problem which was to dog them throughout the campaign and remained an important factor in the community politics of the area: the problem of expertise. Aside from Brian Anson who, as an architect of the original plan, was well-equipped to take on his former colleagues, the CGCA lacked the means to combat the battery of lawyers and experts lined up by the GLC. Moreover, the essential case of the CGCA was founded on a *general* philosophy of what was desirable for Covent Garden. Yet, as a *Sunday Times* analysis stated on 14th January 1973:

> ... the only objections that the inspector would entertain were specific complaints about, say, the exact line of a proposed road—not general questioning of the need for the road at all, or even deeper debating of the GLC's traffic philosophy for the area. Even the objectors who did not fly so high concentrated upon the simple fact that they vastly preferred Covent Garden as it was—a valid point, but outside the inspector's frame of reference.

Thus the community was caught in a cleft stick: it could not present the general or moral case against the plan because that would be ruled out of consideration by the inspector: and nor could it confront the GLC's experts on their own terms and win (a general problem: see Haug & Sussman, Piven, Rein 1969, Ward, S.). The sense of inadequacy over expertise felt by many people in the area contributed to a move towards a neighbourhood council (called the Covent Garden Forum) which might be able to marshall the necessary expertise in face-to-face argument with the planners (although, as is clear from the experience of the Forum, the expertise problem was not solved but re-appeared in a different context).

Strategy and Tactics of the CGCA

After the Inquiry, those who had been to the fore of the activity were thoroughly exhausted and a sense of calm returned temporarily to the area as members of the CGCA recuperated. Something of a political vacuum was created which lasted throughout the period until the Department of the Environment's decision on the inspector's report in January 1973. In late 1971 and throughout 1972 the CGCA tended to turn in on itself and internal political and organisational tensions surfaced. These tensions provide a useful point of entry into an analysis of the changing strategy and tactics of the CGCA, how its role unfolded over time and the external pressures on it. For the

Forum of Representatives had in part its origins in the attempt to resolve the tensions afflicting the CGCA during this period of 'limbo' between the Inquiry and the Minister's decision.

However, it is first necessary to clarify the role and nature of the CGCA. It has always aspired to being a 'community action' group. This suggests a series of connotations which include a strong participatory and self-help ethic together with a commitment to direct action. It also suggests an ideological commitment to a radical notion of community self-management (Barr, Bryant 1972). This concept of community action can be contrasted with what we shall call 'community campaigning' where the main thrust is to generate a sense of community self-awareness, and therefore a threat to the authorities, by an imaginative style of protest and sometimes militant action. While rooted firmly within the community and based on maximum participation of local residents, it is essentially a 'reactive' protest group rather than one geared to a long term goal of community control or community development.

Although the rhetoric of the CGCA gave the impression of a community action group, it was during the first year of its existence a community campaigning group. This is not a matter of semantics since community campaigning groups are ideally suited to reacting to a threat using protest tactics, but are rarely equipped to sustain a long-term programme of community mobilisation. Thus it was that the CGCA was well able to spark off the opposition to the plan but ran into problems when faced with the need to mount a far less dramatic, incremental programme of grass roots involvement. Furthermore, a group based on frenetic action can be highly effective with a specific target to aim at such as the Inquiry, but lack of a clear theoretical perspective can cause problems when the time for reflection sets in and no such clear target is on the horizon.

A split began to appear in the CGCA between those who wanted to adopt a strategy based on 'conflict' and those who wanted one based on 'consensus' (Smith & Anderson). Behind this lay what was essentially a *political* difference between those radicals like Jim Monahan who wanted 'a threatening of the power structure whereby the people in the streets take over' and those whose involvement stemmed from what they would describe as a 'non-political', conservationist standpoint. And, whereas the former tended to adopt the 'class-based' view identified in chapter two on neighbourhood councils, the latter tended towards a liberal position which emphasised a 'community-based' view.

In the early months of the CGCA, a confrontationist or conflict strategy had been adopted, partly by design, partly by accident: 'This confrontationist strategy was not totally conscious—it was a combination of our rather aggressive make-up; remarks from GLC councillors calling us "layabouts"; and hostility from officials. It was clear that it was a battle right from the outset,' said one of the organisers. This aspect of the Covent Garden experience consequently confirms the finding of a study of community action in Glasgow which pointed out that local groups do not necessarily have a free choice over whether or not to adopt a conflict strategy. In that case, as in Covent Garden, 'consensus was not a reasonable alternative available to the people of the area' and they were forced into conflict since the 'alternative was not consensus but complete acceptance of official policy' (Jacob, p. 167, 171). There was however considerable questioning of this strategy.

First there was a feeling that the CGCA's aggressive style together with the somewhat abrasive public manner of its spokesman, Jim Monahan, 'alienated' support in the area. A typical comment is: 'The CGCA seemed intent on picking its nose in public and upsetting people and I sometimes wondered why I was involved myself. Many people were alienated.' This tended to be the view of the middle class conservationist element in the CGCA and, although there seems to be a ring of truth in it, the CGCA's approach would appear to be vindicated on broadly two grounds. So far as local residents were concerned, there was undoubtedly a section of the elderly population who were set in their ways and somewhat scared of anything they saw as 'meddling' in their lives: 'These people wouldn't even open their door for a gas conversion, let alone a CGCA member,' said one community worker. But the indigenous community as a whole was firmly behind the CGCA, as was confirmed by a survey carried out by the Social Administration Department of the London School of Economics & Political Science. It showed a 'remarkable degree of support' for the CGCA. Of the people who said they had heard of the CGCA, 40% had attended its public meetings, which represents a high rate of activism. The CGCA was also the most important single source of information on the plan for local people and 70% of respondents had a favourable view of it: 'The solidarity between the CGCA and the community it serves is obviously very strong. It cannot be dismissed as a sectional or agitationary group containing only minority support from our sample. Indeed the extent of its popular base is one any trade union would envy.' The second justification of the CGCA's approach is that, in order to make any significant impact, it had, in the initial stages at least, to opt for a dramatic, confrontationist approach that would inevitably alienate some sections of the neighbourhood.

The second main cause for internal tensions sprang from the difficulty the CGCA faced when attempting to determine its precise role as a community group. Was it seeking merely to alert people to the threat posed by the plan, in which case there was not much point in further campaigning until the inspector's report on the Inquiry was published and the Minister had pronounced. Or was it seeking to be in some way a radical expression of 'community power' that went well beyond opposition to the plan alone? This was at the heart of a running internal debate in the CGCA that came to a head in mid-1972 after a series of rowdy executive meetings. It was decided to set up two working parties, one to look into the establishing of a social centre that would also act as a focus for informal welfare rights and housing advice; and the other to look into the establishing of a neighbourhood council to be truly representative of residents and workers. The secretary of the CGCA indicated the tensions described above when he explained the reasons for this step in the *Evening Standard* on 20th June 1972:

> In the past it may have been necessary to single out the GLC as a bogey while the association's thinking becomes more precise. The lack of broad policy has made individuals feel that they should do their own thing. Everyone feels very strongly about the future of Covent Garden but we must turn into a body which genuinely represents the 35,000 people who live and work here.

In other words, the neighbourhood council concept was seen by some in the CGCA as a way out of the fairly intractable differences within the group, and as a device which could put an end once and for all to the allegation that the CGCA was 'unrepresentative'. At the same time the social centre was seen as overcoming the problem of lack of resources at the disposal of the CGCA, by providing a permanent and self-financing resource point. (The centre was however subsidised by the GLC by virtue of the low rent the authority demanded.)

Hence one can see how, two years before the Forum of Representatives came into being, pressures on the CGCA were forcing sections of its membership to look towards a Forum-type concept of community organisation. It was one way of resolving the tension between the liberal element in the CGCA and the radical element—a tension exacerbated by the role of the external organisers whose clear ideological commitment allowed them to be portrayed by their opponents as 'outside agitators'.

In view of the picture painted above, it should be stressed that the CGCA was nevertheless highly successful in sustaining its campaigning momentum throughout 1972. Public meetings continued to be well-attended and a regular newssheet distributed. There were planning applications to fight, an empty buildings survey was staged and the preliminary groundwork was laid for setting up tenants' associations The Covent Garden struggle had become something of a model for a rising community action movement throughout the country and the CGCA sponsored a national meeting of about 100 community groups to plan joint action and mutual support in May 1972. In addition, meetings were held with leaders of the Labour opposition group on the GLC. (These meetings later reaped a reward when the Labour group expressed its general sympathy for the disquiet over the plan—a plan, incidentally, that the GLC Labour group had helped to hatch when last in power.) The sheer breadth and rate of activity mounted by the CGCA in this 'limbo' period is most impressive. This is especially the case in view of the fact that the GLC effectively determined the agenda upon which the CGCA had to act. This ability of the statutory authorities to set the pace in such situations can place community groups on the defensive. To retain the initiative the CGCA had to resort to a series of stunts (see Alinsky for a general discussion): 'These were great fun—anything to keep the GLC on the run, to hit them in any way we could.' One practical achievement was to force the resignation of the Chairman of the GLC Covent Garden Development Committee, Lady Dartmouth, in July 1972. Clearly pained at her hostile treatment by the local community—'. . . throughout my whole year in office no-one said a good word about us . . .' (Anson, p. 7)—she had felt increasing misgivings about the destruction of the local environment under the plan.

The DoE turns down the Plan

In January 1973, the Minister of the Environment, Geoffrey Rippon, made his long-awaited statement on the Inspector's report and the future of the plan. Although the GLC put on a brave face, claiming to be 'delighted' with his decision, their plan had to all intents and purposes been rejected by the Minister in a somewhat ambiguous policy statement. Rippon approved the GLC's 'Comprehensive Development Area', but then put so many restrictions within the CDA that the wholesale redevelopment envisaged under the original plan became impossible. He did this principally by 'listing' some 250 buildings of architectural or historic interest and imposing a requirement on the GLC to allow the community to participate fully in drawing up a new local plan within the CDA. It was in no sense a technical decision (he disregarded the Inspector's report which had approved the plan). Rather it was a highly political decision—one designed to get everyone out of a tight spot. By approving the CDA it saved the face of the Tory GLC which had too much prestige invested in the plan to allow it to collapse with the GLC elections only three months away; and by placing the normal CDA powers in such a tight harness it placated both conservationists and the CGCA.

However, the decision was not lightly taken. Rippon had taken extensive soundings over the previous few months and the decision itself was taken by the whole Conservative Cabinet. This showed how successful opponents of the plan had been in making their struggle a truly national political issue. A leading member of the planning Team explained in 1974: 'The plan was defeated by the environmental movement and the CGCA. Party political factors were not important as there was a bigger tide running than party politics. If the Tories had been returned to office in the 1973 GLC elections much the same would exist as now.'

Although the whole of Covent Garden heaved a sigh of relief at the 'defeat' of the plan, there was some uncertainty over the strategy of the community movement now that everything was once more in the melting pot. The dilemma of the CGCA was described by one of its key workers: 'It had all been very sum-uppable in those early days— the battles were clear-cut and the issues obvious. Everybody agreed that the plan was a great big wolf and so they got out their guns and shot it. Everybody agreed with this. But when the wolf died the CGCA lost its way.' A protest or community campaigning group founded on *opposition* and highly competent at banging noisily on the door of the decision-makers found itself in disarray when that door fell open and it was suddenly invited in to sit around the decision-making table. As will be shown, the Forum of Representatives emerged as a means of resolving this further dilemma for the CGCA.

But the origins of the Forum lay not only within the CGCA. There were a number of different strands which all converged to create a momentum towards the setting up of a formal representative body to facilitate the participation exercise stipulated by the DoE decision. The most important of these was the GLC's desire for a consultation mechanism with which it could deal comfortably as a bureaucracy. In diminishing importance, the other strands were: the desire of many activists in Covent Garden to take advantage of any participation on offer; and the loose identification of the GLC Labour group with the community.

The GLC's Role

To a considerable extent, the Forum was the creature of the GLC and its establishment can be viewed as a practical illustration of the theoretical analysis presented in the last chapter which shows, *inter alia*, that participation can be used by representative government to mobilise support for its programmes.

A key figure in the GLC's role was its Assistant Director General, D.L. Blackhurst. At a Covent Garden Development Committee meeting shortly after the Rippon decision he floated the idea of a 'forum'. Although the *Skeffington Report* refers to 'community forums', this appears to have been the first time the term was used seriously in the context of Covent Garden:

> I told the Committee then that the essential problem for participation was the large number of pressure groups in the area. By failing to deal in an ordered and rational way with these groups we were actually encouraging them to make 'large' demands on us. I suggested a 'forum' to bring them all together and get them to resolve their differences amongst themselves and decide their own priorities . . . I hadn't read Skeffington in detail—the idea of the forum didn't come from there. It arose from listening in on the Development Committee to, on the one hand, the ruling Tory group's rejection of consultation and, on the other, the Labour feeling that this should take place. I saw it as a way to get the Committee out of the hot seat and to get the various groups arguing it out amongst themselves. I just took the phrase 'participation' from Skeffington and tried to make it practicable.

Alongside this early suggestion of a forum came a whole series of proposals to allow the community to participate through means of public meetings, surveys and questionnaires.

In the event the new Labour GLC, which assumed office in late-April 1973, decided to hold a public meeting in the area to gauge local opinion. Although the GLC was at pains to point out that it had no preconceived or firm ideas as to what method of participation should be set in motion, the early discussions of the Committee and the formidable influence of Mr. Blackhurst helped to create a momentum from which it was logical a forum would be established.

The first public meeting was held in June and attended by 500 people. It was followed by a series of similar meetings over a period of some 7 months. From the GLC's point of view it quickly became apparent that these meetings were unsatisfactory as a method of participation—'exasperating' was the term used by a member of the planning Team: the GLC was abused, the Team felt it was being made a scapegoat and the high emotion of the meetings was not conducive to the GLC's concept of participation as a joint partnership where disagreements could be resolved on a constructive and reasoned basis. (Ambrose and Colenutt (pp. 153–4) show how the Department of the Environment, too, is unhappy with public meetings, partly because of strong criticisms levelled by the audience at the platform and partly because the meetings format was not amenable to being used as an educative forum.) In addition, a GLC survey carried out later found that, whilst over a quarter of all those interviewed had attended the meetings, of these over a half were dissatisfied either with the content or the outcome of the meetings. At that time, the GLC also had no means of knowing how representative the meetings were: and this question of when and how a community group was truly representative was to be an additional factor that led to the setting up of an elected neighbourhood forum.

At the second public meeting late in June it was agreed to set up a working party to look into the question of establishing formal participatory machinery. This decision followed a motion proposed by a prominent advocate of neighbourhood councils, George Clark, who had moved into an office in the area the previous year as Director of the City Poverty Committee and whose experience with the Golborne Neighbourhood Council in Notting Hill naturally inclined him towards a similar body for Covent Garden. (George Clark was co-opted onto the CGCA Executive in 1972 and convened its 'neighbourhood council working group'. Although he later resigned from the Executive amidst some acrimony, he was an influential member of the Interim Working Party and to that extent can be regarded as another 'external' expert injected into the community politics of Covent Garden.) Although the decision was agreed virtually unanimously, the first signs of discontent from the CGCA about a formal structure for participation came from its leading activist, Jim Monahan, who warned of the dangers of 'rigid' and 'tight' organisations being established that might exclude local people from involvement. The meeting set in train a set of events that ultimately led to the election of a Forum of Representatives a year later.

The CGCA's Role

Meanwhile the CGCA was gripped with doubts about whether or not it should join in wholeheartedly with the process of setting up a formal body. The group's dilemma has been well expressed by Krause (p. 140) who argues that the community group appears to be in 'a difficult position when the bureaucracy offers them a 'citizen participation' ideology. They lose if they participate, and they sometimes lose if they don't participate.'

This helps to explain the basically schizophrenic attitude of the CGCA towards the Forum. For instance, on the same page of the group's annual report for 1973-74, it could claim the setting up of the Forum both as 'a victory for the CGCA' and at the same time stress that the CGCA must continue to play a 'watchdog role', guarding the interests of local residents against an attack from the GLC or a compromise by the Forum. The uncertainty in the CGCA's ranks was caused partly by the more sympathetic stance of the GLC. The onus was now on the CGCA to be 'constructive' and 'positive' whereas it had been born out of a legitimate necessity to be 'destructive' and 'negative' about the plan. In a letter to members in December 1973, the CGCA's Chairman reported a 'significant change in the GLC's attitude to the area' and stated that the CGCA was a 'decisive influence' in bringing this change about. He went on: 'There is little doubt that the GLC are more willing to listen to public opinion now than they have ever been in the past few years. What matters is to ensure that they continue to be given something worth hearing.'

The stress on being rational and constructive tended to wrong-foot the CGCA which, as a group based on protest, was geared up to a fiery oppositional stance. The resulting difficulty is indicated by the situation facing those from the CGCA who were on the Interim Working Party set up by the public meetings:

There were so many situations on the working party where people were pushed by the GLC officials at certain moments into a position desired by the GLC. The GLC would imply or just say that they would not support certain ideas: there was a lot of moulding going on. Our people are not used to committee situations and we all got so exhausted we just gave in. A depression falls on you in meetings like this: you just forget what you believe and sink back. Take a basic moral issue like housing: you end up arguing about the number of bathrooms per acre or some really detailed, technical issue like that.

It is important to understand, however, that the 'moulding' attributed to the officials was in no sense heavy-handed but flowed from the power relationship between the GLC and the community activists, in which the latter tended to assume the role of 'clients' to the GLC's bureaucracy.

As the Interim Working Party's meetings continued, a running skirmish developed over the proportional influence of the residents on any neighbourhood forum that would be set up. The CGCA wanted this influence to be a majority one on the grounds that it was the residents who really lacked power in the area. But other members of the Working Party wanted it to be balanced equally between residents, workers and owners. This division had its roots in the tension discussed above about whether the CGCA was representative of the community or not. (The fact that leading CGCA members later captured nearly half the Forum seats at its first election tends to add to its claim to be representative of the area.) The division was a product of the complex nature of the community in Covent Garden also referred to earlier on in this chapter. With the demise of the plan the tension asserted itself even more sharply. It was easier to bury differences while fighting a common enemy, but when that enemy appeared to defect and join your side, that sense of unity born out of a state of siege disappeared. Although there would be no evidence to support a vulgar conspiracy theory of 'divide and rule' on the part of the GLC, it remains a simple statement of fact that Mr. Blackhurst's original desire to see the various interest groups 'arguing it out amongst themselves', rather than directing hostility at the GLC, had already been achieved.

Such a view is given further credence by the fact that the GLC officials on the Working Party, Mr. Blackhurst in particular, had a considerable influence on its deliberations and the final proposals for a Forum. Part of this influence was exerted through precisely the kind of educational exercise that the GLC had originally had in mind as an attractive attribute of the Forum concept. And, as early as July 1973, Mr. Blackhurst had stated to the Working Party the GLC's desire for 'a consultative/advisory body which would be able to put views and suggestions to the Covent Garden Development Committee . . . ' The term 'consultative/advisory' is crucial for at no time did the GLC envisage a real transfer of power to the participatory body set up.

Labour Group's Role

Despite the fact that the participation tide was stronger than party politics and that a Forum-type body may well have been established anyway had the Tories been returned to power in the GLC, the specific role of the Labour group does have some significance.

As has been stated, Labour GLC leaders had had talks with the CGCA back in 1972 and the Labour GLC manifesto for the 1973 elections expressed solidarity with the community against the original plan. On coming into office, Labour was committed to public participation, albeit in a rather vague way. The new Covent Garden Development Committee Chairman, Tom Ponsonby, had been a local council alderman in Notting Hill at the time when the Golborne Neighbourhood Council was established in early 1971. He was anxious to avoid the clash of sectional interests that caused it to collapse and this led him to override the feelings of his colleagues that the residents should be given a proportionally greater influence on a neighbourhood council-type body for Covent Garden. He wanted a body equally acceptable to *all* interests in the area: 'Everyone's fears had to be catered for through the representation of all groups.' It is also evident that the Labour leadership saw in a participation exercise the opportunity to lower the temperature between the GLC and the residents: 'There was a tremendous lack of communication in the area. What was needed was a public relations effort to bridge the gap.' This latter statement suggests support for 'pseudo participation', that is to say the lower-rung kind of participation that involves no transfer of power but allows for the local authority to obtain a better understanding from the community of the rationale behind its programme.

This rather limited concept of participation was reinforced by the aims and objectives which the new GLC saw for Covent Garden. These were announced late in 1973 and they were substantially the original aims of the CGCA, so that it was reasonable to suppose that whatever participatory body was set up would be more concerned with the detail required to implement the aims, than with an ideological clash over the aims themselves as had been the case prior to the DoE decision.

Agreement on a Forum

After an anguished series of meetings in January and February 1974, the Working Party eventually agreed on a structure for the Forum of Representatives. The final public meeting in early January had endorsed the general scheme, although the dispute over the proportion of residents represented remained. It was proposed to have the Forum elected by popular ballot and consisting of 30 members drawn from the following categories: 9 residents, 9 business interests, 9 'service' interests (e.g. theatres, crafts, welfare and education) and 3 owners of property in the area including resident owner-occupiers. The election was scheduled for April 1974 and it was hoped to begin as soon as possible afterwards with active consideration of the new plan. These proposals were approved by the GLC and a unique experiment in public participation was set in motion.

The role of the Forum will be analysed in chapter six, but it is impossible to understand its role without an understanding of the background against which it emerged, which this chapter has sought to present. The picture corresponds to Cockburn's analysis (p. 103): 'Local people wanted participation; local councils saw advantage in "participation" if it was on their terms. Local people wanted collective strength; local state saw advantage in "community", but one made in its own image.' Thus, analysis of the origins of the Forum appears to validate many of the elements identified at the end of the last chapter as being at the heart of government's stance towards neighbourhood councils. The Forum was certainly born out of a desire by the GLC to 'regulate' the community politics of Covent Garden, by 'mobilising' the different groups in the area, thereby securing a 'legitimacy' for the new plan absent from the old one, and advancing a concept of participation amounting to extensive 'consultation' which it was emphasised must be 'constructive' and which would have an 'educational' value. The 'convenience' of a local forum is also evident in the view expressed by a senior GLC officer:

> The Forum is very convenient from the GLC's standpoint if it works the way I envisage. A great deal of the trouble that has built up over the last few years in places like London is the 'them and us'

mentality of confrontation where the local people simply do not understand the need for priorities, nor the financial problems of the council. It is also a question of getting acceptance from local people and of their understanding of the need for compromise.

5

The Forum is set up

In the name of citizen participation, people are placed on rubber stamp advisory boards for the express purpose of 'educating' them or engineering their support. Instead of genuine citizen participation, the bottom rung of the ladder signifies the distortion of participation into a public relations vehicle by powerholders.
Sherry R. Arnstein, 'A ladder of citizen participation in the USA', *Journal of the Town Planning Institute*, vol. 57, No. 4 (April 1971), p. 177.

. . . it would be naive to suppose, even in a small community . . . that there is ever a perfect harmony of interests, exactly balanced and reflected in a community group. There is more likely to be a conflict, or partial conflict, of interests which will disrupt and fragment any local group which claims to defend the interests of all.
Richard Silburn, 'The Potential and limitations of community action', in David Bull (ed.), *Family Poverty* (Duckworth, 1971), pp. 140–1.

Although the next two chapters principally concern the political role of the Forum over a three year period from its inception, rather than a detailed evaluation of planning issues, it is necessary to be aware of the planning context within which the Forum operated. By the autumn of 1976 agreement had been reached on a new plan and the stages which led up to this can be summarised as follows:

1. May 1974: election of the Forum.
2. June 1974: publication by the GLC of six discussion documents on the main planning areas.
3. Processing of the public's response by means of various consultation procedures, including the participation of the Forum.
4. The preparation of a report on some 120 possible 'Courses of Action' (some of which were incompatible with each other) in the light of the objectives which had emerged from the

public response. This Report was agreed with the Forum and then with the GLC Committee in February 1975.

5. In the six months following July 1975, a series of thirteen policy reports were prepared and submitted for public consultation. These reports examined the various courses of action in a detailed way and presented conclusions on the nature of policies for the plan. The Forum considered each report in detail and submitted written summaries of their response.

6. In March 1976 a 'Policy Options Report' was presented to the GLC Committee. It summarised the results of public consultation on the range of policy options for the area. The Committee was able to choose between options recommended by the Planning Team but which had been influenced by public discussion, and amendments put forward by the Forum and other groups. The decisions taken by the Committee largely determined the policy shape of the plan.

7. Throughout 1976 attention was concentrated on the 'feasibility studies' which were analyses of the physical opportunities to implement the plan's objectives through various sites chosen for housing or amenity gains. As a result of further consultation, alternative approaches to these sites together with preferred options were prepared by the Team.

8. The Draft Plan was published in July 1976 and was followed by a further period of consultation which focused on the feasibility sites.

9. In October 1976 the GLC Covent Garden Committee met to agree the final form of the plan. This was ratified in November by the full GLC Council.

The First Election

The Interim Working Party took responsibility for organising the first election of the Forum which was fixed for 11th April 1974. Mr. Blackhurst, the GLC's Assistant Director-General, was invited to be returning officer and he put a great deal of thought and work into the technical aspects of the election. Although there was sharp criticism from some local people of the part played by the GLC officers, the expertise that Mr. Blackhurst in particular was able to offer was heavily relied upon by the Working Party. It was agreed that the election should be by postal ballot, that a register of electors should be compiled, and that the candidates should stand in four main categories according to whether they were residents, business people, in services or owners. (Details of the electoral arrangements and the category system are described in Appendix I.) Thus, built into its structure was a system of functional representation through which it was intended each local interest could be given expression.

But, as the intended poll date drew near it was apparent that all was not well. Mail in the area was being disrupted by industrial action by Post Office workers, few envelopes were returned, and it later became clear that the registration procedure had not been carried out competently. On the day of the count, 11th April, Mr. Blackhurst sent a letter to each candidate declaring the poll invalid and cancelling the election.

This failure by the Working Party to organise the election meant that the GLC was obliged to step in and take responsibility for it, though still reporting through Mr. Blackhurst to the Working Party. A collection of GLC workers and other helpers was then hurriedly convened under Mrs. Pat Williams who was brought into the Covent Garden Team by Mr. Blackhurst to become 'Forum Liaison Officer'. Work began immediately to compile a fresh register and the election date was fixed for 10th June. Each registration form was checked for reliability (there had been duplication of names and other errors in the first register) and a revised register compiled. On 24th May, 4374 ballot papers and other electoral material was dispatched to voters, the timing allowing more than two full weeks to the closing date of the poll, 10th June.

Meanwhile, 76 candidates had been nominated, spread amongst the 10 different categories for the 30 positions up for election. Reflecting the different electoral categories, the standpoints of the candidates varied considerably. Although these standpoints will be examined more fully later in the chapter, we shall touch briefly upon them at this stage since they set the scene for the conflicting interests that found themselves working together in the Forum.

First, there were radical members of the Covent Garden Community Association who had been unhappy about representation on the Forum of property interests, believing that it should be a body for residents. As one such CGCA member put it: 'I stood because I had been campaigning for public participation for so long that I couldn't really reject what they had done because it was in some ways positive. Politically, we had been outmanoeuvred and we had to get down to helping people register and get on it.'

At the other end of the spectrum was a property consultant to one of the largest land owners in Covent Garden:

I thought the Forum would be an important body. My interest was purely commercial: I had to protect my client's position. I told people I was standing and went around with my secretary and got about 100 people registered to vote. They were all tenants of ours and their employees. I had been totally un-political and had never done anything like it before. Most of the canvassing was done by my secretary. I was very excited: my first taste of politics and the chance of doing something. It was something new.

But between the CGCA and the property owners, there was a disparate collection of candidates—local businessmen, theatre people, community figures, tenants, activists—who relied upon either personal contact or their reputation in the area. One candidate, an antique dealer, printed 10,000 leaflets and mounted a personal publicity drive to get his name known. But such energy and resourcefulness was rare. By conventional political standards it was a low-key election campaign, disappointing one of the GLC officers:

I would have liked to have seen the candidates touting a bit more— I saw no evidence of any great enthusiasm on their behalf. Some of the working class candidates were not fluent. Also, the business people are not soap box orators. None of them had much political background—politicaly they were rookies. Perhaps more publicity by the GLC would have helped.

The 4374 registrations were from a theoretical catchment of 2,800 residents and 29,500 workers. By 5.30 p.m. on the closing date, 1469 ballot papers had been received—a 33.6% poll. The Rev. Austen Williams, Vicar of St. Martin-in-the-Fields, topped the poll, with more than double the votes of the second highest candidate. Others who did well were either prominent in the CGCA or had well-known shops and businesses in the area. Despite the category system however, 'Electors did generally vote "across the board", giving their votes to people they knew and respected and not confining their support to candidates who claimed to represent their own sectional interest' (Blackhurst, p. 8).

If the GLC officers were surprised by the low profile of the election campaign, they were equally surprised to see that only 3 candidates attended the count at the GLC's headquarters, County Hall. As one officer put it: 'We were prepared for the public gallery to be full. But there was no public there—only three GLC councillors! The apathy at the count quite shocked me. I expected the public to be hammering at the doors.' This election apathy amongst the activists suggested that the mechanism of representative politics did not fit comfortably into the *style* of community politics to which those active in the area had been accustomed. It also highlighted the consequences of introducing another layer of bureaucracy into an area already saturated with local pressure groups—precisely the fear of those radicals who, as we saw in chapter two, were opposed to the concept of the neighbourhood council.

But perhaps the major obstacle was that the election was seen partly as 'the GLC's election', for two main reasons. First, elections are irrevocably associated in the public's mind with the local council or with Parliament. Second, the Interim Working Party's inability to organise the election competently made it necessary for the GLC to step in and take the initiative. In the circumstances there was little alternative but for the GLC to intervene and it did so with the backing of the Working Party. As a result the commitment to the election that would have followed had local activists organised it themselves inevitably evaporated. The GLC would have preferred not to intervene but was so committed to a successful election that it was forced to do so, highlighting what was to be a basic dilemma for the GLC Team throughout the life of the Forum: namely, how much it should stand aside in the knowledge that the Forum would not necessarily be able to cope as efficiently with bureaucratic tasks which were part of the day-to-day routine for GLC officers.

The Forum Meets

The inaugural meeting of the Forum was fixed for 19th June 1974. Although within the Team there was no concerted thinking about the direction the Forum might take—most of the officers were feeling their way, as indeed had been true when Lambeth Council sponsored its neighbourhood councils—Mr. Blackhurst *did* have a clear conception of its role. He was able to use his considerable authority, as GLC Assistant Director-General and as someone who had won the respect and trust of the Working Party, to draw up the agenda for the meeting and to prepare a report entitled 'Notes for the Background Information of Members of the Forum'. In it he dealt with the administrative questions which the Forum would have to face and outlined the procedure for communicating with members of the Team and with the GLC as a whole. He made it clear that the GLC would provide financial support for secretarial assistance, office accommodation, expenditure on stationery and hire of meeting halls. And he also covered the future role of the Forum:

a.   To establish means of effective *communication* between the Forum as a whole as distinct from its individual members, and the people of Covent Garden who have elected it. This will require not only regular machinery for informing people about meetings, what is to be discussed and what decisions have been taken, but also machinery by which the people and the various associations to which they belong can bring projects, opinions, complaints, etc., to the Forum for attention.

b.   To establish means of speedy and effective two-way communication between the Forum and the Covent Garden Development Committee . . . so that the views of the Forum including minority views when the Forum was not unanimous on both urgent and longer term matters can be put before the Committee. This means of communication must be able to deal not only with matters the Forum spontaneously wishes to put to the Committee but also with matters, such as applications for planning permission, on which the Committee will wish to know the Forum's views but which have to be dealt with within a statutory time limit.

c.   To make proposals for the future of the Forum itself, specifically for its legal status for the purpose of raising and administering funds; for its composition after the 1975 election; and for any necessary refinements in the method of election in future.

He went on:

It is for the Forum to decide to what extent it will look for advice and information from GLC officers and the Development Team. I assume that the Forum and indeed the Covent Garden Development Committee will wish the Forum to be as independent as possible and, more important, to be seen to be independent. On the other hand, I am confident that the Development Committee will wish the team and officers of all GLC Departments to give such help by way of information and advice and attendance at meetings as the Forum requests.

By placing ten pages of agenda papers in front of the first meeting, the GLC ensured that it transacted its business in a more purposeful manner, rather than waiting to see what course the meeting would take of its own volition. There was no pressure on Forum members to agree with any of Mr. Blackhurst's points—they were in any case presented merely as background material—but the existence of a coherently expressed viewpoint could obviously have been expected to shape what would otherwise have been a somewhat disjointed meeting whose outcome could not be predicted. And indeed, the meeting agreed in full to Mr. Blackhurst's proposal on the role of the Forum and followed broadly his other suggestions for the way in which the Forum should organise itself. (At the second meeting of the Forum it agreed a set of standing orders which it had requested Mr. Blackhurst to prepare.) The degree of participation undertaken by the GLC's Forum Liaison Officer included the smallest detail: 'Forum members were not committee orientated—they were more public meeting orientated. So, to get them thinking and working like a Committee I employed various psychological quirks, for example members' names on boards placed on the table in front of each chair and seating them around a large table.'

The man who topped the ballot, Rev. Austen Williams, was elected temporary Chairman. Simon Pembroke, a university lecturer in Greek who had been secretary of the Interim Working Party, was elected Honorary Secretary. Miss Sheila Malham who represented local theatre groups was elected Treasurer. At the second meeting, Austen Williams was confirmed as Chairman and John Wood, Managing Director of Rules Restaurant, Vice-Chairman. All the officers were unanimously elected, all were middle class and all reflected a 'consensus' view of the role of the Forum: this was to be a significant factor in the Forum's direction.

There was discussion at the first meeting on the role of the Forum officers—a discussion anticipated in Mr. Blackhurst's notes—and the Minutes recorded both how much thought had gone into this and how distant the style of discussion was from the hurly burly of the public meetings of the previous year:

> There was considerable discussion as to what kind of secretary would be in the best interests of the Forum—whether such a secretary should be (a) a mature person, able to guide, contribute, co-ordinate and take administrative action, and paid to do so; (b) a person with legal knowledge who would be able to monitor the legal

planning processes with which the Forum would be concerned; or (c) an administrative honorary secretary, independent of the GLC, with secretarial support paid for by the GLC.

The meeting adopted the third option and agreed to examine the situation more fully at a later date. (A full-time worker was appointed at the end of the year to support the work of the Honorary Secretary and to staff the Forum office.)

It was agreed to set up two sub-committees called the Policy Committee and the Planning Filter Committee. The former would consider long-term policy questions in depth and the latter examine speedily all planning applications submitted to the Forum. Mr. Blackhurst was given a vote of thanks for his work as Returning Officer and was asked to arrange a 'teach-in' for Forum members so that their work could be conducted as effectively as possible; in the event this never took place.

Significantly, discussion on these decisions was initiated and conducted almost entirely by articulate, middle class members. The CGCA activists did not organise beforehand to get one of their number elected as an officer, nor did they give much thought as to how the Forum might be structured. And most members were content to observe the proceedings while they found their feet in what was a new and unfamiliar arena.

In these circumstances it was inevitable that the GLC, the only group involved which had anything like a clear idea of what it wanted from the Forum, should set the pace and partly shape the pattern of the Forum's work. One GLC officer recalls: 'The settling-down period was very difficult: it was like an amoeba. Because it had never been done before, everyone was feeling around in the dark. Even the GLC officers never had a group meeting to decide "how shall we play this lot". We may have known broadly what we wanted but we were unclear how to get it.'

Perspectives of the Participants

From its inception, the Forum's membership divided into five categories: local entrepreneurs; indigenous residents; middle class conservationists; property interests; and radical activists. But although the perspectives adopted by these different groups were reflected mainly in terms of their *ideological* position, their motivation also had a more personal component in that through participating in the Forum they were able to advance their own personal interests (see Weissman).

They can also be regarded as 'neighbourhood politicians' with their own 'leadership styles' in the locality according to the perspective with which they are associated (Yates, pp. 85–102).

So far as the first group, 'local entrepreneurs', is concerned, a characteristic of their explanations on the purpose of their involvement was the straightforward desire to 'save Covent Garden', for a combination of altruistic and self-interested reasons. One member, a middle class antique dealer, put it this way:

> I love Covent Garden. I have lived there for twenty years in a tiny flat on top of an old warehouse. I would eventually want to leave my house in the suburbs and move back to Covent Garden, into a house over a business. I stood for the Forum because this was the way to project my own ideas and interests. A majority of us came to the Forum wanting to make a practical contribution. It was exciting for us. But we have never really sat down and worked out our role.

He was strongly committed to a consensus strategy: 'Confrontation is unhelpful,' he argued. 'A reasoned approach is the only way.' He tended to identify 'confrontation' with 'politics'; for him, being 'reasonable' implied being 'non-political': 'I was disillusioned with party politics like everyone else but I can't say that this was a strong factor in my involvement. I know nothing about politics and I feel I am doing social work rather than political work. I don't want to be part of a power structure—I am not a political animal.' He saw participation in 'non-political' terms, as a fresh way of conducting public affairs: 'Public participation is a new concept. It is an alternative to confrontation and I submit that we cannot allow it to fail,' he told a Forum meeting on 20th February 1975.

At the same time he was frustrated at the Forum's inability to make practical improvements to the area: 'We just sit there and pontificate. But we are not really achieving anything. We must move ahead and *implement*, not just *talk*—the Forum must have resources.' His solution was to establish a 'corporate and legal structure' for the Forum through which it could obtain the necessary resources to mount housing projects and so put its objectives into practical effect. He also believed strongly that the community should be able to influence those decisions that affected it: 'Why should people like the GLC tell us that they know what is best. We know what is best—we live here.' However, that should not be confused with a demand for a radical re-structuring of local government nor for a transfer of political or economic power to the Forum. It was simply an expression of a traditional antipathy to 'big government' and the way it intruded into community affairs in modern urban conditions. Since his overall view of the Forum's role and of his involvement in it was typical of a section of the Forum consisting largely of the self-employed middle class, we shall refer to them as 'local entrepreneurs'.

The second group comprised indigenous working class residents who saw the Forum as a means of fighting for the right to continue to live and work in Covent Garden. They were also anxious to re-create what they felt to be a dwindling sense of community in the area, and tended to be suspicious of working too closely with the GLC:

> I still mistrust the GLC. They promise one thing and then it doesn't happen. It is not that they are dishonest individuals, just that they are scared of developers and owners. They don't work hard enough at the grass roots—they would sooner have lunch with a developer than with one of us locals. They get out of it by machinating with words—they make out they are all for you but nothing gets done. I think too much friendship and talking goes on between the Planning Team and Forum members. It should all be out in the open and above board where we can get it all sorted out.

On the question of political commitment, this resident explained:

> You are on the wrong end of the stick so you tend to be leftish. The struggle of having to survive made us that way: it was part of life. The unfairness of life around me made me politically aware. I have always been sympathetic to the Labour Party, but more will be done through the trade unions than politically. I joined a trade union just before the war and I saw the value of people sticking together. I used to be disgusted with the management's trickery.

This attitude manifested itself on the Forum in a steadfast suspicion of the GLC and a vehement hostility to property developers, which did not fit easily into the consensus atmosphere of the Forum: the desire for a more belligerent and activist role led the indigenous residents to become less and less involved in the Forum. They wanted a direct transfer of power to the area, although the difficulty was that this desire was never properly articulated: they were unable to produce a coherent or workable alternative to the Forum as a method of participation and consequently their demands were sidestepped. Amongst other things, this had the effect of strengthening the consensus style of the Forum and, therefore, its relationship with the GLC.

The third strand was the 'middle class conservationist' element. All the Forum officers could be located within this strand which also determined the Forum's programme and style of working: it effectively dominated the Forum.

Significantly, none of the middle class conservationists had been involved before in political activity and they shared an antipathy to what they saw as the 'cynical manoeuverings' and 'posturings' of party politicians. They found particularly distasteful what they saw as decisions taken according to 'political' rather than 'rational' or 'objective' criteria. 'Political' for them had pejorative overtones, being associated with satisfying 'party dogma' or 'vote-catching'. It was also associated with party confrontation rather than a desired reasoned consensus: 'I know enough members on both sides of the Commons to know you can't get a pin between them. Opposition for its own sake is pointless,' said a Forum officer.

A particular attraction for members of this strand was that they saw local community involvement as being especially productive: 'Whereas one could say one couldn't do anything about, say, the war in Cambodia, the Covent Garden situation was more immediate. One could actually see tangible results from one's efforts.' Involvement in the Forum could thus be seen as a substitute for a broader political involvement that was regarded as ineffectual. Some however extended this and saw what they were doing locally as being of national significance:

> I am not as committed locally as most of the members are—my concern is mainly with a national approach. I put the time into the Forum because I think we have been going astray. I am horrified by the way the country is going. The state of the country is a product of the disease typified by the Covent Garden plan: if you build concrete on euphoria, you still only have euphoria.

Another Forum officer explained why she stood for election to the Forum: 'I suppose I stood because I felt I could make some contribution—do something. I also felt not enough women were involved: men make too many decisions for women. I remember thinking "what am I letting myself in for" when I stood. I had never been involved in anything like this before.'

In common with the other middle class conservationists she saw the

Forum as a vehicle through which all the different interests in the area could accommodate themselves to each others' point of view and agree on a view representing the whole community. She felt this acutely since she was both a resident and businesswoman in the area:

> I believe in overall representation. I don't feel I represent just one group—nor do I want to. I feel I represent the general interest, not a parochial one. I originally supported the concept of the Forum because it would have some sort of official voice. I used to be against compromise of any sort but as I get older I see the necessity for it: if you talk to people you do get co-operation in the end. The Forum has provided an arena for the GLC and the different groups to relate to each other.

The GLC expressed their view of the Forum's role in rather similar terms so it was not surprising that this became the prevailing ethos on the Forum. Flowing from it was a notion of participation as consultation, contrasting with the views of the indigenous residents and of CGCA activists: 'Immediately you have a positive role in taking decisions as we have had through the Forum you also have responsibility. Certain members do not appreciate this. It is inevitably a consultative body alone: it is concerned with seeing that those in power have a better knowledge from the ground up.' This was reinforced by another Forum officer who emphasised the value of rational argument in winning the GLC over to the community's point of view: 'If people concede that they have common interests, that is the important thing. If you achieve a common viewpoint, I don't see how the GLC can resist it then.' Not surprisingly, the GLC endorsed that. In the spring of 1975 a GLC Covent Garden Committee document reported that progress on fulfilling the participation requirement imposed on the GLC could not have been achieved so soon without the Forum: 'Its thoroughness in hearing all points of view is earning it increasing respect in the area.'

The fourth strand consisted of those representing property interests (fourteen out of thirty Forum members owned or managed property in the area in 1976, though not all of them have been included in this strand: some fall more easily into other strands), the most vocal of whom explained his outlook and how it had changed over time. It was abundantly clear that he had stood for the Forum in order to defend his own interests in the area but, equally, the experience of working on the Forum had modified his outlook: while still defending his interests, he became committed to the style of participation generated by the Forum:

> I went to one of the early public meetings before the working party had been set up. I wanted to find out what it was all about: it was something affecting a large client of mine. I was horrified. It was a real 'screw the developers' meeting. I was horrified by the amount of prejudice against developers.
>
> In following up the issue I was just doing my job: nothing more than that at that stage, though it has become so since. My initial feeling was that the GLC was setting up the Forum as a cul de sac for dissent. A significant number of the GLC Committee still see it that way. Cynicism more than anything made me feel that: I don't normally touch politics. I was worried at the time—and still am—that the Forum idea could become yet another hurdle, a classic excuse for bureaucrats to do nothing.
>
> But joining the Forum is like joining a team: you start shouting for it. Being on the Forum and being part of it means that I find myself working with people whose ideas are totally at odds with mine. I went in with a heart filled with hate and they still get my temples banging. I have had a go at quite a few of them. I am prepared to modify my views. They really aren't: they have completely closed minds—however I can accept that this is a good strategy from their point of view as they do achieve something by this approach.
>
> We all thought it was a bad plan. I don't think the GLC are competent to control anything. Also I have always been an anti-planning person. Planners are not competent to plan: everything that people like about this country was not planned. I want people to be able to take the initiative and make money. That is the only way things really creative get done. I would rather see planning come up from the bottom: from the consumer, except on obvious things like height limits of buildings. Since being on the Forum my attitude to the GLC has not really changed. But I have come to admire some of the work bureaucrats do.
>
> It has been very rewarding being on the Forum. You meet people you would never have met otherwise. I don't think I am really guarding my client's interests. I don't even know why I am putting in all those long hours! I suppose it is because it fascinates me and also because I want to prevent the area from dying. I am consciously part of something unique.

He added that this involvement was part of a 'middle class revolt' (King & Nugent, pp. 1–22) against being 'pushed around' by politicians, trade unions and radical protesters.

The fifth strand was what may be called the 'radical activists'. They were loosely left-wing in disposition, although there was a notable absence of activity in the area by left wing political organisations. Little if any of the rhetoric of the Left was heard in Covent Garden and the radicals could only be said to have a common ideological commitment in the broadest sense: in favour of 'grass roots community control' and against remote centralised decision-making; in favour of working class interests and against property developers; and prepared to by-pass conventional methods and adopt protest tactics.

The GLC's Programme

Before analysing the Forum in more detail it is necessary to appreciate the GLC's general programme for the area. At a meeting of the full Council on 18th December 1973, the GLC agreed a report from its Covent Garden Development Committee stating the aims and objectives of the new plan. It was founded on a different premise from the original plan. Instead of a rigid, grand design, the aim was more modest: to establish a series of priorities, fitting within a cohesive pattern and to be attained as part of an evolving programme that would tackle each problem successively, with enough flexibility for modification according to circumstances as they arose: 'What we envisage is a guide for a programme of the regeneration of the whole comprehensive development area and, although we aim to make it firm in broad principle, we aim also to make it flexible and adaptable in its implementation.'

The report went on to endorse a number of principles for which the local pressure groups had fought in opposition to the original plan. There would be no increase of office floorspace and existing hotel space was felt to be adequate. Once the market had gone, the report argued, the existing street pattern would be sufficient for local needs. Priority was to be given to increasing the amount of rented housing and to providing tenants with proper amenities; some buildings which had been illegally converted to offices could now revert to residential use; and in the limited cases where redevelopment was to be permitted 'it should be for housing or other socially desirable purposes'.

Consultation was built into the programme from the outset—and not simply through the Forum. Six attractive discussion papers were published in June 1974 on the main themes of the plan—'Context', 'Living', 'Working', 'Finance and Resources', 'Conservation & Development', 'Roads, Traffic & Transport Management'. Their aim was to attract public comment and a questionnaire was included in each copy. The reports were unusual for the GLC in that they were purely officers' reports and were made available to the councillors on the Covent Garden Committee at the same time as to the public.

In addition, meetings were held on a continuing basis with other groups in the community, with planning and professional bodies, and with members of the general public. Questionnaires were distributed and, at the Planning Team's office which faced onto the old central Market building, there was an information centre which promoted interest by various means including lunchtime slideshows. Finally, an interview-based survey of the area was conducted, and GLC interviewers visited over 1000 homes. Thus, in its concern to identify the 'real public' (Hoinville & Jowell), the GLC employed an array of consultation techniques which would have gladdened the hearts of the Skeffington Committee on public participation in planning, and the Covent Garden planners were apparently influenced by Skeffington in this respect at least. The GLC felt unable to rely exclusively on the Forum for facilitating consultation, partly because the percentage of voters in the Forum election was relatively low (though it was high by local election standards) and partly because some groups in the community had specialist interests and needed to be approached separately (for example, theatre and industry).

So far as the Forum was concerned, it was to receive similar servicing from the GLC Planning Team to that given by the Team to the Covent Garden Committee—an unprecedented step in a local authority. The Forum Liaison Officer, brought in to organise the election after the initial debacle, was to work fulltime on maintaining contact between the GLC and Forum members. Administrative support in the form of providing facilities for duplicating documents was also always given and the GLC later agreed to make an annual grant of £5000 to the Forum to cover administrative expenses.

From the outset, a central feature of the relationship between the GLC and the Forum was the presence at Forum meetings of the principal Team officers. Between five and ten officers were normally present; since only three or four were there in an advisory capacity, the remainder came out of their own interest—and none of them received overtime payments, even for meetings which frequently lasted from the early evening to after ten o'clock at night.

The Forum in Action

Forum meetings were conducted according to a conventional agenda, although within an informal and sometimes jovial atmosphere. Discussion was on the whole polite and orderly. It tended however to be disjointed and to lack a clear purpose, especially in the early stages.

A striking feature after the Forum had met for the first few months was the detailed nature of the debate which was invariably conducted on a relatively technical level. For example, a Forum meeting in October 1974 spent an hour on the question of the period for which temporary planning permissions should be given before coming up for review. A motion was introduced by a prominent local shopowner proposing that planning consents should be changed from 3 years to 'a minimum of 7 years so as to make it economic for necessary renovations to be carried out'. However, several Forum members representing residents expressed the view that this was too long since the tendency was for temporary permissions to be renewed at the end of the period and that a 7 year period would therefore allow temporary permission to become semi-permanent by default. Two amendments were moved suggesting more flexible variations on the existing 3-year rule but the voting on both these tied and so, somewhat in desperation, the Forum turned to a GLC officer for advice. Finally, a compromise amendment was agreed substituting the words 'for a reasonable period', for the words 'for a minimum of 7 years'. This was carried by 11 votes to 7, the vote partly reflecting à straight split between the business lobby on the Forum and a combination of local residents and the CGCA activists. After this long drawn-out procedure, a local resident present in the audience remarked sardonically: 'They are wasting their time here. The business people wanting to set up their businesses will use their influence to get their own way regardless.' This remark partly reflected the obvious feeling of frustration by local people attending the meeting at the technical level of much of the argument which they found difficult to follow and thought was somewhat irrelevant. In fact, very few local people did attend—perhaps one or two on average—although there were plenty of outside observers.

A typical agenda for the Forum might include consideration of a major planning application or redevelopment project, during which the applicants or their architects may be present and answer questions from the Forum; there might be a discussion on a particular policy area such as open spaces or housing; and GLC attitudes towards the vacated Market Building or its other properties would be closely scrutinised. Although a proportion of the agenda items would be there at the request of the GLC and although meetings sometimes appeared to have their agendas dominated by GLC-initiated items, the GLC did not normally 'run' the agenda. The Forum sometimes originated items at an earlier stage which required some action from the GLC and which they then reported on some time later. But it remains true that, effectively from the beginning, the Forum played a predominantly reactive role, responding to GLC consultation requests and only rarely initiating substantive issues itself.

A characteristic of Forum meetings was that discussion amongst members often deferred to the knowledge and expertise of the GLC officers who sat on one of the meeting table's four sides. It was notable how discussion was to a large extent shaped by the presence of the officers who intervened intermittently, usually (though not always) at the request of the meeting, and during the first half year of the Forum's life this sometimes provoked open irritation. For example, at a meeting in October 1974, a leading figure in the indigenous community, Sam Driscoll, raised the question of a compulsory purchase order in a street near his home. He maintained that the people had lived there for 25 years, yet they had not even been informed about the planned CPO. Backing up Driscoll, Jim Monahan, the CGCA activist, suggested that the Forum copied the application and distributed it to the tenants who would be affected. But a GLC officer pointed out quickly that this would be against the terms of normal legal process. He did however suggest that the Forum could write to the tenants telling them to ask the GLC about the future of their building and the GLC would then be able to reply, supplying them with the information. Monahan retorted that the Forum should not be seen as the 'mechanic of the GLC' and that the Forum should simply send the information directly to the tenants. This tension between the Forum's aspirations and statutory law and procedure surfaced frequently in the early Forum meetings and on another occasion one resident remarked in frustration at being told that the Forum was not able to intervene in law to stop a particular application for office use: 'The Forum should be concerned with the good of the people in the area, not with legal detail.'

Throughout the period under examination, GLC officers were

privately exasperated by what they saw as the disjointed and unproductive meandering of much Forum discussion—a view shared by local people who sat in on meetings. This resulted partly from lack of experience in committee-type deliberations. But loose chairmanship was also a factor. The Chairman saw his role in terms of a referee, to maintain a sense of balance between the conflicting interests on the Forum and thus the debate often lacked direction. However, as time went on and as some of the dissident voices from the CGCA drifted away, this failing was to some extent remedied.

Another failing was not. Perhaps because they were overwhelmed by Forum paperwork and in meetings of such frequence that active members of the two sub-committees could find themselves attending two or three a week, the Forum took virtually no *action* as a collective body. In the 18 months between the first and second elections, only one public meeting was held to report back to local people and virtually no practical work was undertaken. Apart from the production of an irregular newspaper, there was no attempt to achieve publicity or to project the Forum's work to its constituents, and no funds were raised. This failing will be analysed more fully in the next chapter, since it does raise the question as to whether the kind of interlocking consultation with the GLC practised by the Forum was incompatible with an activist programme.

However, before moving on to discuss in detail the activity and the ideology of the Forum, it is necessary to be clearer about the relationships between the GLC and the Forum and about the organisation of the Forum itself. This will be dealt with in the next three sections which also reveal the key role played by the individual GLC officers.

Forum/GLC Relationship

The channels of communication between the GLC and the Forum are depicted overleaf. The main channels are from the two Forum subcommittees through the full Forum to the Team and then onto the Committee upon which two Forum members were represented.

In addition there was considerable contact outside these formal channels. First, GLC officers sat on the Policy and Filter subcommittees and a two-way process of dialogue occurred even before the full Forum was reached, through which the GLC was able to feed in its ideas and proposals. Second, the Forum Liaison Officer played a crucial role in keeping the lines of communication unblocked and in

Forum/GLC Relationship

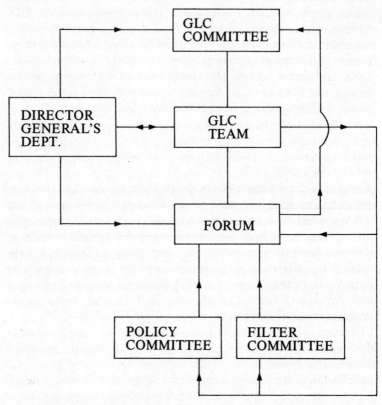

building a close working relationship between the GLC and the Forum. She advised and serviced the Forum, and acted as a go-between, ensuring that tensions were removed and that each side understood the other's point of view. So crucial was her role that it is doubtful if the experiment could have proceeded as relatively smoothly as it did without her. She was strongly committed to the Forum and because she had been brought in as a fresh member of the Team, and thus had not experienced the traumas of the 1970-74 period of conflict, she was better able to appreciate the Forum's point of view and was trusted by its members. Her feelings about her role show the extent of her commitment: 'I have a love-hate relationship with the Forum. It is almost like having a family: you get very ashamed when they misbehave in public but you constantly have to bear in mind their difficulties.' Her role was however far from one-sided in the sense of seeking to mollify the Forum or of acting as an apologist for the GLC. Indeed she often had to cajole the GLC officers, to ensure that they did not slip back into their traditional methods of working but gave a priority to consultation with the Forum. A third informal channel of contact was through the Assistant Director General of the GLC, Mr. Blackhurst. The Forum was to a large extent his brainchild and without his active involvement in its affairs it is again doubtful whether the relationship with the GLC would have been as harmonious or as productive. He had the personal commitment to give close attention to the Forum's affairs. He also had the authority to speak for the GLC and to commit it to a course of action which cleared away obstacles standing in the way of effective and speedy consultation. Whenever the Forum got into a procedural difficulty or a policy dilemma he was on hand to give valued advice.

The elected councillors played an almost negligible part in the week to week process of participation: they were confined to a 'long stop' role at Committee meetings. Significantly the CGCA newssheet contained regular attacks on members of the Team, often couched in personalised terms, yet councillors were rarely criticised—a recognition of their relative unimportance in the day-to-day participation process (confirmed by Christensen, pp. 100–3, Jenkins 1973, p. 54, Cockburn, p. 36, pp. 169–72). The GLC officers were well aware of the way in which they were 'short-circuiting politics' (Meynaud, p. 269) by being taken out from behind their desks into the front line of public contact and controversy through public participation schemes (see Worskett, Gyford, pp. 133–43, Rabinovitz), and recognised the implications of this: 'As a planner one is coming into more direct contact with the people and therefore one's role is more political—and it is not particularly comfortable.' (However, this argument over the limited role of elected councillors in Covent Garden should be qualified at least in respect of Labour councillors in the London Borough of Camden. It will be recalled that part of Covent Garden lies within Camden Borough and the CGCA were able to foster close relations with Camden councillors and exploit their antagonism to the the GLC as an institution to exert pressure through Camden which expressed itself at committee and senior officer level.)

Broadly speaking, the Team was impressed with the feedback they obtained from the Forum and although Team members were initially irritated at having to deal with 'yet another body' which slowed down

their work, they quickly came to appreciate the value of the Forum:
'Now that we have accepted that we have to consult and work with the
Forum, there is the final satisfaction of knowing that, while the whole
process does slow you down, you are not making enemies along the
way. So your natural irritation is submerged by satisfaction at the
end.'

The Filter Committee

The planning Filter Committee met shortly after the first meeting of
the Forum. The size of the Committee varied between six and eight
members, balanced between residents and business representatives.
Its purpose was to sift through each planning application submitted to
the GLC and to recommend support or opposition to the full Forum.
Once the Forum had decided, the GLC officers then put the Forum's
comments alongside their own recommendations to the full GLC
Covent Garden Committee. Since the Filter Committee was concerned with the detail of planning law and procedure, it was agreed
that it should have a rotating membership, so that each Forum
member could gain experience and knowledge of planning technicalities from participating in the work of the Committee. Meetings were
not held in public, but an applicant could apply to sit in when his own
application was considered and could have the opportunity to put his
case to the Forum members. Several GLC officers were normally
present to give advice on technical questions.

The GLC officers attending the meetings regarded the Filter
Committee as the most successful part of the Forum. Often frustrated
at what they saw as the time-wasting and 'negative' rhetoric of full
Forum meetings, the officers were impressed by the 'constructive'
and 'realistic' approach of the Filter Committee. It was undoubtedly
the most productive aspect of the Forum's work, principally because
it was concerned with immediate and tangible issues which Forum
members could easily tackle, in contrast to more abstract policy
questions: both Forum members and GLC officers agreed that the
concept of participation advanced by the Forum expressed itself most
effectively through the Filter Committee. From the GLC officers'
point of view, an important aspect was the educational effect on
members of the Filter Committee and their gradual though grudging
acceptance of planning law constraints. All applications were circulated
by the Forum Liaison Officer at least a week in advance of the meeting
so that members could go and see the sites personally: 'Our intention

is to get them into an arrowhead of thinking,' said one officer early on in the Forum's life.

One Filter Committee meeting in November 1974 was typical. There were eight properties on the agenda and a GLC officer began by introducing each application, summarising the position. He was then closely questioned by Committee members and, as discussion amongst members proceeded, he was continually consulted on technical aspects of the application. He appeared to maintain a scrupulous detachment from the argument, not seeking outwardly to prod the Committee in any particular direction, yet he undoubtedly dominated the meeting and few decisions went against his advice. Although the members were frequently unhappy at not being able to take a particular decision on account of planning law or procedure, they did not have the expertise with which to contest the advice being given by the officer.

The meeting was relaxed and informal and periodically a member would rise to peer at a map on the wall. There was a low-keyed and practical job-of-work-to-do atmosphere and some of the contributions were based on personal knowledge of the properties concerned. It was apparent that they took greater care over their decisions than might typically happen on a local authority—a point which impressed the GLC officers.

The Policy Committee

The Policy Committee contrasted with the Filter Committee in that it comprised professional or middle class members alone. Its role was geared virtually exclusively to consideration of the GLC plan. This was initially presented to the Committee as a series of options which, after consultation and debate at Policy meetings, went to the full Forum.

A meeting of the Policy Committee in January 1975 provided an insight into its role. Earlier meetings had been concerned with the Forum's general policy stance and with responses to the GLC discussion papers issued in the middle of 1974. But this particular meeting was the second one to consider the options in the proposed plan. The GLC officers had spent the previous three weeks re-drafting these options in the light of comments at the last Policy meeting. The Planning Team Leader, Geoffrey Holland, introduced the options paper and described the procedure envisaged by the Team. The Policy Committee, if it was agreeable, would take a reconsidered version of the Team's options paper to a full Forum meeting and 'recommend' it. The Forum would then recommend it to the Covent Garden Committee. (This was the procedure adopted with all major policy reports.) He was anxious that it should proceed through these stages smoothly and saw the advantage of the Policy discussion as being to iron out queries and clarify potential areas of disagreement. 'There is such a consensus between the Team and the Forum on conservation and housing that we should concentrate on physical planning areas,' he said. Then, in a relaxed and conversational atmosphere, followed a detailed discussion on specific issues, Forum members being visibly concerned that the paper should be presented neatly and cogently so as to avoid wasting time at the full Forum meeting.

When the Forum met a week later on 30th January 1975 it had before it the paper of options agreed by the Policy Committee. Attached was a note by the Policy Chairman, Leslie Ginsberg, stating that the Policy Committee felt that in its present form the options paper 'does represent the views of the people living or working in Covent Garden . . . This paper provides a positive and viable framework for action, and the sooner we can get it through the cumbersome procedures within the GLC the better.' He recommended that it be accepted by the Forum for submission to the GLC Committee whilst reserving 'the right to discuss and amend proposed courses of action, in the light of feasibility studies when these have been prepared.'

The Team's paper introduced the options by outlining the procedure that was being followed in drawing up the plan. The first stage had been the publication in June 1974 of the Discussion Papers. Then followed a process of intensive consultation with the Forum and through the other means referred to earlier in this chapter. The result of this consultation was 'general agreement on the direction the new plan should take and the issues it must seek to resolve.' Consequently the paper set out the various options available within the context of this general agreement, explaining that the next stage in preparing the plan would be to examine in detail the effectiveness and feasibility of all the possible courses of action. The outcome of these studies would be presented for further debate 'to inform the choices which will have to be made between alternative courses of action'. The paper also made it clear that in the meantime urgent action on, for example, housing matters, would not be shelved. The objectives of the plan were listed:

1. *Social and Economic*
A   to safeguard the existing residential community and provide for a substantial improvement in housing conditions
B   an increase in the residential population achieved through an increase in the stock of rented accommodation and a greater provision of family accommodation
C   improvement of local services to meet the needs of the residential and working populations
D   to strengthen the economic character and vitality of Covent Garden by promoting the growth of new and traditional uses appropriate to the area
E   urgent re-use of buildings and land previously in market use with activities that will give the area new vitality and focus

2. *Physical*
A   safeguard and improve the existing physical character and fabric of Covent Garden
B   restrict vehicular traffic, and give much more emphasis to pedestrians and access to public transport

The courses of action to meet these objectives were also set out:

  i Action through policies controlling development and change of use either using existing policies or seeking additional policies to encourage certain uses and activities.
 ii Action through a programme of public acquisition and subsequent rehabilitation or redevelopment.
iii Action through lettings policies for properties in Council ownership.
 iv Action through constructive co-operation with the private sector to achieve planning gains where desirable and practicable.
  v Action through negotiation and co-operation with other authorities (e.g. ILEA, DHSS), and in particular Westminster and Camden.
 vi Action through information and promotional activities to encourage and attract new uses consistent with the character of Covent Garden.

These objectives and courses of action were then set out in a detailed fashion in a table attached to the paper, making a 26-page document. When it came up for debate at the Forum meeting, all the preparation that had gone into it paid off handsomely: it was accepted unanimously after only 15 minutes' discussion which revolved around queries of detail rather than of substance. The lack of opposition could perhaps be attributed to the very general phraseology in the paper, but it was in fact fairly normal for Policy reports to go by unchallenged at Forum meetings (in contrast to Filter Committee reports which were queried and contested with an excruciating eye for detail) because of the real consensus between the GLC and the Forum on broad policy objectives.

6

The Forum in Action: 1974–77

The greatest danger that confronts residents of deprived areas is ... that their leaders should be sucked into middle class, professionally dominated bureaucracies as representatives of the poor, the deprived, the consumers. To involve residents in management bodies, steering committees, area councils and the like, has the appearance of participation, gives the impression of shared control, but in fact is the surest way of drawing the teeth out of any form of community action. A meeting can be structured in such a way that residents have little opportunity of raising the things which are important to them. If local people are to have power and influence then they must determine the agenda and the setting in which it is discussed.
Harry Salmon, 'The Hillfields Community Association: A Case Study', *CDP Occasional Paper No. 3* (CDP, October 1972), p. 32.

During the first year of its existence, Forum meetings were frequently characterised by clashes between the interests of residents, and of the business representatives and property owners (although such clashes recurred throughout the Forum's existence, they became more muted after this initial period). The meeting on 31st October 1974 was an example. Sam Driscoll was one of the most articulate and active of the indigenous residents and his interventions at this meeting had exhibited growing exasperation with the complexity of planning, producing the following clash with Alexander Moss, an eloquent and equally forthright property consultant:

Moss: Nobody ever mentions 'justice for owners'—you are always impugning their motives. You must approach owners personally and not stand on your dignity. The Forum represents *all* the community, owners included.

Driscoll: Never mind the owners. *Locals* have no bloody legal rights at all.

Moss: Balls, Sam! All the Rent Act paraphernalia protects
                   tenants. Don't shout at owners and landlords, talk to
                   them.

Chairman: We must talk to owners. One of our common
                   dangers is to opt for confrontation. We must go for
                   understanding.

A different side of the same conflict appeared at a Forum meeting in
March 1975 where there was a discussion about an application for a
late night club in the area. A representative of the club was present in
the audience and intervened several times. In the end the disagreement
boiled down to the difference between residents who did not want late
night noises and those who thought that city-centre dwellers must
expect that kind of inconvenience. It was in one respect a classic
conflict between the narrow interests of the local people and the wider
interest of the whole city. It also illustrated what was a principal
feature of the residents' role on the Forum: namely, to resist almost all
change that disturbed their pattern of life. In the course of the
argument, Alexander Moss accused the residents: 'What you want to
do is have Covent Garden die. Covent Garden residents must be the
most selfish people in England!' (Outbursts from residents). The
Forum split straight down the middle on the issue, voting by 10 to 9 to
oppose the application—even though the GLC planners told the
meeting that they did not think there were any statutory grounds for
refusing the application.

On 30th January 1975 the problems of the Forum's role as a body
to be consulted, rather than a body which possessed certain powers,
was highlighted by discussion over a development at Seven Dials in
Covent Garden. The project was explained to the Forum by an
architect, with the aid of an attractive visual display. As soon as he
had finished, the CGCA activist Jim Monahan intervened rather
testily. He took exception to the appearance of the building and then,
after others had commented, asked the Forum to oppose demolition of
the old building and not to be diverted into considering the aesthetics
of the proposed new one. But Mr. J.C.G. Cook, a GLC officer,
quickly stepped in to point out that applications for demolition were
dealt with by the Historic Buildings Board, a sub-committee of the
GLC Planning Committee, and at present not submitted to the
Forum, so that it was pointless to contest the demolition (the Forum
only enjoyed direct consultative status through the Covent Garden
Committee of the GLC and not with other Committees). Moreover,

outline planning permission had been given the year before, so the
Forum were being faced with a *fait accompli* in more ways than one.

It was obvious from the views expressed that virtually all the Forum
members were unhappy in one way or another about the details of the
scheme; they felt in particular that it did not blend adequately into its
surroundings. There was also a good deal of annoyance at their
apparent inability to influence matters, as opposed to voice criticisms.
The Chairman, Austen Williams, tried to calm the meeting by
summarising their objections and suggesting that the next item on the
agenda be taken. But Monahan challenged this:

Monahan: Why are we not making a decision one way or the
other?

Williams: Are we in a position to make a decision?

Discussion then took place on whether they were *able* to make a
decision in view of Mr. Cook's statement, and Austen Williams asked
the GLC to bear in mind the Forum's 'grave' objections to the
scheme. Two GLC officers also intervened:

Cook: What you have said this evening goes beyond the
terms of reference laid down. The final decision is
with the GLC.

Holland: But we must have a firm statement on this matter
from the Forum. We shall have to face the fact
sooner or later of disagreement between the Committee and the Forum.

However it was clear that the Forum was not satisfied, as two of its
members made clear:

Montgomery: We are left rather with Hobson's choice. If we make
too much fuss about it we will delay more housing. If
we don't, history will not thank us.

Monahan: This is disgusting. We are yet again being made
irrelevant by GLC procedure which brings it to us
far too late in the day.

That view was echoed by others and a wrangle with the GLC officers
followed, at the end of which Austen Williams said to them: 'Do you
recognise the strength of feeling? I want a complete assurance that this
will never arise again.' And that was about as far as the Forum was
able to take the matter.

A similar example, though one about which there was far less
strength of opposition, was the GLC's plans for a housing development on the Odhams site. The GLC's Chief Housing Architect

presented a Forum meeting on 14th November 1974 with models, photographs and plans of the scheme proposed: 'It would be a very human, sensitive, environment,' he said. He was persistently questioned about very detailed issues such as the size of rooms in the dwellings. And in answer to criticisms he appealed to the Forum not to delay it further by querying the basis of the scheme in any fundamental way. Answering a request for more family accommodation in the scheme, he said: 'This is a finely tuned scheme. We wouldn't like it disturbed too much. To get to this design stage takes 5 to 6 months. If we want to change the family/couple ratio it will delay it a further six months.' After this he explained that he had to leave early, and received a clap in thanks from the meeting. Then followed an exchange between a Forum member and a senior GLC housing officer from County Hall.

Member: Is it a *fait accompli* or can we give comments?

Officer: We have literally to fight the Department of the Environment all the way since it is such an expensive development. But if we can say we have the whole-hearted support of the Forum, our hand will be strengthened enormously. Otherwise the civil servants will block it. We must fight together: not fight amongst ourselves. I beg you to give us some support.

The Forum was in a dilemma. There was very general approval of the scheme, but a number of detailed reservations. Yet, in view of what the GLC had said, unless the Forum backed up the scheme fully then it might be blocked by the DoE. Just as the Planning Team sometimes used the Forum's backing to persuade the GLC Committee to a particular point of view, so the GLC now sought to use the Forum as a lever against the DoE which, after all, had imposed the participation requirement in the first place. Not surprisingly, the Forum decided to express 'qualified approval of the scheme, while reserving detailed comment for a later discussion.' After the meeting had ended, a GLC officer remarked that Forum members had 'asked better questions than the GLC councillors when the scheme was put to the Covent Garden Committee.'

The discussion on the Seven Dials and Odhams developments underlined the Forum's status as a *consultative* body rather than one which wielded power. Many members (though not all) felt constricted by this status and it expressed itself in a different way over a proposal from a member, Rex Montgomery, for the Forum to set up its own Housing Association. He had tried to get this raised before and was given the opportunity to do so at a meeting on 20th February 1975. In a leaflet circulated to Forum members beforehand, he stated:

> One of the main criticisms of the Forum to date has been its lack of teeth—political and economic power—and we have heard many propositions in Forum ranging from requests to the GLC to 'delegate' its powers (which it is not likely to do) to the opposite extreme of 'usurping' those powers. Either of these propositions is in my view unrealistic and I can only see us achieving any worthwhile objectives if we ally ourselves to the rolling programme through a corporate structure with legal status. A Housing Association would give us such a structure. It would put the Forum at the focal point of the GLC's rolling programme with funding from many sources . . .

Elsewhere in the leaflet, he wrote of the need to give the Forum 'teeth' and 'credibility'. Otherwise, he argued, public participation would fail: 'Public participation is a new concept. It is an alternative to confrontation and I submit that we cannot allow it to fail . . . any programme of housing in Covent Garden should be kept within the controlling influence of the Forum . . .' After he had introduced it, an interesting debate followed, involving a variety of members and centering around the Forum's 'credibility'.

McLeish:	If the Forum can be seen to be implementing and not just talking, it will be very good for our credibility.
Loew:	There is no consensus of opinion on the Forum: the moment we move beyond a demand for 'more housing' and start establishing for whom, where and when, we all disagree.
Pembroke:	Our credibility derives from the strength of our argument. We have a certain amount of 'unofficial power' through this. We don't really want to control everything in Covent Garden. It is a question of power versus influence—we have influence.
Spence:	This is an opportunity for democratic grass roots control through the Forum.

A fairly heated discussion ensued and it was apparent that the obviously important issues at stake were to some extent being overshadowed by suspicion on the part of the officers of the Forum and others as to Mr. Montgomery's motives (this suspicion dated from several years previously and concerned a somewhat parochial conflict over the legitimacy of a Housing Association with which he had been associated). Making a rare partisan intervention, the Forum's Chairman, Austen Williams, argued forcefully: 'Our impartiality will be at stake. We shall be in danger of losing support from some people because we shall be *committed* in a particular way. The role of the Forum is at stake.' After discussion had got rather acrimonious, the Policy Committee Chairman, Leslie Ginsberg, intervened skilfully on a conciliatory note and asked for a considered reaction from the GLC on the role of housing associations so that the Forum could reassess the question. Once more the Forum had backed away from an important issue by relying on the GLC to find a solution and on this inconclusive basis the discussion ended and the proposal was later shelved.

Another example illustrating limitations on the Forum's influence arose over the use of the Jubilee Market Building. A motion was proposed at a Forum meeting on 20th February 1975 supporting the application of two local groups, Street Aid and the Covent Garden Community Centre, for use of space in the building for recreational and educational purposes. But Forum members were in some difficulty as they did not know the relative merits of the other contending alternatives for use of the building—and a GLC officer quickly pointed out that this was not possible as by law details of tenders were confidential. This provoked the following retort from Austen Williams: 'That means the GLC could do anything under tender and then present it to us as a *fait accompli*. We could be removed from the scene almost totally until after a decision is made. We do really want to participate. We don't want to be excluded.' As a compromise, the meeting agreed to drop the original motion and asked the GLC to defer a decision until the Forum had had a chance to consider the options, even if they were presented to a Forum meeting without the financial details that would accompany an application. The issue of confidentiality of tenders was one frequently raised by the Forum.

Participation

The first four months of the Forum's existence saw frequent and sometimes heated clashes between the CGCA activists (Jim Monahan in particular) and GLC officers. Essentially this reflected a clash between the 'conflict' and 'consensus' models discussed earlier, and a large number of Forum members were unhappy about what they saw as unproductive and unnecessary skirmishes which merely diverted them from the detailed issues they had to deal with; they were also annoyed by Monahan's aggressive manner. Underlying this was some confusion over what exactly the Forum's role was and what 'participation' really meant. At a round table conference on 26th September 1974, the future of the Forum had been debated and the Forum's Chairman asked Mr. Blackhurst to put forward some ideas and proposals for 'improving methods of communication between the Forum and the GLC', since there had been a 'breakdown of communications'.

Mr. Blackhurst prepared a thoughtful paper entitled 'Communications' which he presented to the Forum meeting on 31st October. (It will be discussed more fully in the next chapter and is reproduced as Appendix II since it is a significant and coherent statement on a local authority's concept of participation.) The paper began by referring to an 'us and them' attitude which had surfaced through the Forum:

> Some members of the Forum talk and write about 'Participation' but some of the same members (not all) persist in regarding the GLC, The Development Committee and the officers as fundamentally hostile—a body which has preconceived (and sinister) intentions to make changes in Covent Garden against the wishes and interests of the community. There can be no 'participation' between two groups of people when one regards the other as an enemy who cannot be trusted. 'Participation' means sharing, in particular sharing the responsibility for decisions by making a contribution to the process of choice between alternative policies and courses of action. It does not and cannot mean a complete transfer of responsibility from the GLC to the Forum . . .

He went on to elaborate on his view of participation and suggested various ways through which communications might be improved. But the issue was in essence a political one concerning the stance of the Forum and its relationship to the GLC, not one which could be resolved by easing the channels and procedure of communication. This was borne out by the ensuing discussion at the meeting. Jim Monahan followed immediately on Mr. Blackhurst's introductory remarks by challenging the assumptions behind the paper, and other Forum members expressed their views:

Monahan:	The GLC looks to the Forum as a means of being kept informed. The Forum has been dominated so far by things the GLC thinks we should discuss. The aim must eventually be to usurp the GLC's power. The GLC is too large and amorphous to be kept in touch with people. The Forum must *determine*, not just influence or be consulted. We need to have the attitude on this Forum that we, emotionally and morally, are the people in power. The Forum's time spent arguing around legal constraints has been wasted: we might need on moral grounds to go outside these.
Clark:	But if we are in a position of authority, as we are, we must have a responsible attitude—otherwise we shall muck things up.
Gey:	We are the Filter Committee of the GLC Covent Garden Committee—much of what we suggest is rubber stamped by the Committee.

Debate then ranged around the Forum's lack of 'teeth' and 'resources'. It was clear however that there was considerable agreement with Blackhurst's viewpoint, although less so amongst indigenous residents:

Driscoll:	It is frustrating sitting on this Forum. I feel like getting hold of all these papers and throwing them (he picks up his agenda papers and gestures appropriately) . . . What's the bloody use of all this talk unless we have the wherewithall?

There was disagreement as to whether they should first try to work through the system and improve it, or to try for an immediate change in their relationship with the GLC.

Monahan:	Unless power is transferred to the area, it is not 'participation' but merely 'communication'.
Montgomery:	A 'them' and 'us' situation is completely destructive and deplorable.

Then followed an open clash between Monahan and Blackhurst. It was unprecedented for a GLC officer to intervene on such a pointed basis and take direct issue with a Forum member. But Mr. Blackhurst had sensed the majority feeling of the meeting and timed his intervention skilfully, when the discussion was beginning to be somewhat abstract and irritation was shown at Monahan's aggressive persistence in challenging the GLC's view. As Mr. Blackhurst was later to remark in an interview:

The confrontation with Jim was a deliberate tactic. I went for him because he had been more than pin-pricking: he believes in dramatic confrontation. I thought I had the majority of the Forum on my side and he made the mistake of often coming up with issues which were not well researched and which I could easily explain and justify to the Forum. But it does no harm to have the Jim Monahan's there: his enthusiasm and hard work is very useful provided they don't always go along with him.

As frequently happened when the Forum discussed questions about its general role, it backed away from facing up to the implications of its position and fell back on procedural proposals which would not disturb the delicate consensus between the divergent interests represented in its membership. It was decided to have a public meeting and to follow up Mr. Blackhurst's suggestion that the Forum could have the right to sit on the GLC Committee meetings, though not the right to vote. Later, the Chairman summed up:

Williams: There is a certain sense of being unable to arrive at a statement of clear policy because, of necessity, the Forum is continually listening to expert advice.

Monahan: We are expected to behave like civil servants.

The result of the discussion, however, was to steer the Forum towards an acceptance of Mr. Blackhurst's concept of participation and it was this above all that led to a growing estrangement of CGCA activists from the Forum.

By this time too, it was apparent that the overriding objective of the Forum was to arrive at a style and method of working geared towards maintaining a consensus—however fragile—between the diverse series of views and interests represented on it. And an important feature of the Forum was that it *did* become an arena where the different groups and interests in the community could 'argue it out amongst themselves and get the GLC out of the hot seat', as the GLC's Assistant Director General had envisaged would be the case. As a result the Forum tended to produce what may be called a 'lowest common denominator consensus'—that is to say it tended to arrive at a position over which there was a minimum of disagreement rather than a maximum of enthusiasm or support. This inevitably inhibited the Forum from adopting an aggressive or bold approach to both policy and strategy and consequently tended to harmonise its objectives and activities with those of the GLC. Another result was that there was considerable pressure from the Forum officers not to do anything which might injure what the Chairman called the 'impartiality' of the Forum. Indeed, the Forum's officers gave the impression of mini town councillors, being sticklers for orthodox procedure and believing in the technique of a quiet word in the GLC's ear rather than open and if need be aggressive pressure. Both GLC councillors and officials were surprised at the passive role of the officers. Their middle class image was respectability personified, and this was partly responsible for the fact that no coherent alternative was advanced to the concept of participation on offer from the GLC. Consequently the Forum drifted into a style of working and of decision-making that conveniently meshed into the GLC's structure: but although this drift appeared to be occurring by default rather than by a series of conscious or explicit decisions by the participants, it was rather a direct product of the GLC's role in structuring the Forum's *modus operandi*.

The Forum's Role

Throughout the period under study, Forum members regularly attempted to get to grips with what their role should be. Most of these attempts were inconclusive, but a fresh move was made in the spring of 1975 to generate a debate by the Chairman of the Policy Committee: 'Immediately there is a policy committee I get a flood of bumph from the GLC: you just get bogged down in it. So at one policy meeting I said "Let's put everything on one side and just discuss the role of the Forum".' The result was that he drafted a memorandum suggesting issues for consideration, such as whether the Forum was really representative; what policies should be given priority; what format the GLC plan should take; and the Forum's relationship with the GLC. On the latter, he wrote:

> To date most Forum activity has been in response to GLC papers and proposals. A few individual problems have been highlighted and pressed . . . but major matters . . . have not been pressed hard by the Forum, and have met a cool reception from the GLC.

When he presented this to a Forum meeting called specifically to discuss policy, there was an interesting debate between Forum members from which extracts are reproduced below. They reveal both differing conceptions of the Forum's role and an overriding commitment by the majority to a consensus strategy and to a constructive relationship with the GLC. The debate was essentially between the CGCA activist Jim Monahan and the mainstream of the Forum.

Monahan: The Forum is basically a mimic of the GLC—which is very convenient for them. It has achieved nothing beyond a lot of information from the GLC which we wouldn't otherwise have got. The Officers of the Forum have a consensus view that has prevented it operating properly as a body. What practical work has been done has been by individuals on the Forum, not the Forum itself. The GLC has just defused the situation. A lot of Forum members have no business being on it—through their financial power they have their own channels direct to the GLC anyway. Participation is a movement of power. What has happened is a stagnation of power. We don't have any real power—we are just a talking shop.

Ginsberg: But we have finished the battle—now we are doing things constructively.

Pembroke: There is no alternative to consensus. It is the method by which all government works.

Williams: Is the alternative to consensus really minority rule? What do I do as a Chairman?

Monahan, however, was not able to specify with any conviction what exactly his alternative was, except to suggest that the various sectional groups on the Forum should organise themselves so that members were 'active working delegates' from their groups. He maintained that local residents' interests were still being ignored.

Smith: Covent Garden has had more exposure than any other area in the country and if local people haven't had the gumption to press their case then to hell with them.

Wood: We are out of the situation where pressure groups could corner their portion of the cake. There will be no cake to go round if we all don't pull together.

GLC Officer: Yes, the Forum has been useful to the GLC. But the Team has been considerably influenced by it.

Williams: I do not believe the future holds any hope if the Forum disintegrates. It is essential as a means of discovering a method of working together.

No firm decisions were taken by the meeting, although there was a general feeling that a number of working 'action' groups should be set up so that the Forum could make more public impact and have a more immediately practical influence on events.

This was taken a step further after another paper from Leslie Ginsberg, the Policy Committee Chairman, discussed at a full Forum meeting a month later. It was decided to set up a series of study groups to examine such questions as housing, recreation and shopping, as well as promotional activities to encourage businesses to move into Covent Garden (in fact, with the exception of a trade promotion group, these never met). It was clear from the discussion that the concept of a self-help approach based on co-operative enterprises was attractive to the whole Forum. This particular concept reflected both the Forum's commitment to localised participation and its view that the deteriorating economic climate meant that of necessity there would have to be a return to a more self-dependent, self-sufficient mode of economic life.

Ginsberg: We are working with an antique system of local government based on the limitless growth of technocracy. The GLC has become a dinosaur. The Forum should help create a new philosophy of urban living. But the Forum is in danger of becoming like a political caucus on a local authority, representative only of itself.

Albery: We should pressure the GLC to direct funds to self-help projects. We must also work with private enterprise.

Overshadowing much of the internal debate on the Forum's role was the role of the Covent Garden Community Association (CGCA). During the first year of the Forum's existence the CGCA had faced something of a crisis. It was not even able to elect a fresh committee as it had done each year since its formation. This was largely for two reasons and they both had to do with the Forum. The first was that the issues in Covent Garden were not as dramatic or sharply formed as they had been previously, partly because the original plan had been abandoned and partly because the GLC was now actively co-operating with the community through the Forum. The second reason was that the energies of the principal CGCA activists had been channelled into the Forum so that they were no longer campaigning with their earlier verve (10 of the 12 strong CGCA Executive were Forum members in 1974–75).

Jim Monahan, for example, found himself slipping into a stalemate position: he could neither give the CGCA the attention it needed, nor perform the role he would have wished on the Forum. He held a minority viewpoint on the Forum and to obtain the support of a majority of members he needed to do a considerable amount of preparatory work. Yet he often came to meetings of the Forum inadequately prepared, reacting to particular issues or arguments of other members rather than adopting a coherent strategy which might have forced the pace on the Forum. The result was that the credibility of the CGCA's standpoint was undermined as he gave the impression of an individual sounding-off somewhat shrilly from the side-lines rather than being in the thick of the Forum's decision-making process.

Matters came to a head at the CGCA's annual general meeting on 18th July 1975. In the organisation's annual report for 1974–5 its dilemma was spelt out:

> To some extent the CGCA is responsible for its (the Forum's) creation, its successes and failures. What has emerged is that despite the Forum, the CGCA is still desperately needed to do the nitty-gritty pressurising, and to indicate new ideas for the area . . . In comparison to past years, the CGCA has not been so publicly active due in part to the fact that a number of its Executive members have also been members of the Forum. Now that the Forum is established as a negotiating body, the next year must see the re-emergence of the CGCA as a strong local pressure group.

The annual meeting was attended by some fifty people, spanning middle-aged to elderly working class residents and young middle class radicals. The main topic was a motion that 'Officers and Executive Committee members can not stand as candidates for the Forum'. The debate was by no means one-sided however and a number of CGCA members who were also on the Forum opposed it strongly:

Monahan: We must be seen as separate bodies. The Forum is better at negotiating with the GLC. The CGCA is better at pressurising. The CGCA cannot claim to be as representative as the Forum but it is better for action. These roles must be clearly distinguished from each other.

Gey: This motion must not be passed. Jim has been very important to the Forum. He has bitten into the developers where others of us have lacked the ability

	to do so. We also need to bridge between the two bodies.
Mackay:	We don't want to be liked. If we were we would not be doing our job. We are a pressure group. We must be a sore on the body politic. I foresee a situation where GLC and local authority bankruptcy leads to the developers moving back in and if that happens the CGCA must stand ready and prepared.

In a heated, though cordial, debate there were calls to 'by-pass' the Forum, accusations that the GLC was employing a policy of 'divide and rule' between the Forum and the CGCA and counter arguments that the CGCA must be represented on the Forum like any other interest group and that this could best be done by CGCA officers. Austen Williams was in the chair, having been the CGCA's figurehead since its inception, and he made it clear that he supported the resolution, even though it meant he would not re-stand as Chairman and would give his whole time to the chairmanship of the Forum. The motion was finally carried by 26 votes to 19.

The decision visibly upset the GLC Planning Team, since it represented a failure of the original objective of the Forum as the GLC saw it: namely that all the pressure groups in the area should be thrashing out their differences within the confines of the Forum.

Finance and the Plan

Early on in the life of the Forum, some of the Team officers were concerned about the consequences of the deteriorating national economic situation and the effect this might have on Covent Garden: 'What worries me is that at the end of it all a good plan will be produced but not implemented because of lack of resources. It is going to be very difficult for the GLC to turn around to the community and say 'sorry', all your effort has been shelved for the present.'

In the spring of 1975, Mr. Blackhurst addressed the Forum for 25 minutes on the financial position facing the GLC and its implications for Covent Garden. He explained that whereas revenue expenditure would be unaffected for the next year, it was probable that capital expenditure would be severely affected. For the year 1975–76, £1.3 million had been allocated to Covent Garden, of which 80 per cent (i.e. £930,000) would be spent on loan charges for property acquisitions. £115,000 could be spent on managing GLC properties, £200,000 on the Covent Garden Team's Office and salaries, £25,000 on publicity and £25,000 on site improvements. Rental income from GLC properties in the area would be £300,000 divided between residents (40%) and business or commerce (60%).

Most of his talk took the form of a highly informative lecture on the nature of local government finance and the great problems faced by the GLC. The Forum gave him their close attention and it was something of an educational exercise, fulfilling one of the GLC's original desires—namely, that it would be able to make local people through the medium of the Forum aware of the constraints involved in regenerating Covent Garden. Then Mr. Blackhurst came to the point:

> It is possible that we may have to consider a move towards the original plan, that is towards projects which will produce a market value rent. We also have to decide on the allocation of resources as between other areas and Covent Garden. But the GLC does give a high priority to Covent Garden because it is in the city centre and because we want to show how a city centre can be rescued.

As always, Mr. Blackhurst did not beat about the bush with the Forum: he told them bluntly that they would have to face up to economic 'realities' as the GLC saw them. The Forum received his comments in a somewhat subdued fashion: 'We have had our honeymoon with each other—our fun with the GLC,' said one member, 'We can't indulge ourselves anymore. We have to come to some accommodation with the GLC: this is emphasised by the financial plight.'

At the end, the Chairman said that Mr. Blackhurst's 'revelations' were welcome and he thanked him for attending. The meeting agreed to 'discuss the practical consequences of the new situation at a later stage', so effectively sidestepping the implications of what they had been told, in particular Mr. Blackhurst's statement that something closer to the financial base of the original plan might have to be attempted. For this placed a question mark over the effectiveness of 'participation' in the face of an economic system orientated to profit rather than to the interests of the indigenous community.

In this respect the views of Brian Anson, the former GLC planner who left the Covent Garden Team after identifying himself with the community, should be noted. He argued in rather scathing terms that the 'indigenous working class people have once again been used as a pawn in a trendy middle class game with the system.' He pointed to the influx of middle class residents in the 1970s and the simultaneous decline of the indigenous community, the rise of 'trendy' shops, boutiques and health food restaurants and the decline of traditional small businesses and cheap cafes. In short, he believed that, although the physical environment threatened by the original plan had been saved, the pattern of economic and social life had changed radically, threatening the existence of the indigenous community who were finding it increasingly difficult to afford to live in the area: 'It is no use defeating a £200 million plan if you destroy the fabric of an area in the process anyway, through gentrification.' (See also Christensen, pp. 131–8, Jenkins 1975, p. 238, Pitt, Ambrose & Colenutt.)

If the problem of finance imposed severe *external* constraints upon the Forum's impact, there were two *internal* constraints, partly self-imposed, partly thrust upon members by the Team, which critically affected its role. They were to some extent interlinked and concerned, on the one hand, the Forum's response to professional expertise and, on the other, the need to maintain contact with the community.

Expertise

Throughout its life the Forum was dogged by the problem of expertise: of how to get to grips with the technical nature of much of the argument presented by the GLC in the voluminous reports prepared by the Team. As has become apparent through the chapter, Forum discussions were often conducted on a relatively technical level and this was a major source of confusion for many of the non-professionals on the Forum, especially new members elected at the second and third elections who had not undergone the educative experience of those who had been members since the Forum's inception.

From the outset there were two different views on how the problem of expertise could be resolved. One view was expressed by a Forum officer: 'The crux of the matter is expertise: we need to match that of the local authority.' A contrary view was expressed by one of the radical members: 'The problem of the forum is that the GLC want it to be right in detail, whereas it should be right in general. The Team has consistently manipulated the Forum by posing the issues in technical terms.

In fact, the Forum did not face this problem head on and instead slipped almost unconsciously into conducting a dialogue with the Planning Team in the terms in which the Team presented its reports and proposals. It is doubtful however if the Forum could have done this without having amongst its members a number of professionals who could cope with the level and style of discussion that ensued. The most articulate of these was the Policy Chairman and himself a consultant architect–planner. He explained the dilemma of his role:

> When I was first asked to get involved in the Interim Working Party in 1973, I said 'no' because I believe these committees shouldn't have professionals on them. If you have a professional planner in a neighbourhood association facing a professional in the local authority, this can thwart involvement by local people. If you want real local participation it shouldn't be left to the planners to argue it out: you must do it in a way everyone understands.

But he *did* get involved, and later his initial reservations were shown to have been prophetic:

> I was elected to the Forum and to my surprise a lot of the community people have urged me to stay on because of my ability to translate planners' jargon into ordinary terms. I worry about this. I find myself acting as an interpreter at times: because I am there maybe some conflict is avoided which would have been healthier out in the open. Maybe this is the reason the GLC ring me up before each Forum meeting to discuss what is coming up.
>
> The purpose of these meetings should be participation, not for one to get involved in technical debate. The planners tend to use me as a kind of buffer between them and the public. I also try to translate the Forum's at times inarticulate views to the planning officials.

However, the fact that he was so pointedly aware of the dilemmas of his situation did not prevent him playing an important role on the Forum which to some extent became dependent on his technical advice and advocacy. And the fact that the Forum conducted its discussions with the GLC on a largely technical level further strengthened the consensus style of the Forum, since the detailed arguments on the technical issues debated left little scope for the intrusion of larger policy issues. Whether this could have been avoided is of course another matter because the GLC submitted so many reports and documents for the Forum to discuss that members hardly had time to read them thoroughly before meetings, let alone raise what in the circumstances would have been somewhat abstract issues over whether to break free of the technical argument and stick resolutely to general policy issues.

Contact with the Community

If the conflict which had preceded the setting up of the Forum was about anything it was about the GLC's failure to consult and involve the people of Covent Garden. It was therefore notable that the Forum did very little to maintain contact with those same people—the people it claimed to represent. (In fact, the GLC Team officers formally reminded the Forum twice about the necessity contained in its standing orders to maintain close contact with the community.) The main reason for this lack of active contact would appear to be that the Forum was so preoccupied with attending meetings and coping with the paperwork processed through by the GLC, that there was no time for action or for direct contact with the community (although such an excuse from local councillors might not be expected to be sympathetically received by community activists). It was a regular criticism of the Forum that it was 'all talk and no action', this being said by CGCA activists and GLC Officers alike.

The Forum was in fact committed by its standing orders to hold at least two report-back public meetings per year, but it was not until it had been in existence for five months that it held its first meeting (and the only one in the two-and-three-quarter years covered by this study). On 17th November 1974 approximately 120 people attended a Forum-convened public meeting. About 60 per cent of those present appeared to be from the indigenous community. The atmosphere was orderly and the Forum's vice-chairman, John Wood, began proceedings by stating: 'We have successfully entered new ground and achieved communication with a local authority that has not been achieved elsewhere. I wish to thank the GLC officers for helping the Forum and for giving us their time and advice.' Austen Williams added: 'We are no longer facing a vast bureaucratic machine—we are face to face with officials where we can argue practically and reasonably. But we have as a body difficulty in achieving clarity of mind and we are always in danger of boring each other!'

As the meeting was opened up for discussion there were rumblings of discontent from the tenants: it was claimed that they were not being consulted by the Forum and that they didn't even know where and when Forum meetings were held. Austen Williams conceded: 'We have not taken sufficiently seriously our representative role. We have also fallen down on communications with the people of this area.'

To loud clapping, one tenant said angrily: '*Make* Westminster pull the buildings down. Don't just sit there explaining the Council's difficulties.' In response to this, the Forum representatives became rather defensive and apologetic—which merely increased the discontent in the meeting. It was noticeable how confidently and competently those in the body of the meeting spoke and contested what was being said from the platform. Most of the people doing the talking were local working class women who were also more articulate than the men (this contrasted markedly with Forum meetings where, apart from the Treasurer who was a woman, the other women members spoke very rarely if at all).

The style of the meeting also contrasted with Forum meetings in a way that could not be explained simply by the fact that it was a much bigger gathering: a rumbustious style with considerable involvement from working class residents, as opposed to the more sedate style of the Forum with its middle class language and procedure. Some activists in the area held the view that the Forum's style was incompatible with high working class participation, as these comments indicate: 'The Forum just does not connect with ordinary people's ordinary feelings: and by the time an ordinary person has made it with the Forum, he becomes a piece of paper.' And: 'Most people in the area don't know what the Forum is. Working class residents are very action-orientated in a practical way and will turn out in force on, for example, a protest like the one we held against the closure of the local Sainsburys. But they feel the Forum meetings are too high-powered and, anyway, they are not interested in endless waffle.'

Forum meetings were certainly confusing to observers and the gap between it and the community was illustrated by the reply of an old working class resident who was asked how he felt having sat through his first Forum meeting: 'I can't figure out who's who. The CGCA lot are at one end, I know. But where is the Forum? Where is the GLC? . . . Oh—you mean everyone is the Forum and the GLC are at the far end of the table? . . . I can't understand it. Why are businessmen on?'

The Forum is Re-elected

Covent Garden faced a second Forum election in November 1975. It was again organised on a postal vote basis, with voting closing on 17th November. As the election approached, there was considerable anxiety amongst the GLC officers as to whether it would be successful. One officer said:

The situation was still fraught before the last election, but not so now. The bulldozers didn't come and this time the community is not fighting bulldozers it is fighting blight which, although it doesn't seem as dramatic, is possibly even more serious. Apathy has set in, but to avoid the danger of the Forum and the GLC being 'hand in hand', I can't do anything to stir up interest. This is terribly frustrating because the election really needs a good PR job to project it properly.

The last two meetings of the old Forum were certainly not conspicuous by their dynamism. The second last one achieved a quorum only twenty minutes after it was scheduled to start and the last one only half an hour afterwards. At the first of these, the Forum's Chairman appealed for more nominations for the election, 'otherwise all the work of the past year will be undone'. That the Forum still saw the election as the GLC's responsibility was underlined by an exchange at the meeting. In answer to a question from a member as to what would happen if there were not enough candidates, the Forum secretary, Simon Pembroke, said that that was 'the GLC's problem' and a GLC officer replied that she would need to consult Mr. Blackhurst who was again Returning Officer. The GLC's Forum Liaison Officer had been forced to organise the election on her own, obtaining virtually no support from the Forum, and was understandably saddened by this: 'I constantly have to treat them as if they were thirty children. I have to tell them what to do. For example, I nagged them until I was silly to get them to organise registrations of voters; I also nagged them to get people to stand; now I have got to push them to get people to vote.'

In fact, the election went relatively successfully. There were more than enough candidates: 57—19 down on the previous year. Registrations were up from 4374 to 5360. In 1974 the electorate was made up of people who completed a registration form entitling them to vote. This resulted in an electorate of 25% residents and 75% other categories. For the 1975 election all 2891 residents on the Parliamentary Electoral Register were automatically included on the Register, plus 2469 persons in categories other than residents and who had completed a registration form. The poll fell from 33.6% in 1974 to 27.3% in 1975, suggesting that there was still considerable interest locally in the Forum. The Returning Officer argued that the fall could be accounted for by the inclusion in the 1975 register of about 1500 residents who received a ballot paper without expressly asking to do so by virtue of being on the electoral roll.

Mr. Blackhurst, as Returning Officer, conducted a survey based on a random sample of 100 ballot papers for which subsequent checks indicated a sampling error of less than 5%. This showed that, as in the first Forum election, the total votes cast for each group of candidates matched almost exactly the proportion of seats on the Forum held by that group. Moreover, this survey showed that over 60% of voters had voted for candidates in one or more of the categories, suggesting that they voted for *individuals* as well as for *interests*. This finding in the GLC's eyes tended to vindicate the Forum as a body which resolved the conflicting interests in the area and expressed a common viewpoint.

The new Forum was a more professional, middle class body in composition. The voice of the indigenous working class had in any event been muted for some time because Sam Driscoll had contracted a severe illness which prevented him being active and was later to lead to his death in 1976. In addition, the CGCA's decision not to permit its Executive members to be on the Forum deprived the Forum of a radical element (although a different radical element did emerge later). The officers remained the same, with the exception of Treasurer where Miss Christina Smith, a local businesswoman and resident, replaced Sheila Malham.

Agreement on the Plan

The final stages of agreeing the plan took place throughout 1976, beginning with a special meeting of the GLC's Covent Garden Committee on 17th March. The Committee had taken the unprecedented step of switching its meeting from its normal venue at County Hall to a hall within Covent Garden (a decision vindicated by a large public turnout). Its purpose was to consider the policy for the new plan and a report had been prepared setting out the policy options for decision; this was distributed in advance to the Forum and to members of the public at the meeting. Included were the views and recommendations of the Forum and of other bodies (for example, the CGCA) which had responded during the consultation process. The Forum members on the Committee intervened to argue the case for a higher density of housing than was proposed by the Team: people in the city centre were accustomed to living close to each other, they argued, and a higher density could accommodate more homes. After a discussion in which views were exchanged with some vehemence, the

Committee agreed to the Forum's position. The Forum also opposed widescale pedestrianisation of streets because it believed people in the area were 'used to traffic'. Most of the Forum's recommendations proposed only marginal changes in the options presented and, by and large, the Committee accepted the Forum's views. It was clear that the consultative process of the previous two years had produced a considerable area of agreement between the Forum and the GLC on major policy questions. Indeed, that agreement on general policy extended even to the CGCA.

However, when it came to the question of *implementing* these policies, the participation experiment in Covent Garden was stretched to its limits. It was one thing to agree on a series of policy objectives, but quite another practically to express them, especially when the physical implications of policies had been largely neglected during the previous two years of discussion.

The GLC introduced the physical dimension through what were called 'Feasibility Studies'. In essence, each study examined a particular site in Covent Garden in order to see how it could fit into the general policy plan. Three options for each site were offered: (1) total redevelopment, (2) partial rehabilitation and redevelopment, or (3) infill development and rehabilitation. But although the Forum had agreed in early 1975 to feasibility studies being conducted into chosen sites and they had then been processed by the GLC Team, these studies had receded into the background as Forum members grappled with policy issues. It therefore came as something of a shock to the Forum when, without prior notice, the Team produced a Feasibility Studies Progress Report at the February 1976 meeting of the GLC's Covent Garden Committee. When this report came up for discussion, there was an angry intervention from Jo Hanlon, a worker in the area and one of the radicals on the Forum, who was sitting in the public gallery. An uproar developed (significantly, the two Forum members who sat as of right on the Committee played no part in the incident; their role tended to give credence to the view shared by some Forum members that they were largely ineffective on the Committee since they consistently adopted a passive stance). It appeared to Forum members that they were being by-passed by the Team and that there had been an attempt to present them with a *fait accompli*, especially since the Committee had appeared to be proceeding towards a decision before Hanlon's intervention. In fact, it was not the Team's intention to have a decision made and they were merely presenting the

Report to draw attention to the feasibility dimension of the policy in the plan. But the issue was evidently mishandled and resulted in considerable acrimony and tension between the Forum and the GLC officers. The nett effect was to sour the atmosphere in which discussion took place over the feasibility studies.

Between the outburst at the February GLC Committee and May of that year, very little progress was made on consultation over the feasibility studies, as the Forum dug in its heels over the issue. It would appear that the delay also reflected the Forum's basic confusion over the feasibility studies and its inability to handle practical decisions over sites in the area. In addition, the Planning Team was in a quandary. When the senior planners in the Team re-examined the studies they found that there was much to be desired about the work of the architects who had analysed the sites and formulated alternative courses of action. There were mistakes in the architects' calculations, discrepancies and a general lack of consistency between the various studies. Unlike the planners in the Team, the architects involved had little direct knowledge of Covent Garden and their work was not as thorough as that of the planners.

Because of the technical issues involved, some Forum members believed that it should hire its own architect and produce alternative schemes that could, technically, match those of the GLC point for point. But this idea did not progress very far, partly because the GLC was not prepared to see its money used to employ architects who would vet their own architects' work. However that was precisely what the CGCA were able to do. The group had received a grant from the Sainsbury Trust and used it to employ two architects, one of whom was Jim Monahan, to work fulltime on rehabilitating short-term housing in the area which the GLC had decided it was not financially viable to undertake. With these resources the CGCA also produced its own detailed schemes for the feasibility sites, creating some resentment towards the CGCA from those within the Planning Team who saw in the CGCA's initiative a slur on their professional ability. The CGCA consequently set the pace on community reaction, partly because the Forum lacked the resources and ability to do the kind of detailed and expert work that was required.

Nevertheless the Forum did play a crucial role. A radical faction had come together on the Forum, comprising several new members elected at the second election and Jo Hanlon who had formerly edited the Forum's newspaper. Initially the Forum confined itself to examining the sites chosen by the GLC. But, under pressure from the radicals, the Forum began to look beyond the GLC sites, to form a fresh and comprehensive view of all the physical opportunities that existed in Covent Garden for implementing the policy of the plan. The fact that it took the Forum some time to adopt this approach is indicative of how constrained it felt itself to be by the proposals of the GLC; conditioned by the consensus role it had played since its inception, the Forum tended to see its role as being to improve upon such proposals rather than to consider whether the assumptions upon which they were based were acceptable.

In addition, the radicals on the Forum were concerned that it should assume a more belligerent role. A similar view was held by the Forum's fulltime worker, Janet Sutherland, who had been appointed at the start of the year and who saw her role in a more activist and interventionist light than her predecessor. This group of radicals proposed that the Forum should organise meetings on the sites of the feasibility studies, partly to inform and involve those affected and partly to assist the Forum to form a coherent and comprehensive view on what should be done with each site: 'We saw it as a means by which the people affected could come up with their own proposals, as a means of extending participation,' said one. The Forum accepted this basic proposal although it was clear that it saw the site meetings in the liberal terms of a two-way information process, rather than a means of enabling the people affected to be the key element in deciding what the policy should be. That is to say, the mainstream of the Forum saw its role as to make decisions on behalf of the community whereas the radicals saw the potential of allowing what they called 'grass roots power' to express itself.

The opportunity for such direct participation arose after the publication in July 1976 of the GLC's draft plan for Covent Garden, which was accompanied by a revised report on the feasibility studies. They were made available for consultation and the GLC announced that a public meeting would be organised for September, in time to assess public reaction before the final plan went for decision to the GLC Committee in the autumn. The Forum Policy Committee prepared a detailed series of recommendations for amendment of the policies in the draft plan, but it was clear that there was general approval for its contents.

However, it was the feasibility report which resulted in the most contention and it consumed much of the Forum's energy over the summer. As originally proposed by the radicals on the Forum, a series of meetings were organised on each of the sites chosen for a feasibility study. These proved to be one of the most rewarding parts of the Forum's work, as a high involvement of the occupants of the sites was achieved. Initially, the Forum convened a meeting on each site and encouraged the occupants to form their own group and come to a considered view on what should be done with the site. A chairman of each site group was elected from the first meeting and liaised with Forum members—predominantly from amongst the radicals—together with the Forum's fulltime worker who also attended the site meetings. These were well attended by site occupants, and the CGCA and GLC were also present to give their respective views. On each site, the principal focus for discussion was the three proposed options from the GLC for total redevelopment, partial redevelopment or extensive renovation. But it soon became apparent that these options were frequently all unacceptable. There was also a questioning of whether the GLC had chosen the correct sites for action (they had in fact been taken from the rejected 1968 Plan rather than looked at afresh). The CGCA representatives tended to press the case for incremental development and rehabilitation—that is to say, rather than deciding to demolish sites and redevelop them, it would be preferable to modify, renovate and improve the properties step by step.

For the Forum, the experience of engaging in participation with the occupants had both advantages and disadvantages. Whilst the radicals on the Forum were enthusiastic about the occupants' meetings, Forum officers were much less so, fearing that this direct liaison could injure the 'impartiality' of the Forum. For example, the procedure adopted was for the occupants' meetings to agree a response which would then be put to meetings of the Forum's Policy Committee. But most members of the Policy Committee did not attend the site meetings and so were out of touch with occupants' feelings. There were also disagreements on the Committee about whether representatives of the occupants' associations should be present at Policy meetings which drafted recommendations for the full Forum to discuss. A proposal from the Policy Committee Chairman (then a property consultant) that the second half of its meetings on the sites should be in camera with occupants excluded so that the Committee could be 'detached' while forming its recommendations, was in fact defeated. But it pinpointed a dilemma which the Forum felt about its role: should it engage in 'direct democracy', acting as a conduit for the occupants' views, or did it have some large 'representative democracy' function, deciding what *it* felt was the best policy, consulting the occupants but not being bound by their views? In one case, the Policy Committee decided on a course of total demolition and redevelopment, going completely against the occupants' view and causing conflict with the occupants who felt the Forum ought to represent *them*.

This attitude contrasted with that of the CGCA which, having agreed a view with the occupants, then saw its duty as being to represent that view. It is indeed somewhat ironic that the Forum played a role in relation to the occupants rather similar to the GLC's role in relation to itself. Faced with the differing aspirations of the GLC, the CGCA and the occupants, the Forum chose to arbitrate between the interests involved in decisions over the sites. In fact, there was eventually considerable agreement between the Forum, the CGCA and the occupants, and also a common disagreement with the GLC's proposals which were thought to be ill-conceived and inadequately prepared. Certainly, the GLC's proposals contained anomalies which could only satisfactorily be explained in terms of an abject lack of detailed knowledge about the sites. For instance, one of the feasibility studies proposed the demolition of a site containing one of Britain's leading silversmiths. The GLC's architects were apparently unaware of the company's existence and the property could have cost several millions to purchase; and, to make matters worse, the Forum's fulltime worker discovered a site just across the road with an old empty London Electricity Board building which could have been demolished relatively cheaply.

Notwithstanding the fact that almost all the GLC sites contained similar, if less extreme, anomalies, the Forum collectively felt hidebound by the fact that the GLC was asking it to comment on a series of specific sites. Used as it had become to reacting to GLC proposals rather than initiating its own, the Forum initially felt constrained when dealing with the feasibility studies into restricting its comments and proposals to the GLC's recommended sites. As one member put it: 'We were incapable of thinking laterally when that was exactly what was needed.' Eventually however the Forum did draw up a list of vacant sites in the area as alternatives to the GLC's proposals and which they said should be given first priority in any development or rehabilitation work. It also suggested a concept of 'parallel phasing' in such work: that is to say, instead of setting a series of future dates on which major works would begin on each site as the

GLC proposed, the Forum wanted work to start on all sites, with part of it being started immediately and part later, so as to cause minimum disruption and also to get some progress at least throughout Covent Garden rather than concentrated on a few sites. Thus, the Forum came to adopt a strategy over the feasibility sites which contrasted markedly with its general response on the GLC's policy proposals where it typically saw its role as being to modify rather than suggest an alternative. It ended up backing a 'least disturbance' policy for the sites which was in fact largely accepted by the GLC (although by that time the GLC would have had grave difficulty in financing its original extensive demoliton and redevelopment proposals, and so the Forum's viewpoint was not the sole factor encouraging it toward such a policy).

By the time the GLC's public consultation meeting took place on 8th September 1976, the plan was in the last stages of being finalised. The meeting was attended by some 250 people. A roving microphone was provided and, after an introductory speech by the Covent Garden Committee Chairman, Jean Merriton, a lively discussion took place. It was clear that local people wanted a change in the *style* of planning and Jim Monahan was loudly clapped when he said that there was no real disagreement with the objectives or with the overall policies of the plan: 'The real villains are your professionals. A lot can be achieved with very little. Use local initiative. Plans are meaningless—what we want is action. At the nitty gritty level you on the Committee and your officers can't cope.' This view was expressed more comprehensively in the CGCA pamphlet *Keep The Elephants Out of Covent Garden*. And much the same position was adopted by the Forum in its publication *Less Planning More Happening*. The distinctive concept of planning that evolved through the Forum had been well summarised in part of a broadsheet it produced in March 1976:

> In many cases, the planners are still indulging in the grandiose thinking that led to the old plan; *improved street parking* would be better than the suggested underground car park and would be £100,000 per year cheaper; *filling empty flats and vacant sites* would provide housing sooner than long term plans for large blocks of flats; a *doctor's surgery* now is more important than a large health centre later. The GLC and their planners must learn to think small, and think about the present.

On 20th October 1976 the GLC Committee met to agree the final *Action Area Plan for Covent Garden*, and the full GLC Council ratified this in November. Broadly speaking, the plan reflected the views of the community; even the CGCA regarded it as a 'victory' for local people. Although it would have been surprising if it did not have strong local support in view of all the time and effort that many local people had put into it, there could be no doubting their sense of satisfaction, well expressed by the Forum's Chairman:

> The new plan . . . marks a watershed in the history of Central London. People may have their reservations, but to compare this plan with its predecessor is to discover that something truly startling has happened. A plan that, blindly and perversely, took no account of the wishes and feelings of the local community, that would have utterly destroyed the shape and texture of its life, has given way to a plan in the making of which the local community has played an unprecedented part. To call this simply a successful exercise in protest or participation would be to miss the real point of what has happened. A community has begun to discover and to recognise itself in a new way, and rightly to demand full recognition by the very powers which, only a few years ago, were set to destroy it, as so many communities have been destroyed in other great cities.

But the Forum's work had not finished and no sooner had the process of consultation on the plan ended than a third Forum election loomed on the horizon. It took place on 28th January 1977 and marked a new phase in the Covent Garden participation experiment, also providing a convenient 'cut-off' point for this book.

Changes in the Forum's Role

One of the most notable changes in the Forum over the period under review was its gradual albeit grudging acceptance of the financial, legal and practical constraints within which the GLC operated, and, with this, a greater readiness to defer to the GLC's viewpoint. That had in fact been one of the objectives of the GLC when it initiated the participation experiment. As one senior GLC officer put it:

> It needed an all-out effort to see whether public participation worked. Essentially, participation is in direct conflict with representative institutions: I think basically it is to do with size. Elected representatives cover a wider area and have responsibility for the 'public interest' and for establishing priorities. Ultimately, responsibility must always rest with the elected representative or

the public interest will lose out. So all we can ever hope for with public participation is that the local community understands the constraints within which we all have to operate.

The forum had hardly been in existence nine months when the Chairman of the GLC Committee was able to say with satisfaction:

The education of the local community has been extremely useful. Whereas previously people were blasting away from a position of ignorance, the Forum has made them aware of the problems and limitations the GLC face.

However, a consequence of the mutual understanding that developed between the Forum and the GLC was a marked estrangement of the indigenous working class residents from the Forum which occurred for three main reasons. First, as we have seen, the Forum's adoption of a consensus style went against the more belligerent instincts of the residents. Second, the technical and detailed level of discussion at Forum meetings seemed to residents to be remote from their day-to-day concerns and their perception of what was required to revitalise the area. Third, the Forum's failure to undertake practical activities led to a feeling in the community that it was 'all talk and no action'.

All these reasons are inter-linked and flowed from what may be conveniently described as a 'middle class style' of community organisation. As one working class Forum member put it rather caustically: 'The Forum is a very middle class body, the whole way it is organised. More truth comes out of people who have butterflies in their stomach at the thought of talking at a Forum meeting, than all of those careerists and fast talkers. In the relaxed atmosphere of, say, a pub you can really talk—but not on the Forum.' Community workers active in Covent Garden corroborate such a view, although whether it is entirely fair does not strictly matter in this context, for the crucial issue is the working class residents' *perception* of the Forum. The composition of the Forum certainly appeared to become more middle class over time. Statistically, the class representation of its members remained fairly constant, but the indigenous residents became less vocal and influential and, consequently, the Forum gave the impression to an outsider of being an almost exclusively middle class body— an impression strengthened by the fact that the officers were thoroughly middle class, stamping the Forum with an image that was altogether proper and conventional.

The officers formed a cohesive group which effectively controlled the internal affairs of the Forum: they determined the composition of both the agenda and the minutes, and exerted considerable influence at Forum meetings, especially in the second and third years when the Forum included newer and less experienced members. Moreover, the fact that they conducted Forum meetings in relatively formal language (which one working class member described as 'posh') and according to an etiquette which placed a higher premium upon graciousness rather than substance during debate, had the effect, especially when coupled with the insistence upon a consensus style, of being tant-amount to an *ideology* of running the Forum. Those who did not conform to this ideology—as was the case for working class residents and for the radicals—lacked credibility and therefore influence on the Forum's direction. Not surprisingly, therefore, both groups became steadily disillusioned with it.

The procedure under which Forum business was conducted (and for which the Forum officers in concert with the GLC officers were largely responsible) also meant that, in the words of one member, it got 'bogged down in its own bureaucracy and was unable to cope with issues'. As a consequence the Forum was forced to adopt an ideological stance favouring the status quo. This is illustrated by the problem of squatting which came up for debate at a Forum meeting on 10th June 1976, over an occupation of Trentishoe Mansions, an empty building in the area. Fifty people had moved in and elected their own management committee, with each occupier paying £3 a week towards running, repair and cleaning costs. The radicals proposed that 'the GLC be urged to licence their continued occupation until such time as the future of the building may be determined'. Despite a suggestion from a GLC officer that the GLC, while not able to grant a licence without committing an offence under the Public Health Act, might nevertheless be prepared to turn a blind eye to the occupation, Forum members expressed vehement oppos-ition to the squat. An unusual alliance of property developers and indigenous residents opposed the motion. 'Can we really put our name to an act which is illegal?' asked property consultant Alex Moss, 'These people have stolen someone else's property. I find the motion personally repulsive.' Resident Kathy Francomb saw squatting as a threat by outsiders to working class residents like herself who were struggling to remain in the area. But the Forum Chairman was at great pains to avoid taking a decision about the principle of squatting. To do so on such a controversial topic would be to infringe the consensus ideology under which the Forum operated and he pleaded for a decision on the 'merits' of the particular case without taking a view on the question of squatting as a whole. Eventually it became apparent that the motion had little support and it was withdrawn.

It should be noted that the radicals on this occasion as on others displayed a certain amateurishness in their conduct on the Forum and their criticisms of its role. But this, as Saunders (1979, pp. 229–30) shows in his discussion of the way in which the interventions of the young radicals in the minority Labour group on Croydon Council could also be portrayed as 'amateurish', was principally because they were forced to reject 'the informal and private rules of the game'. Those rules were commonly accepted between the Forum's officers and the Team officers. The radicals also had cause to be exasperated by what they saw as the conservative direction given by the Forum's officers and the refusal of the Forum to stand up to the GLC and to the growing influence of property and business interests on the Forum.

The contrast with the CGCA was vivid. Although the CGCA, too, was controlled by a small group (of radical activists) it had high working class participation and support, manifesting itself at public meetings, at its annual general meetings, on protests and community projects, in the Social Centre which the CGCA had initiated and through the tenants' associations it helped to establish. The CGCA was undoubtedly closer to the residential community, or to be more precise, closer to those residents active in community affairs. This was partly because the CGCA saw itself as directly representing residents' interests, and partly because its commitment to participatory methods of action and protest attracted interest and enthusiasm: it enabled people to get involved in a tangible and practical way. The CGCA also took up individual grievances and problems, gaining the reputation as a body which 'got things done' and with it the allegiance of local working class people. By contrast to the aloof and informal style of the Forum, the CGCA's style was extremely formal and down-to-earth. It was the more approachable of the two bodies. Decisions and discussions would often take place in the Social Centre, over a pint of beer, and public meetings were lively and informal and characterised by frequent interventions from working class residents, especially women.

It is in fact difficult to analyse the changing role of the Forum in isolation from the activities of the CGCA, for the latter's existence as an aggressive pressure group accentuated the Forum's tendency to adopt a consensus strategy. Had the CGCA not existed and instead had its activists channelled their energies into the Forum, it may well have had to adopt more of a pressure group posture simply in order to prevent a vacuum opening up in the community politics of Covent Garden; the role of the Forum may then have been quite different. As it was the CGCA played something of a pressure group role in relation not merely to the GLC but to the Forum as well. It had most impact on the Forum during the feasibility studies controversy when it helped persuade the Forum to adopt a position much the same as its own; indeed it is doubtful whether the Forum would have adopted the radical position it did on the feasibility sites without being prodded by the CGCA which, as we have seen, was able to take the initiative and produce its own options.

Nevertheless, however much the CGCA may have influenced the Forum from time to time, this did not rival the influence of the GLC through the Team's officers. Far from this influence decreasing over time, as the Forum became more experienced and confident, it increased. This was because the closer the Forum and its officers became wedded to the GLC's style of administration and decision-making, the more dependent they became upon the Team. Its officers soon came to appreciate the full advantages of such close co-operation as opposed to the distant relationship of a pressure group. Eversley comments (p. 155) that 'the planner's traditions make him a paternalist by nature' and, working mainly through the Forum's officers, the Team was able to influence them considerably, as one member of the Team admitted: 'The Team does 'lead' the Forum officers to a surprising degree, and they do seem rather naive at times.' Another Team member extended this: 'If you realised the extent to which we as GLC officials control the flow of information and regulate it as to whom we give it and when, you would be surprised.' And yet a further Team member elaborated on the way in which information was presented to the Forum for decision: 'The whole approach of the Team was almost to evade the real issues involved. This was not a conscious policy in the sense of being discussed and formally agreed at meetings of the Team's officers. But it was delib-erate nevertheless—almost a natural way of working for us.'

The nett result was that the GLC through the Team was able to control and regulate the activities and impact of the Forum. But it is important to understand that whilst this was not a crude or heavy handed form of control, neither did it simply 'happen'. Even though both GLC councillors and officials were quite insistent about their desire not to 'impose' any style of participation or any specific policy on the Forum, the nett effect of their role was normally to do precisely that. It was a natural bureaucratic consequence of the inter-locking consultative relationship between the Forum and the GLC, reinforced by the lack of time, resources and back-up facilities which made it difficult for Forum members to resist the steady drip-drip effect of GLC attitudes and views seeping through the many reports which the Forum had to consider. One Team officer explained:

> The way the Forum was set up and is now manipulated by the GLC is not a process of conspiracy in the normal sense of the term. It is the whole value judgement selective process used by officers, the regulating at the point at which they feel they may be out of control. The *instinct* was always there to control the Forum: a very ingrained, deep instinct. Nobody, least of all officers, are prepared to operate out of their depth. Therefore to attempt to control the Forum is a natural reflex: a conservative, inhibiting, regulating influence and therefore a conspiracy in that sense.

Influence of the Forum

In principle the scope for the Forum to influence the GLC was considerable. It had extensive access to GLC decision-makers and therefore possibly the greatest opportunity that any neighbourhood council has so far had to influence a local authority in Britain. The GLC officials consulted it at every stage and in exhaustive detail. The Forum's views were incorporated in reports discussed at GLC Committee meetings and two Forum members had the right to sit on the Committee and to intervene in debates. The Forum had the unique opportunity to scrutinise planning applications before they went to Committee. In addition it had, for a community group, relatively large resources (virtually unlimited access to the GLC Team's photocopier, to give only a small example) and its members were relatively articulate and experienced in (to use Donnison's terms) 'micro politics'.

In practice however the situation was more complex and a full analysis is necessary before an attempt can be made to assess the influence of the Forum.

First it is necessary to acknowledge that the Forum's influence was necessarily limited at the outset by the economic forces which determined property values and regulated the business life of the area as well as the housing situation (CDP, *Profits Against Houses* and *The Costs of Industrial Change*, also Broadbent). Acute limitations were also placed on the Forum's ability to influence by the financial and legal constraints accepted by the GLC. These observations are made in passing merely to emphasise that the community politics of Covent Garden cannot be divorced from national forces impinging on the area; it is beyond the scope of the book to attempt to quantify the precise impact of these forces in restricting the ability of local people to exert influence over the future of their area.

Nevertheless, by its very existence, the Forum was able to mitigate the impact of property developers because the GLC had to recognise the Forum as a further constraint on *its* decisions. As a senior GLC officer explained:

> Of course it helps to have the Forum operating the way it does. It tends to highlight those things that we in an institutional sense cannot do and so has an educative effect on the community. But, on the other hand, they do push us (for example, the compulsory purchase order on Centre Point had no case in planning law but was won on political grounds). There is a new kind of feeling in planning and one can threaten developers with this.

Such a view is borne out by the way in which developers came regularly to Forum meetings anxious to justify their projects and head off potential opposition from the Forum. But the nett result of such consultation should not be exaggerated. As was demonstrated earlier in the chapter, the Forum was often placed in a position of accepting a *fait accompli* when faced with a property developer. In one case, a developer had obtained planning permission in 1965 for an office block which the Forum would have opposed, but in the event they were only asked to comment on the elevation of the building.

The Forum was also frustrated in its aim of restoring housing on the many sites in the area which had had an illegal change of use to offices, businesses or shops. This was partly because of the lengthy process of local authority bureaucracy: the relevant local authorities were both reluctant and slow to take enforcement action to insist that the owner converted the property back to its original housing use. Additionally, financial interests have exerted a disproportionate overall power at the expense of the jobs and homes of working class Londoners (Ambrose & Colenutt, pp. 79–103), and Covent Garden proved no exception. A further area in which the Forum felt itself trapped by property forces was where premises were altered on a piecemeal, ad-hoc basis. This process of incremental change which slipped through loopholes in the law encouraged a creeping gentrification of the area throughout the period of the Forum's life—and the Forum was powerless to check the growth of new boutiques, health food shops and expensive restaurants which, largely because they could afford higher rents, replaced the old corner shops, small traders and cheap cafes used by the indigenous residents.

In terms of its influence on the ground in the day to day pattern of economic life the Forum's effect was at best marginal. However, when it came to formulating the GLC's plan for the area the Forum came more into its own. It is clear that the Forum (as well as the CGCA) did manage to shift the emphasis of the plan radically, from a comprehensive demolition and development approach to a more incremental step-by-step approach. The influence of the Forum can be summarised as follows:

1. From a careful reading of the GLC documents during the period under study, a steady and cumulative influence of the Forum is discernible and is evident in the agreed policy report.

2. In a very high percentage of the planning applications the Forum's views were accepted; where the GLC took an opposite point of view, this was usually in terms of legal or procedural obligations under planning law. The result was the accretion of what one GLC officer referred to as the 'equivalent of Judge-made law: we came to know what the community would stand for'. It should however be recalled that, as was shown earlier in the chapter, the planners were able to exert considerable influence over the Forum's Filter Committee through which the applications were initially processed.

3. The Forum secured definite amendments to the plan: for example a passage in a policy report on entertainment uses, which encouraged massage parlours, was struck out in the final version.

4. Forum ideas such as that for an 'entertainment route' through the area were incorporated in the plan. So was a proposal to have open spaces of a smaller size than the single large one first suggested by the GLC.

5. A major success was achieved in switching the focus on a number of feasibility sites for the physical implementation of the

plan, to taking whatever opportunity arose in the area to achieve housing gains.

6.   The Forum undoubtedly changed the attitudes of the Covent Garden planners, if only because the latter for professional reasons had to take account of the Forum as a constraint upon their activities.

Consequently, under the Forum's influence, the GLC opted for a plan of minimum disturbance rather than wholesale redevelopment. It might plausibly be argued that such a change from the original plan merely reflected the changed economic climate and the collapse of the property market after 1973: that the low-profile of the new plan would have occurred anyway because the restriction on private capital and the limitation on public finance inevitably required a plan geared to rehabilitation rather than demolition and redevelopment. However the situation was not as straightforward as this. Merely to argue that market forces would have produced activity without any plan rather similar to that which was taking place in Covent Garden around the time the plan was being agreed, may say something about the real impact of such physical planning (participatory or not) but avoids explaining the specifically political factors which produced the change in the nature of the plan. Moreover, in the absence of the plan it is likely that the process of change in the area would have slowed down still further while owners opted for temporary renovations and short term leases in anticipation of cashing in later on a property boom. With the plan agreed there was the opportunity to exert some control over such a boom.

Not the least of the Forum's impact was on the planners themselves, as one of the Team's members explained:

> People will argue that the planning work dragged on as long as it did because of participation. This is not so. Local people were saying the same thing at the end of 1976 as they were at the public meetings back in 1973. It isn't the community that has changed its attitudes: it is the GLC. The process was so slow because the GLC and the planners needed educating. One of the failures in planning is that, partly because of the professional training of planners and partly because of the way a local authority operates, we can be deaf to the wishes of the community.

The success of the Forum in influencing the plan must, then, be balanced against its inability to check market forces and there remained a crucial battle still to be fought: whether the plan would be implemented according to the community's wishes or whether economic pressures would render much of it redundant. Excluded from the plan were many supplementary issues, for example, management policy on who would be able to rent property or who would get the new housing planned. In that context the words of a member of the Team at a public meeting on 14th March 1977 in retrospect seem uncomfortably prophetic: 'The plan excluded the "how things are actually done" issues, as opposed to rather woolly things like housing mix etc. Nobody lives in a 150 page plan, or eats in it or works in it. It is how it is implemented that really matters.'

In short, the Forum was able to influence, in some significant respects, the 'paper' content of the plan. But it is very doubtful whether in the translating of that plan from paper to practical reality, the Forum's influence will prove to have been very great. In the period after my detailed research was completed, the advent of a Conservative controlled GLC encouraged private sector market forces within the area which quickly demonstrated just how marginal was the Forum's influence. 'Who would have believed when we were set up in April 1971 that eight years later we would still be here fighting the same fights? . . . that old alliance of planners, politicians, and property developers is back at work . . . Money counts again, not people,' said the CGCA's Annual Report for 1978–9. In addition, although the experiment in Covent Garden extended public participation in a novel and comprehensive way, there were important failures in this. Working class residents were not involved to any significant degree. Nor was the level of participation higher than the lower rungs of Arnstein's ladder, partly because no transfer of power or resources to the Forum was ever envisaged by the GLC and partly because the dominant thinking in the Forum adopted a liberal and consensus position which did not seek such a transfer. The Forum's policy achievements were thus even more prey to fluctuations in the property market and to changes in the political direction of the GLC or of the Department of the Environment, a suitable epitaph being provided by a member of the GLC Team: 'Participation is the casting of small crumbs to people as decisions get bigger and bigger.'

Part Three

CONCLUSIONS

7

Participation and Mobilisation

> The potential control of the state increases the more closely the
> working population is knit to the state system. We should think for
> the moment not of overtly repressive control but simply of
> management of the working class, its 'families' and 'groups' in the
> business of reproduction of the labour force and of capitalist
> relations.
> Cynthia Cockburn, *The Local State* (Pluto, 1977), p. 101.

Before drawing on the lessons of Covent Garden and attempting to
establish a fresh perspective through which the practice of participation
can be evaluated, it is as well to review what the preceding chapters
have revealed about the nature of participation. In a nutshell, the aim
has been to contrast the aspirations and indeed rhetoric of advocates
of participation with an examination of recent practice. Towards that
end, the argument has progressed through a number of stages. First it
was shown that participation advocates divided broadly into two
camps: liberals and radicals. Then the experience of neighbourhood
councils in England was surveyed, demonstrating the inadequacies of
both liberal and radical theories of participation but confirming the
general validity of the distinction made between them. Next, the
perspective of government was analysed and it appeared that
participation was being officially sponsored in order to secure popular
legitimacy for government programmes. Moreover, the official perspective identified appeared to correspond closely to the practice even
of the 'non-governmental' neighbourhood councils described in
chapter two. However, since the analysis at that stage relied
predominantly upon interpretation of official publications and secondary sources, it could not be claimed with any certainty that the *desire*
by government to regulate participation reflected itself in *practice*.
Nor, without additional research into the specific processes of public
participation through neighbourhood councils, could it be confirmed
that the findings suggested in chapter three had a general validity. In

summary, then, the argument prior to examination of the Covent Garden experience suggested that public participation, far from producing a transfer of power or at least influence from government to citizen, actually appeared in practice to be more explicable in terms of a process of mobilisation of consent.

Against that background a detailed analysis of the Covent Garden Forum was presented. It was shown how the authorities, facing considerable local hostility, agreed to the establishing of a neighbourhood council which then became an important mechanism for securing legitimacy and consent over the future development of the area. The chapters on Covent Garden further underlined the gap between the theory of the participatory advocates and the reality of participation. However, far from there being a gap between the practice and the *authority's concept* of participation, they in fact tended to coincide, and it is therefore of interest to spell out more clearly how exactly the authorities conceived participation in Covent Garden.

Sponsored Participation in Covent Garden

That conception is perhaps most clearly expressed in a paper referred to in the last chapter, by the GLC's Assistant Director-General, Mr. Blackhurst. It is reproduced as Appendix II and in it he argued that participation meant 'sharing the responsibility for decisions by making a contribution to the process of choice between alternative policies and courses of action. It does not and cannot mean a complete transfer of responsibility from the GLC to the Forum.' He went on to distinguish a participatory body such as the Forum from a pressure group such as the CGCA:

> Pressure groups do *not* 'participate'; they are 'consulted'. It is the proper function of a pressure group to make 'demands' on behalf of its members and to support these demands by every kind of argument and agitation, without regard to the merits of rival 'demands' by other pressure groups representing different social interests. This leaves the responsible public authority to judge between the claims of rival pressure groups and to make a final decision which will please some and disappoint others.
>
> If 'participation' is to have any real meaning, it calls for a body which will contribute to the process of judging between pressure groups and their demands—a body which will use its local knowledge and its opportunity to listen to and question the

spokesman for special interests to help the GLC find a solution which is genuinely the best possible, taking account of all the facts and opinions. Without such a body there is always a danger that the GLC's decisions will be either 'remote' (i.e. not sufficiently responsive to special local circumstances), or on the other hand, too much influenced by whichever of the pressure groups is best organised to make a loud and persistent noise.

I hope the Forum will come to play this role—testing the arguments put forward by individual pressure groups and passing on the 'demands' with its support only when it has satisfied itself that they are realistic and are in the best interests of Covent Garden as a whole. If the Forum does behave in this way it will gain real influence over decisions by the GLC, but it will also come to be regarded—by disappointed pressure groups—as part of 'the Establishment'. This is an inevitable consequence of real participation.

The significance of this was that it saw participation as an arm of government: the Forum had to act as an arbiter between conflicting interests and 'help the GLC find a solution'. This, in itself, could mean using the Forum to discover the genuine needs and wishes of the different parts of the community. In practice it meant that, to a considerable extent the GLC was seeking to *mobilise* the Forum, to assist it with the process of obtaining legitimacy for the plan. His conception of participation was also a 'pluralistic' (see Kay 1974, p. 200) one in the sense that he saw the Forum's role as being to arbitrate between competing interests and views, rather than to represent the views of those excluded from the system of decision-making and economic power. To that extent, it echoes pluralist writers who envisage participation as a control mechanism operating through 'intermediate groups' which both regulate popular pressure and provide a system of checks and balances for competing interests (Kornhauser, pp. 78, 81, Sartori, p. 256, Eckstein, p. 191).

Mr. Blackhurst was later also to spell out in a letter to the author more clearly why he never saw it as being possible or desirable to make any transfer of power to the community:

This . . . is a question crucial to the whole idea of participation, and one that I have thought about many times in the last three years. I have not yet been able to envisage any way in which real power can be transferred from a body which raises and disposes of public money and is responsible to the electors for its conduct to a less formal body which is *not* responsible in any constitutional way to the people who provide the money. This is especially true of Covent Garden which cannot be given the help it wants and needs without the injection of far more money than the local community can find.

That is to say, his justification for the necessity of a 'lower rung' level of participation is that a higher level is incompatible with the system of representative democracy—a point to which we shall return at the end of this chapter. At this point, however, it remains to confirm that in general the limited notion of participation supported by the GLC was in fact the one which predominated through the Covent Garden Forum. Thus, the argument as it had been advanced prior to the Covent Garden chapters is reinforced. But what is now required if a more precise attempt at understanding and explaining public participation is to be made than the one which emerged earlier, is a closer analysis of how and why events occurred as they did in Covent Garden. As will become clear in this chapter, such an analysis suggests an alternative perspective, certainly to the approach of activist and reflective advocates of participation and even to the approach which stresses mobilisation. For the latter, whilst injecting the crucial dimension of the role of government, nevertheless are posited at a level of abstraction unable to grapple with the detailed processes of urban participation and mobilisation required to be better understood.

The Local State

One of the principal lessons of the Covent Garden experience is that it is not possible to understand the function of public participation without taking account of the structure of power, the distribution of resources and the nature of class conflict in the context of which participation occurs. As the life of the Forum unfolded it was clear that the indigenous working class residents on it became more muted and that their interests became less and less represented compared with those of business or property. This process is indeed confirmed by an analysis of Inner London's housing crisis (Kay, Mayo & Thompson, p. 135): '. . . that one group of people, the traditional residents of the area, continually lose out at all stages of the process, and that another connected group of interests, landlords, speculators, banks, insurance companies, builders, employers, owner occupiers and local authorities consistently gain from the changes.' Participation through the Covent Garden Forum did not stop that process. Indeed, to the extent that the Forum failed to tackle the creeping gentrification of the area or even saw it as an issue, and to the extent that one of its major preoccupations became commercially to revitalise the area (with an admitted emphasis upon small businesses), the Forum actually legitimated that process. Additionally, it was concluded at the end of the last chapter that the Forum's influence was marginal and that it did not compare with financial and property interests in the area.

It is therefore important to make a break, not only from mainstream analyses of participation or mobilisation, but also from the approaches which stress either organisational characteristics (e.g. Kramer & Specht, Barr) of community groups, or opportunities for individuals to participate in them (see Pikvance 1976, pp. 198–9). The French structuralist tradition of urban sociology has recently begun to attempt this, notably in the writings of Castells, and was influential in re-orientating the study of urban politics in Britain in the mid-to-late 1970s (Pikvance, Harloe, Hawley). Broadly, they conceptualize the urban system as the other side of the coin of the system of *production* in that its purpose is the *reproduction* of labour power. Moreover, through the process of *consumption* it services the productive process and its power relations therefore reflect those of capitalism (Lamarche, p. 86).

Castells also develops the theme suggested by the Marxist or neo-Marxist writers discussed earlier in chapter three, when they provided a general characterisation of modern government intervention and sponsorship of participation as the product of a particular stage in the development of capitalism, namely when the state begins directly to manage the productive process (in Harloe 1977, p. 64):

to the extent that . . . means of collective consumption are generally managed by public authorities (the state at its different levels: national, regional and local), the entire urban perspective becomes politicized, since the organisation of hospitals, schools, housing and transportation are at the same time fundamental determinants of everyday life, tightly linked and interdependent networks, and political options linked to the class interests which form the social structure. Consequently, the state becomes, through its arrange-ment of space, the real manager of everyday life. But, on the other hand, the politicization of the urban question also politicizes the consequent social conflicts: urban movements become one of the axes of social change in advanced societies.

Thus, we have the rationale for the encouragement of neighbourhood councils by both government and local activists. But the experience of Covent Garden endorses the critique of Castells and his fellow structuralists mounted by Saunders (pp. 180–9). He argues, *inter alia*, that the problem with these writings is less in terms of possible theoretical weaknesses than in their applicability to understanding empirical situations (pp. 13–27). It is furthermore not sufficient to assert that local government is an agent of capitalism—however welcome a shift that represents from previous orthodoxies. Rather it is necessary to specify in what ways capitalist forces transmit themselves into urban politics. For example, no understanding of the process of participation in Covent Garden and therefore of its influence on the forces at work in the locality is possible without examining the role of the GLC officers, the constraints within which they were working, the control they exercised over the participants from the community and the manner in which the Forum effectively became a creature of the GLC. Other studies, of the impact of community groups on the local decision-making process have also emphasised the importance of forces internal to the local authority (Ferris, Lipsky 1970, Muchnick).

The Covent Garden case illustrates how crucial a local authority's role can be in relation to external factors. To be sure, the GLC and through it the Forum was subject to market forces, as the structuralists rightly help us to explain. The GLC was also required to meet certain procedures for participation and so on, set down by central government in the form of the Department of Environment. But within that context it had considerable autonomy in decisions over *policy*. And since a localised group such as the Forum could only ever hope to influence policy—for wider structural matters were plainly beyond its scope for influence—that level becomes crucial to an assessment of the impact and nature of public participation. In his study of North Kensington, Dearlove (1973, p. 20) argues that 'local authorities are by no means the passive agents of the central government but have scope to develop their own policies'. And he emphasises something which as we shall see played an important role in determining the impact of the Forum: the fact that council policies are geared to what he calls 'the defence of commitment and the control of disturbance' (pp. 226–36). For the fact is that at no time was it necessary for the GLC to act in an 'oppressive' manner, insisting that the Forum follow a particular course or that it subjugate itself to dominant class interests. The process that occurred was a great deal more complex and subtle than this, not least in the role played by 'organisational resources' (Pikvance 1976, 1977) of the various community groups which the structuralists tend to underplay in concentrating upon whether urban social movements have a coherent political commitment to working class struggle rather than in emphasising the resource constraints affecting them (Dunleavy, p. 6).

Moreover, whilst the central motivating force on urban relations may be the market economy, within that context, the 'local state' is left in a position of some autonomy (Broadbent, p. 128): 'The local state does not only gain its income from the local economy but also from central government; it is thus more 'relatively autonomous' with respect to the local economy than is the national state *vis-à-vis* the national economy.' Or, to put the argument another way: the 'underlying dynamic of capitalism' clearly shapes the urbanisation process, but 'we have to seek for many of the technics and mechanics for the reproduction of the capitalist social order within the complex fabric of the urban process itself' (Harvey 1977, p. 138). Dearlove summarises the approach which will be adopted in the rest of this chapter when he argues (1979, p. 242): 'we need an analysis which is sensitive to the limits of that (central) control and to the problems of its assertion.'

Towards that end, we can draw on recent analyses of urban politics in Britain which have been conducted in terms of the study of *political economy* and have described the notion of the 'local state'. Their starting point is an analysis of modern capitalism which, rather like the structuralists, conceives the urban system revolving around related forces: production and reproduction. In urban systems, *production* is carried on, requiring the *reproduction* of labour (for the production process) which in turn involves the *consumption* of goods and services as provided both by the market and by the state. One activist, Jan O'Malley puts it this way in her analysis of community action in Notting Hill (p. 174):

> Though under capitalism, production and consumption, work and the home, workmates and family appear as two separate spheres of social experience, they are indissolubly linked. It is as members of the community where they live that workers consume, so providing the market which capitalism requires. It is also within the

community that the labour force upon which capitalism depends, is reproduced and serviced.

However, she ignores the fact that publicly provided goods and services account for a considerable proportion of workers' consumption (even though, prior to the actual point of consumption, these may have been provided to the state by the private sector). But Cockburn distinguishes this clearly (pp. 54–6) and it follows that, just as modern capitalism requires Keynesian and post-Keynesian techniques of state intervention and management of *production* (Kidron, Harris), so the state has a twofold interest in managing *consumption*, both of private sector goods and of its own goods and services. And, so far as the city is concerned, it has (Hill, R.C., pp. 215-6): 'increasingly been delegated managerial responsibility for facilitating the process of capital accumulation and mitigating the contradictions emanating from the unremitting quest for private profit.'

Hence we have the rationale for government sponsorhip of public participation in terms of a necessity to manage and control the urban process. For although the Covent Garden case may appear to be the result of a straightforward tactical judgement on the part of the Minister for the Environment that participation be stipulated in drawing up a new plan, such an interpretation begs a number of questions. Was it simply a prudent response to the public clamour over the first plan, in which case there was presumably also the option available to the Minister of ignoring the community opposition, safe in the knowledge that the tendency was for community action to be unable to sustain itself over a long period (Dearlove 1974). Or is it really possible to ignore the broader political context within which that decision was made? For Covent Garden undoubtedly typified the 'urban crisis' which came to a head in Britain in the early 1970s. And the requirement for government to control and manage activist participation was made more urgent by that urban crisis which threatened the stability of the city as an economic, social and political unit. With Cockburn we can characterise the modern urban crisis in terms of a contradiction between, on the one hand the financial crisis of capitalism from the 1960s onwards, and, on the other, the necessity in the process of reproduction to maintain and indeed expand local services (p. 64):

The city is as necessary to capitalist reproduction as the factory is to capitalist production. It is for this reason that the financial crisis of the state at local level has been experienced most acutely by the local authorities of big cities, where the rate base was static or declining yet the nature of the physical environment and the condition of the population demanded above-average public spending.

It is argued that the major factor in the urban crisis has been the decline of the old manufacturing sector which provided the economic base of the city (CDP, *Costs of Industrial Change*). Certainly, that decline was very pronounced in Covent Garden: between 1966 and 1974, floorspace in industrial and manufacturing use declined by nearly half. The important point about this kind of decline however is that, although its immediate impact was felt in the locality, its cause is external. A study of the economy of the London Borough of Wandsworth (M. Ward, pp. 6-8), for example, showed that seven-eighths of the job loss in manufacturing industry in the Borough between 1971 and 1975 was caused by the departure of ten large firms, eight of which were subsidiaries of national or multi-national companies.

Thus we can characterise the urban crisis, not as a technical, but as a political crisis. As Katznelson (1973, p. 466) argues, the mainstream literature on urban problems has by-passed 'core political questions' of power, dominance and social control: 'For those basically at ease with present structural patterns, it is far more congenial . . . to conceptualize the urban 'crisis' in terms of discrete, technical micro-issues of finance, housing, transportation, and the like, and to formulate policy solutions to each of the diagnosed 'social problems'.' In fact, he argues (p. 474), we have an 'urban political crisis of control'. For the collapse of the economic base of the inner city has produced a shortage of finance and hence a dependence upon central government and the surburban taxpayer which, in turn, has led to urban politics becoming 'a politics of dependency' (1976, p. 219). This weakening position of urban politics has coincided with the decline in 'urban legitimacy' and as a consequence 'urban political mechanisms became terribly important as mechanisms of social control' (1976, p. 223). For Cockburn, this produced a necessity on the part of the focus of her study, Lambeth Council, to exercise control through both corporate planning and participation programmes, which she sees as different facets of the same mechanism of urban management (p. 66 and Benington).

Thus, urban politics is concerned with control—the attempt to cope with the ungovernability of the modern city. Katznelson (1973, p. 471) goes on to conceptualize a social control apparatus 'as an interlocking set of buffers that soften the impact of basic social contradictions'. He describes how, during the period of migration and urban growth in the USA, the political party machines 'acted as social buffers linking their clienteles and dominant elites' (p. 473), thus mobilising potentially dissident groups through their participation in politics, and integrating them within the prevailing urban structure. But, he shows, the contemporary shift in the locus of power from party organisation to bureaucracies left something of a vacuum in that nobody was 'organising participation'. Hence the creation of 'linkage organisations'—that is, neighbourhood bodies of a semi-public nature—to fill that vacuum (p. 475): 'these organisations structure participation and establish administrative mechanisms for reaching a client neighbourhood on elite terms, leaving the existing structure of power and resources largely intact.'

That, in general terms, captures the essence of the Covent Garden Forum, and Cockburn offers a more refined version of much the same perspective. Relating her analysis to the British experience and, specifically to Lambeth, she argues that the decline of working class political activity through the Labour Party created something of a vacuum in the local political system. The sponsorship of neighbour-hood councils and other participation projects was an attempt to fill this vacuum. For her, the creation of 'buffer' organisations is directed specifically at the working class (p. 101): 'The potential control of the state increases the more closely the working population is knit to the state system. We should think for the moment not of overtly repressive control but simply of management of the working class, its 'families' and 'groups' in the business of reproduction of the labour force and of capitalist relations.'

The task of urban management has consequently become central to the purposes of the local state. Cockburn describes in detail how Lambeth experimented during the 1970s with both corporate man-agement techniques and with participation as part of that task and it is clear that public participation has been used as a tool of urban management on a much wider scale (CDP reports, Malpass, Benington).

It seems reasonable therefore to consider this analysis in the context of Covent Garden. Certainly, in the GLC's conception of the Forum—as expressed notably by Mr. Blackhurst and as practised by the Team's officers in its dealings with the Forum—the latter's role can be interpreted in terms of a 'buffer' institution between the GLC and the community. And, indeed, the same is true for other community forums in England (Humble & Talbot 1974), as well as for community associations concerned with race relations (Hill & Issacharoff, pp. 280–1). Significantly, the CGCA's Vice-Chairman actually described the Forum as a 'buffer between governors and the governed'.

It is important to establish, however, that the approach of social control and urban management does not support any crude concept of the state-as-oppressor. As both the Lambeth and Covent Garden experience show, the process is far more complex. In Covent Garden, the authorities 'muddled through' in an at times desperate attempt to secure community consent for the development of the area. In Lambeth, corporate management was tried and found wanting. Thus, while this control thesis appears to fit the experience of neighbourhood councils and other participation programmes, it must not be taken to imply an unlimited view of state power (Broadbent, p. 47). Initiatives of this kind by the local state are, as in Covent Garden, signs of weakness. Problems of inner city areas like Covent Garden are a product of class and power inequalities not only beyond the control of activists, but also of the local authorities and their officials. Consequently, the latter's overriding aim becomes '*the management of the consequences of their inability to solve urban problems*' (Katznelson & Kesselman, p. 408). Attention needs therefore to be given to the limitations on the state's power, to the means it has available and their precise impact. In Covent Garden, for example, the central role within the local state was played by the fulltime officers. (Whilst Saunders (1979, p. 223) would qualify this by reference to the important role of the leading councillors who may effectively form a 'political elite', that was only valid in Covent Garden to the limited extent of general policy guidelines (about which there was a general consensus in the area anyway). Leading councillor influence was not felt in the participation process itself.) The interests and objectives of these officers, as we saw, did not always coincide exactly with local property developers. That is not however to suggest that their role endorses the 'managerialist' perspective of 'urban managers' and 'technical experts' acting autonomously from dominant class interests and sources of capital (Pahl, 1977, pp. 55–7). Indeed, in Covent Garden, whilst the fulltime officials enjoyed considerable scope to determine the nature of the participation which occurred they were nevertheless constrained by wider economic forces, and in their own ideological dispositions reflected dominant interests (see Miliband 1969, p. 123). They had a certain autonomy over local policy questions and in managing community groups, but they were not autonomous in relation to the wider structure of power.

The Process of Bureaucratic Control

Exhibited sharply in Covent Garden and reflected in the general neighbourhood council movement, were a number of features which have been documented elsewhere, illustrating the role of participation in urban management. The tendency for participation to 'become another vehicle for the extension of bureaucratic control' (Cloward & Piven 1969a) was evident, partly resulting from what a local councillor in Lambeth described as 'the need to key the demands of neighbourhood councils into the committee system of local government.' The latter point was important in Covent Garden because it was more than anything the daily contact between the GLC and the Forum which, particularly under the pressure of work needed to be processed, led for administrative convenience to Forum members being educated into the procedures operated by the GLC, thereby overcoming the undoubted problems of 'trying to harmonise the claims of public participation with those of existing institutions of local government' (Gyford, pp. 147-8). As we saw, also, the planners and other fulltime officers, though retaining a residual superiority by virtue of their professionalism and expertise, nevertheless came to see advantages in terms of their own work in the device of the Forum. There was certainly a real sense in which the planners 'co-opted' their challengers through the Forum, but a different form of co-optation occurred than either the more usual absorption of individuals into the local political establishment or the absorption of a whole community association. Instead, the GLC co-opted a whole group of people onto a body which they endowed with official legitimacy and which was given a priority over others with claims to speak for residents or workers. However, if the CGCA had been lifted bodily into the role performed by the Forum perhaps that co-optation framework would have been more successful; as it was the CGCA continued to operate independently. Moreover, those radicals from whose co-option the GLC would have perhaps benefited most, in fact chose to abandon the Forum rather than to accept its mode of participation.

As was shown—and, indeed, admitted by Team members themselves—the GLC officers controlled and regulated the activities of the Forum to a considerable extent. One Team member went so far as to say that they 'manipulated' the Forum, and their publicly 'apolitical' stance actually concealed what became, out of necessity more than personal desire, explicit political intervention and bias (Benveniste, pp. 63–5). Certainly, they collectively evolved what had been described (Lambert *et al*, p. 169) as a 'style of urban managerialism . . . [which had a] . . . potent ideological force in shaping and reinforcing the dominant pattern of power, influence and profit.' It rested essentially upon claims to superior technical expertise and administrative ability, but also relied upon the support of the councillors— even if the latter's was a largely passive role in the partnership.

It is important to note however, as has been shown of another but similar situation, that this style was 'not simply repressive and coercive, but a mixture of toleration, flexibility, seeming generosity, participation and opportunity—but ultimately controlling . . .' (Lambert, p. 170). Thus, although (as we saw) one Team member referred to their controlling function as being a form of 'conspiracy', it is important to understand the precise context in which that term— with all its polemical connotations—can be used in order accurately to describe the process which occurred. It was not a deliberate, conspiratorial plan to subvert community participation which took place, but the product of a series of factors. The principal of these was what has been described as a 'bureaucratic impulse to stability and the least possible fuss and change' (Sills, p. 124). The Team wished to ensure that the Forum operated according to the procedures and attitudes with which the GLC officers were familiar and in which they could therefore have confidence. One result was what Saunders calls the 'routinization of bias' and he makes the point that whilst it is necessary to qualify such terms as 'conspiracy', it is equally necessary to be aware of the consequences and purposes of local state intervention through its officials (1975, p. 37): 'The "routines of ruling" are . . . governed by the informal and unexplicated rules of the game evolved by decision-makers themselves. The bias may certainly be unconscious, non-deliberate, and non-conspiratorial, but its beneficiaries are nonetheless also its originators and perpetuators.'

A further factor was the attitude, unsurprising in a fulltime official, expressed by the first Team leader: 'It is responsibility we want: not negative opposition.' Similar sentiments were expressed by Mr. Blackhurst in the stress he laid upon participation being about realism and his warning that the Forum could 'come to be regarded—by disappointed pressure groups—as part of "the establishment".' (A warning which showed some insight since that was exactly how the CGCA at least came to view the Forum.) In these circumstances however it says something, both for the professional competence of the GLC officers and the consensus ideology of the Forum, that relations between the two were on the whole remarkably harmonious, contrasting both with the situation prior to the Forum's inception and experiences elsewhere. In Lambeth, for example, relations between the senior officers and the neighbourhood councils which Lambeth Council had sponsored were strained. The officers expressed antagonism to the neighbourhood councils, trying on occasion to stop the distribution of newsletters which were partly funded by the local authority but which the officers felt to be overly critical of them, and even isolating the Neighbourhood Development Workers employed by the Council from normal inter-departmental contact within the Town Hall; these Workers were regarded as being too sympathetic to the neighbourhood councils which they were employed to service. In Covent Garden it may well be that it was the fact that the GLC officers rather than the councillors who devised the Forum in consultation with the community which was the crucial factor (in Lambeth, by contrast, it was a Labour Party manifesto proposal which led to the neighbourhood councils being set up and it was clear that the Lambeth officers never really accepted them).

A further factor which was important in the GLC's relationship with the Forum was the authority's conception of the Forum as a mechanism for resolving conflicting interests in the area. This was crucial to Mr. Blackhurst's concept of the Forum and it was the dominant view of the Forum's own officers. For both, the crucial problem in Covent Garden was the management of conflict (see Schattschneider, p. 71 for a general analysis), and for the GLC in particular the Forum was seen as a broker of competing demands (see Dahrendorf). For that purpose, it was necessary for the Forum to be constituted and run in such a way that it presented 'organised claims' (Lowi 1967, p. 18) to the GLC—claims that the GLC's own administration could respond to and which were clearly articulated. It was not sufficient to make generalised political demands: they had to be specific and realistic in the GLC's eyes.

However, that pluralistic conception of politics also had other consequences. Since such a high premium was placed upon reconciling conflicting interests, the Forum was not able to take up political issues because that would jeopardise what its Chairman referred to as its 'impartiality'. Its use for the GLC was also that, by appealing to a notion of community, class conflict in the area was regulated (see Heraud, Cowley *et al*), although, as we saw from the Forum's discussion examples, that regulation was far from 'impartial' as it tended to be at the expense of local working class interests. There is moreover considerable evidence that an attempt by a public agency to act as a 'referee' between competing interests, as the Forum tried to do, in reality leads to it systematically favouring the stronger at the expense of the weaker interests (McConnell, Miliband, Playford 1971, Kariel 1961). In short, by ascribing to the Forum the task of managing conflict in the area, the GLC ensured that it did not challenge the wider structure of power but rather acted conservatively to encourage legitimacy for that structure. Planners and other officials tend to reflect the interests of capitalism in the way they work and Covent Garden was no exception. Whether however that would have been so successfully achieved in a period when property investment was soaring is another matter, for it may not have been as easy in that climate to contain the community.

One of the effects of both the management control exerted over the Forum and its role as a buffer between the GLC and the interests in the community, was that it became a vehicle for the 'mobilisation of bias', that is to say, 'a set of predominant values, beliefs, rituals, and institutional procedures ("rules of the game") that operate systematically and consistently to the benefit of certain persons and groups at the expense of others' (Bachrach & Baratz, p. 43). Certain issues were not taken up at all (the squatting example to take just one) even though they were considered. Others did not even reach the agenda for discussion (including many local issues about housing, shopping, children's playspace and so on which were taken up by the CGCA and were often of more immediate and direct consequence to local residents than the paper content of the plan). The Forum's role was almost entirely geared to the agenda set by the GLC and the sheer pace of consultation required meant that it seldom if ever had time to consider what other issues might be discussed (Parenti, pp. 128–9). What this meant was a cumulative pattern of 'non-issues' and 'non-decisions' (Bachrach & Baratz, Crenson) which favoured both the status quo in Covent Garden and the interests of the GLC. Broadly speaking, these can be broken down into three areas: those that threatened the *ideological consensus* on the Forum; those that required it to take *action*; and those that necessitated an intervention into the system of *resource allocation* (for instance, the Forum's refusal to consider setting up a housing association).

There is also a sense in which the pattern of decision-making—fed into the Forum by the GLC in order to satisfy the Department of Environment's requirement for participation in drawing up a new plan—meant that the Forum was preoccupied with 'symbolic' rather than 'substantive' issues (Edelman). And that, as has been shown (Parenti, Lipsky 1968), is very convenient from the standpoint of those in authority. While it certainly cannot be said that either all the issues pressed by the Forum for inclusion in the plan or the concessions made to them by the GLC were 'symbolic', it may have been that the *plan itself* was 'symbolic'. This was suggested in the last chapter when it came to assess the influence of the Forum. Certainly, the real weakness of the planning system is that its ability to control social or economic forces is greatly limited compared with its ability to cause physical changes in the environment (Ambrose & Colenutt, pp. 60-7). And the evidence available does point to the probability that the whole exercise of consultation over the plan was symbolic in its effect on the major property and market forces at work in Covent Garden, even if it may have been substantive at the level of marginal issues such as the idea of an 'entertainment' route running through the area.

The Politics of the Forum

So far in this chapter, the role of the state and its agencies has been highlighted in attempting to explain the nature of public participation experienced in Covent Garden. But the politics of the Forum itself contributed to many of the tendencies toward bureaucratic control identified, and at the very least *complemented* those tendencies.

An important factor determining the politics of the Forum was what will be termed its 'middle class style', as distinct from a 'working class style'. As we saw, the Forum was dominated by middle class members. This was simply accepted by both the GLC and the Forum officers as a regrettable but apparently inevitable 'fact of life'. Certainly, studies of community participation projects have pointed to them being mainly middle class in composition (Dilys Hill 1970, Weissman, Wilson, D. 1975). But that does not tell us *why* this should be the case, nor if indeed it is inevitable, particularly in an area like Covent Garden with a large and traditional working class population. Yet the reasons are fairly clear. First, working class individuals lack the personal resources and the time that comes from flexible working hours, and which was so important to the Forum officers for example (Yates, p. 120, Williams, p. 166, Beresford). Thus while they were sometimes characterised by GLC officers or Forum leaders as 'apathetic', as Repo has shown of another participation project, it was not necessarily a voluntary form of apathy. By contrast however working class participation in the CGCA was relatively high, suggesting that in a sympathetic environment the supposed apathy disappeared.

This leads us to a second factor that discouraged working class involvement in the Forum. The GLC officers operated what has been described as a 'middle class model' of meetings. That is to say, a model based upon a formal committee type system with conventional procedures, rules of debate, moderate and carefully expressed language, requiring considerable time to be spent reading papers written in relatively complex and technical prose. Certainly, it was clear that working class residents were generally bored with Forum meetings to which they could not relate either as spectators or participants; yet CGCA meetings were well attended by indigenous people and they operated on a much more open, informal and vocal basis. Furthermore, it was noticeable that whereas middle class members of the Forum were more prepared to listen to the views of GLC officers or invited property developers, that was far less so for working class members whose interventions, rare though they were, tended to be in strongly expressed language. They also tended to be saying an abrupt 'no' to some proposal rather than seeking to modify it (see Repo, p. 54), suggesting that if working class residents had been in control of the Forum then it would have found itself in greater conflict with the GLC; that is to say, the consensus style of the Forum was pre-eminently a middle class style. Or, as an analysis of the American government sponsored Community Action Programme of the mid-1960s put it (K. Coit, p. 300): 'Participation has been one means of giving middle-class attitudes, middle-class values, to the working class and the very poor . . . once the poor accept middle class "decorum", they may become less rather than more effective.' Even though that objective may not have been wholly realised in practice (partly because of the CGCA's role), the nature of the participation expressed by the Forum has been characterised as follows (Repo, p.

54): 'Unlike labour negotiations, where at least workers are making demands about wages, benefits and working conditions, there is nothing to "negotiate" in urban renewal areas, because the working class has not asked for urban renewal in the first place. Participation in that context is like being allowed to choose the colour and texture of the rope that one is to be hanged by.'

The third element in the middle class style of the Forum was its failure to take *action*. As we saw, it was a frequent criticism of the Forum that it only discussed and never acted. It was also clear that working class activists in the area were attracted to the CGCA because of its wide programme of activities and its relative impatience with discursive meetings. They did not share the view implicit in many middle class participants that Forum meetings were intrinsically of value in that the GLC was being forced to sit around the same table and listen to local views (which is not however to pretend that middle class members of the Forum did not get exasperated at its at times long-winded and meandering proceedings). A similar tension existed in Lambeth, and the emphasis for working class people upon *action*, and *informality* and *loose* and *flexible* structures was identified in the debate on neighbourhood councils. The Forum, being the very opposite, it followed that working class residents were not comfortable working within it, thereby enabling the GLC to exert more control than might otherwise have been the case.

Covent Garden also confirms and explains how, as suggested in the analysis in chapter two, a liberal conception of neighbourhood councils negates working class involvement. The Forum was an expression of a liberal ideology as opposed to a radical one. It consequently did not see its role as being to challenge the structure of power or to take up political issues. No links were forged with working class organisations, notably trade unions, and when the Forum did feel frustrated (for example, when it was presented with a *fait accompli* over a development) it tended to blame, not the system of power and of resource allocation, but *individuals* in the GLC. That, again, was manageable from the GLC's point of view whereas a challenge to the system itself would not necessarily have been so easily contained, at least without considerable cost to the close relationship between the Forum and the GLC.

The final component to understanding the Forum's politics is related to the first two of class and ideology. It is in essence what we shall call a 'community consensus style of politics'. Community action and participation is in general said to express a new form of 'non-political politics' (Dilys Hill, p. 151) or 'anti-politics' (T. Smith 1972, 1973). And, certainly, the consensus style of the Forum where 'votes almost never occur' is expressed in other community groups (Ridley & Banks, p. 19). One of the factors encouraging a consensus style is that, once a 'large' battle with the authorities is over and community activists turn (as they did in Covent Garden) to the business of day to day participation with the local authority, there is a tendency for the issues with which they are concerned to become more technical and detailed, so discouraging attention on larger political questions. In addition a 'localist' orientation on the part of activists can lead to conservatism, since it becomes more important to maintain a consensus within the community than to tackle issues which might provoke controversy and division (K. Young, Bell & Newby). Thus, as we also saw of neighbourhood councils in general, one of the key characteristics of this community consensus style of politics is that for the activists involved, it is anti-ideological in *conviction* (which is not to say it is anti-ideological in *effect*). It is also anti-party—a form of non-competitive, non-dogmatic politics to which many of those involved can relate more easily than political parties. Two people involved in Lambeth's neighbourhood councils (the first a fulltime worker, the second a chairman of one of the councils) put it this way:

> Part of the basis of involvement in a neighbourhood council is that it is not committed to anything in particular—that is, it is free of political dogma. There is also no competition in neighbourhood councils in the way that occurs, for example, in the Labour Party. Also there is no boring old stuff like collecting subscriptions. The whole style of party politics puts people off. The neighbourhood council is about your street, not some distant issue. It is also easier to get absorbed into the neighbourhood council machinery, because of its informality, than it is to get involved in the whole party apparatus.

and

> In the Labour Party, my party, you tend to get involved in committees and internal council work—you forget about ordinary people. The neighbourhood council is a way of getting out amongst the people. So many things don't get done because of party-political pressures. Whereas the neighbourhood council can rally support from *all* opinions: that is the most important issue.

Interestingly, this desire to 'take community out of politics' has clear affinities with a desire to 'take economics out of politics' by pursuing a consensus-based strategy for economic goals, as in the attempts to introduce planning in Britain in the 1960s. The initiatives taken by-passed Parliament (T. Smith 1979, Shonfield) and appealed to 'rationality' rather than to ideology as a basis for decision-making (Harris, Crosland), in order to secure a consensus amongst extra-parliamentary interest groups that could overcome the tensions and conflicts of a form of party politics in Britain that seemed incapable of building the required consensus. The Chairman of the Prices and Incomes Board between 1966 and 1970 hailed this as the arrival of the 'politics of non-partisanship' (A. Jones, pp. 173-87).

What needs to be emphasised is that this notion of non-partisan, consensus politics, just as when applied nationally helps national government to exercise control, so when applied locally encourages the ability of the local authority to exercise control (Malpass, p. 15). This is partly because it increases the ability of planners and other officials to claim justification for a controlling function (Heraud, p. 50) and partly because it encourages a style of organisation which 'reproduces' the structure of the local authority itself (CDP, Neighbourhood Democracy). That certainly occurred in Covent Garden, where the Forum began to assume a relationship to those individuals in the community outside its membership rather similar to the one for which the GLC had been bitterly criticised prior to the Forum being set up. The significant point about this however is that the community consensus approach of the Covent Garden Forum was as much a product of the activities of the GLC's officers and of the Council's relationship to the Forum, as it was of the voluntary decisions by Forum members.

Conclusion

Thus it can be seen that the case of Covent Garden, in the context of a wider analysis both of neighbourhood councils and public participation in general, cannot be interpreted as the orthodox approaches have done, either simply as a process of participation from below, or simply as a process of mobilisation from above. These are not discrete processes but part of a single relationship, just as the conventional characterisation of power as a division between an 'influence perspective' (of activists) and a 'social control perspective' (of authorities) ignores the reality that they are products of a single relationship (Gamson, pp. 2-19).

This single process of participation and mobilisation can be depicted as a *power struggle* in which both the pull of participation from below and the pull of mobilisation from above are always present. At the neighbourhood level, the activists try to pull the locus of power down towards themselves; although, as we have seen, they may not wish to, or be prepared to, pull 'hard enough' to alter to any significant degree the balance of power. At the local state level, there is *always* a mobilising drive, either conscious in the sense of a deliberate desire to control and regulate, or unconscious in the sense of the natural reflex action of a bureaucracy which—as identified in Covent Garden—wishes to marry any external agency with its own preferred objectives and patterns of activity. However, the evidence and analysis has also suggested that this participation/mobilisation power struggle is not somehow evenly balanced. It is likely that the participants will always lose out to the authorities, certainly if they continue to adopt the strategies and be prompted by the ideologies identified in the research. This likelihood is not simply for the reasons of comparative lack of resources and political legitimacy often referred to. It is pre-eminently for two reasons. First, because the whole *raison d'être* of the local state is now to manage and control the urban system through direct intervention. And second, because the structure of representative democracy simply cannot permit participation at anything other than a lower-rung level and still remain intact.

However, that is not to say that participation is necessarily in conflict with representation. Indeed, the crisis of representative democracy required participation (albeit of a liberal nature) to bolster it. Even for radical participation, there is precious little evidence that it poses a serious challenge to representative democracy in practice—although it may well appear to do so in theory. We are thus left with major and perhaps fatal questionmarks over the quality of the theories of participation, whether these be of an activist or reflective variety. Not the least of their failings is an inability to take account of the class and other interest conflicts which were shown to have been so critical in determining the role and impact of neighbourhood councils.

So far as neighbourhood councils are concerned, they play the role of buffer institutions providing at once a forum for the participation of activists and their mobilisation by the authorities to secure consent for state programmes and policies. Furthermore, such mobilisation is inevitable. There can be no significant distribution of power to the activists—at least whilst the predominant ideology of these neighbourhood council activists continues to specify a concept of organisation and of strategy which conforms to all intents and purposes to what in Chapter 3 was termed 'official attitudes'. On the other hand, this is not to argue that neighbourhood councils are politically impotent or that they can have no influence at all. Clearly, they can influence local authority policies and, in the case of Covent Garden, in ways which are felt to be of some importance to local people. What is being argued is that, for the neighbourhood council model of organisation, the extent of influence is marginal, particularly from the standpoint of advancing working class interests for which the usual neighbourhood council model is clearly unsuitable. In fact, neighbourhood councils tend to act against those very interests and to favour the status quo to the extent of legitimising it.

8

Neighbourhood Struggle, the Workplace and Politics

> The struggle for a better quality of life increasingly has to challenge the false divisions between people's role at work as producers, and in the community as consumers. The greatest potential for change may lie in new initiatives which create alliances across the neighbourhood, the factory floor and the local political parties.
>
> C.D.P., *Coventry CDP Final Report Part I* (Coventry, Community Development Project, 1975), p. 67.
>
> Unless people actually participate in change, unless through struggle their consciousness of society is clearer, then society will not be transformed for the better. Many political changes and reforms can be brought about for people, or on their behalf, by elites, minority pressure groups and 'parties' but without the physical and thinking involvement of the mass of people, then those changes and reforms are merely improvements in the management of a passive population, not their liberation.
>
> Tom Woolley, 'The politics of intervention', in J. Cowley, *et al*, *Community or Class Struggle?* (Stage 1, 1977), pp. 210–21.

If, then, the neighbourhood council movement has been unable to fulfil even its own limited objectives, let alone larger demands for a basic redistribution of power and resources, does that imply that the neighbourhood council in particular or community action in general offers no prospects for achieving radical change? To those steeped in either conventional party politics or so-called revolutionary parties, the answer may be 'yes', that the analysis of this book has merely confirmed their existing prejudices about community organisations. If so, however, they would be seriously mistaken. For the real issue is not to accept or reject the legitimacy of community organising, but instead how to respond to the experience of community action since the late 1960s and the limitations of neighbourhood councils.

The Case for Community Organising

The 'new politics' which has asserted itself over the past decade in community and pressure group campaigning cannot simply be dismissed because it has shortcomings. Quite apart from anything else, the available alternatives—whether political parties, trade unions, or left wing groups—have not exactly been conspicuously successful either. Nothing can take away from community groups (neighbourhood councils included) their impressive record of involving huge numbers of people in struggle and campaigning. Many of these people would otherwise have lacked a vehicle for their aspirations and community action has given them the confidence and ability to defend and struggle for their interests. Moreover, important successes on local issues have been achieved. Similarly, single-issue campaigns, whether on racism, the environment, abortion or international questions, have achieved an impact and levels of activity which traditional political methods and parties have been quite incapable of generating.

Above all, however, there is still the opportunity of challenging the power of the local state through the participation/mobilisation process of struggle characterised in the last chapter. Indeed, it can be strongly argued that, by seeking to incorporate urban movements within its apparatus, the local state is making itself more vulnerable to being challenged, rather as the capitalist economy is now more vulnerable than at any stage of its previous development to industrial action and disruption by workers' organisations. As Cockburn (p. 101) puts it: '. . . incorporation of the population is a two-edged sword for the state (and the working class). Because the closer the working class come to inclusion within the state system, the more dangerous is any disruptive behaviour to the equilibrium of the state. The state has reduced the risk in one way but increased it in another.' That is to say, the mobilisation inherent in government's approach to participation offers the opportunity of a 'Trojan Horse' strategy, providing of course that community groups have a rather clearer political perspective than was displayed for the most part by neighbourhood council activists. At the very least, 'participation can be used to unmask the present system and accelerate the pace of action against it' (Loney, p. 103). Advances can be made, limited victories can be won, the political awareness of those active can be raised, and it would be shortsighted indeed to ignore this.

Moreover the validity of community organising from the

standpoint of those wishing to achieve social change and advance the interests of working class people stems essentially from an understanding of the nature of capitalism, particularly in its modern form where state intervention plays a key role, not least at local level. As was shown in the last chapter, political struggle should not be confined to the system of *production*, but extended to the associated system of *reproduction* as well. That being the case, the issue of workers engaged in struggle within the productive process should not be pursued to the neglect of those who are part of the reproductive system. And the latter are not confined, for example, to women at home, pensioners and the unemployed—all of whom are wageless and are most obviously excluded from involvement in direct production. *Every* worker plays out a role in the reproductive arena, even if only in the sense of being affected by levels of welfare and the state of the housing system for example. Exploitation occurs not simply at the workplace, but through reactionary officialdom, inadequate welfare, bad housing, hostile police and so on. Equally, what may be seen as relatively narrow issues of workplace concern, such as safety and amenities, are in practice intimately linked not merely to profitability but to wider environmental issues. For instance, building workers facing injury or death whilst working on high buildings have a coincidence of interests with environmentalists seeking humanely sensitive architecture (P. Thomas, p. 7).

The suggestion therefore that area-based struggles are somehow secondary and of marginal importance needs a firm rebuttal. For there is a strong tradition on the left which elevates industrial action into a position where everything else is deemed either irrelevant or so peripheral as to be worthless. That tradition has been strongly criticised by recent socialist writers on community action (Cockburn, Corrigan) and even Marx pointed to the need to move beyond 'economistic' industrial struggles and to engage in action in the wider community.

That need is sharply underlined by the position of women. Cockburn (p. 177) has pointed to the 'key role' played by working class women in housing action in Lambeth. And it was notable that in the community politics of Covent Garden (and the activities of the CGCA particularly) working class women played a prominent role.

Evidently, community issues affected the majority of women who were home-based far more immediately and directly than workplace issues (see also J. Smith, pp. 33–4, Mayo). Partly of course because of male/female role stereotyping, local shopping opportunities, children's playspace, playgroups and even housing, were all issues that appeared to concern local working class women more than men. It also appeared that those of their husbands who were active trade unionists felt their own priority to be participation at their workplace. Given limitations of time, energy and resources, it was perhaps understandable that, relatively speaking, men were less visibly active. It can be argued therefore that to ignore community action is to ignore opportunities for women specifically to organise. According to Rowbotham (pp. 95–6), the experience of the women's movement during the 1970s has placed many:

> ... at odds with the stress of workers' control. For it obviously excludes women working in the family just as it excludes other groups who are not on the cash nexus, children or old people for example. It also tends to disregard areas of life which are crucial in women's lives, around welfare legislation for instance, or around personal and sexual relationships. It does not illuminate the inter-connection between different forms of power which men's groups, the gay movement and women's liberation have begun to discover ... By focussing on class struggle at work other aspects of power relationships become of secondary importance. There is also a tendency to see workers possessing a true consciousness intact underneath the encrustment of treacherous leaders and the beguilements of the leaders. (This can be transplanted to women.) Once the crust is cut off the true consciousness becomes apparent. This implies that the people cutting the crust off are somehow not part of the problem.

Workplace Links

For these various reasons therefore the legitimacy and indeed necessity for community action ought to be clear. But that, in turn, should not obscure important limitations of community-based organising, some of which are sharply illustrated in the experience of neighbourhood councils. These limitations have been well summarised by Tim Young (1976, pp. 118–9):

> It is the structural roots of ... major problems which require tackling if ... an effective transfer of power and resources to the disadvantaged is to take place. However, many community action groups lack an adequate perspective on the ultimate nature and

sources of the problems affecting them ... The essence of the
problem for these groups is their lack of power and resources. As
consumers of social welfare ... community action groups lack the
power and resources enjoyed by workers and by their trade unions
at the point of production ...

Such problems for the 'alternative politics' (Hain 1975) of community
action, the women's movement and single-issues, have been exacerbated by the impact of economic recession. It is notable that local
campaigns successful in the boom period up until the mid-1970s have
since been undermined by public expenditure cuts in particular. Many
groups built their success on an ability to squeeze more services or
resources out of the local state through imaginative and sometimes
militant methods of protest and participation. The cuts however have
severely restricted the scope for such pressure to be able to deliver the
goods.

As a result, there has been a clear shift in the perspective, certainly
of radical community activists, away from area-based organising
alone. From the mid-1970s on, the way forward was seen as being to
'bridge the gap between community politics and industrial politics'
(Coventry CDP, p. 61. See also Woolley, Bryant 1974, Cowley *et al*,
pp. 185–246, Craig, Mayo & Sharman). Whereas previously community activists had been either hostile or indifferent to the trade
unions and the labour movement as a whole, it was now felt that the
linking of community and industrial action could strengthen both, by
enabling a more comprehensive challenge to be mounted against the
existing system of power and resource distribution.

The evidence available suggests that this can occur. Community
based campaigns are given extra muscle when allied to trade unions,
as was demonstrated by the example of rent strikes in 1915 on the
Clyde and in Glasgow; these were largely successful, partly because
of an industrial threat by munitions workers in support of the rents
campaign (Moorhouse). There are other examples of effective
alliances like this, notably in New South Wales, Australia, where the
Builders Laborers' Federation 'blacked' new property developments,
particularly office blocks, which threatened the position of local
working class communities and which were opposed by environmentalists (P. Thomas). These so-called 'green bans' were extended to
include social issues. For instance, in June 1973 the builders even put
a ban on new work at Macquarie University over the exclusion of a
homosexual student and at Sydney University over the authorities'

refusal to agree a course on feminism (P. Thomas, p. 54).

Forging such links does not only benefit community groups however, but strengthens workers' struggles as well. For workers' occupations fighting redundancies or closures, the active support of the local community can be crucial in determining whether or not the law is invoked against them, and also in circumscribing the role of the police (T. Clarke, p. 95). Similarly struggles by Asian workers in London's East End were strengthened by community support (Morris). In a broader sense, the whole perspective of trade unionism—normally confined in Britain at least to narrow issues of wages and conditions—is strengthened by a community dimension. When the highly skilled workforce at Lucas Aerospace was threatened with redundancies, for instance, they looked to outside communities for support and ideas in drawing up their own corporate plan for the company. They came up with a commercially viable programme for utilising their skills and resources to create socially useful products, as distinct from the manufacture of sophisticated armaments to which their skills had previously been harnessed. As a result, they began to discover ways in which the whole notion of workers' control could be extended to cover not just self-management but control over *what* products their skills were utilised to make (Benyon & Wainwright, Cooley). Potentially, this represents a major extension of workers' power and yet it depends upon a strong community link to ensure the production of goods actually needed by people. The threat it posed to established authority patterns was underlined by the blanket opposition their initiative received, not just from their employer, but the existing trade union establishment as well. A similar story unfolded in New South Wales over the Builders Laborers and it is instructive to note how they responded to criticisms that in 'blacking' certain developments they ‚were depriving their members of much-needed work. As the Secretary of the New South Wales branch, Jack Mundey, put it (P. Thomas, pp. 56–7):

> . . . Yes, we want to build. However, we prefer to build urgently required hospitals, schools, other public utilities, high-quality flats, units and houses, provided they are designed with adequate concern for the environment, than to build ugly unimaginative architecturally-bankrupt blocks of concrete and glass offices. Likewise, we wish to build for those aged people who gave their working lives to improve our country only to end up in some pent-up squalid room . . .

Trade unionists as traditionally organised may be effective on matters such as pay and conditions of service, but are normally ineffective in servicing members when they retire, when they are made redundant or are on strike—still less in servicing members' families in their home situation. It took a separate initiative, the National Unemployed Workers Movement, to organise the unemployed in the 1920s in Britain (Edwards), just as in recent years Claimants Unions have been needed to fight for the rights of those dependent upon social benefits (Jordan, East London). In the case of the latter, there has been some hostility from trade unions—yet the working class movement as a whole would clearly be strengthened by a more comprehensive perspective of trade unionism including community links. As one trade unionist active in a tenants' association in Glasgow put it (Liddell & Bryant, p. 92): 'If you're going to fight the boss for a pound it seems logical that you should then resist the landlord trying to take it back off you.' Another by-product of community action is that it tends to broaden the political horizons of those involved. It can encourage greater involvement, in for example trade unions, by previously apathetic members, as happened for instance in Glasgow tenants' associations (Bryant 1974, p. 29).

The issue therefore becomes how to fashion such workplace/ neighbourhood links. That is easier to resolve in the context of a crisis situation, such as a factory or hospital closure on the one hand, or a rent strike in a tight 'occupational' community such as Clydeside on the other. For these cases involve rearguard actions with a high public profile, seeking to resist unpopular measures being imposed from above. But it is less easy to make the transition to day-to-day, non-crisis circumstances, and cement links which could be formalised and gradually extended into a struggle for both community and workers' control. One way out of this dilemma has been to suggest trades councils as forums for community/workers links (O'Malley, p. 179, Colenutt, p. 252). Another proposal has been for trade unions to sponsor community groups and programmes. However, both of these require radical changes in conventional trade union attitudes and practice. Whilst some trades councils—in Leeds, Coventry, Tyneside and South Shields, for example—have begun to develop into positive forums for uniting local struggles, the wider picture is less encouraging. And even trade unionists sympathetic to and involved in community groups are sceptical about the extent to which trade union sponsorship of community action is feasible in terms of available union resources or desirable in terms of the *quid pro quo* union bureaucracies might require and which could restrict the political scope of the sponsored group (Liddell & Bryant, pp. 95–6). In some of the advocacy (E. G. Gavin & O'Malley, pp. 208–9) of trade union links it is possible to detect a certain romanticism on the part of community activists which tends to expose their ignorance of the nature of contemporary trade unionism which is for the most part economistic and narrowly self-interested. Some left-wing community activists have fallen for what has been characterised as 'the soft option syndrome' where 'the left, while rejecting the last illusion, invents the next.' (J. Smith, p. 30). Whilst that over-states the argument, it adds a useful cautionary note.

The Political Dimension

Therefore, unless some hard thought is given to a way through these dilemmas, we may well come back after some years of exploring community/industrial links to embark on the quest for a further fresh political perspective on neighbourhood organising. To avoid that, it is necessary at this stage for a specifically *political* dimension to be fused together with the community/industrial link. For it is one thing to point with justification to the growth of groups and initiatives outside orthodox parties (Wainwright, pp. 9–10), but quite another to duck the crucial question of political organisation.

To be sure, there have been suggestions for 'socialist' community action embracing trade unionism and including links to the labour movement (O'Malley, pp. 171–2, Corrigan). But these remain on a fragmented basis and are sometimes expressed in the kind of rhetoric all too reminiscent of the radical advocates of participation identified earlier, camouflaging more than it reveals about strategic and tactical possibilities and problems (Cowley, p. 226, CDP 1975). For community activists can no longer avoid the question of seating their activity within a broad political movement. Which is not to say that community action must necessarily be subsumed under a specific political group, nor to imply that existing groups on the left will be able easily to relate to the new urban politics of the last decade. Indeed the experience suggests they are far from being able to respond to that politics Rowbotham *et al*). Rather, the argument is that, just as community action cannot be divorced from industrial action, so both will remain fragmented and limited unless linked to a political movement. Analysis of successful local action in Italy has pointed to the importance of left wing political leadership (K. Coit, pp. 303–4), whilst as Benyon argues of the position of trade unionists (Benyon, p. 300):

> Without the backing of a vigorous socialist movement, capable of relating particular sectional struggles to each other, and extending struggles beyond the particular factory, the radical trade unionist finds himself in an insoluble dilemma. He fights by the rules of a system that he hardly approves of, within an organisation that has proved itself manifestly incapable of changing those rules.

The question therefore becomes: which political movement? Saunders expresses the central dilemma when he argues (p. 135): 'if urban and industrial struggles are to be brought together then this can only be accomplished through the existing institutional framework of the labour movement. At the present time, however, the labour movement in Britain shows little sign of being able or willing to forge such an integration.' But there is an additional issue in this dilemma. Most socialist community activists who argue for links with the labour movement define the latter in such a way as to exclude the Labour Party. For them, the 'labour movement' is the rank and file of the trade unions together with other socialist groupings. However that notion is typically vague in its formulation. It also avoids facing up to political reality in pretending that the Labour Party and the official structures of the trade unions can either be ignored or bypassed. Experience tells us different, despite the many defects of both institutions. Recognition of that apparently leads Saunders (p. 136) to acknowledge a further dilemma when he argues: 'There is, it seems, no realistic alternative to the Labour Party, yet that party poses no alternative.'

Unfortunately, that view—widely held amongst radical community activists and other socialists—leads to a position of political stalemate. The logic of the argument points irrevocably to links with the Labour Party, yet the act of attempting to do so is felt to be tainted and unpalatable. That may be understandable in view of the Party's record, especially in office, but it cannot become an excuse for immobilising any attempt to place community action upon a firmer political footing. The onus is surely upon those who disagree to suggest a feasible strategy capable of transforming community action from its defensive posture that tends inevitably towards its absorption by the local state, as we saw strikingly in the case of neighbourhood councils.

Otherwise, there is an inescapable need for 'overall solutions such as can only be canvassed by nationally structured political and social organisations'—which means revitalising the Labour Party (Silburn, pp. 143–4). That being accepted, a radical change is required in the Party's politics. For, as conventionally organised, both Labour and the unions have become part of the very system which radical community action has sought to challenge; indeed, it was partly Labour's post-War failure to advance working class interests which created a political vacuum community activists have tried to fill.

Revitalising the Labour Movement

The Labour Movement therefore needs to learn from the experience of radical community action and orientate itself firmly towards extra-parliamentary politics so that this becomes the base of its activity within the Town Hall or Westminster systems (Hain & Hebditch, Hain 1980). Such a strategy would avoid the historic limitations of Labour's 'parliamentary socialism' (Miliband 1972). Given the nature of politics in Britain, there is no practicable alternative but to press the capitalist system and its parliamentary structure to its limits—a strategy which allows for a marriage of parliamentary and extra-parliamentary methods of change (Hodgson). In that context, community groups could seek the kind of alliance with the Party which trade unions have historically enjoyed: whilst still retaining their autonomy, they could become the wing of the Party intervening in the arena of *reproduction* just as trade unions intervene in the *production* system.

Also required as part of this process will be far-reaching change in the nature and style of political activity and organisation, learning specifically from the women's movement, as Hilary Wainwright argues (p. 13):

> ... because of the form of oppression which it confronts, the women's movement has radically extended the scope of politics and, with this, has changed who is involved in politics and how. Much of the oppression of women takes place in 'private', in areas of life considered 'personal'. The causes of that oppression are social and economic, but these causes could only be revealed and confronted when women challenged the assumptions of their personal life ...

Just as community action emphasises that apparently parochial issues both concern people deeply and provide a means of allowing them to relate to wider concerns and thereby a point of entry into politics 'proper', so the women's movement has highlighted that the politics of everyday life must be the cornerstone of any new form of politics.

Similarly, broadening the scope of trade unions to include political and community issues encourages rank and file activism and demands for accountability and democracy (P. Thomas, pp. 63–70), thereby helping to overcome many of the bureaucratic and political obstacles which restrict the ability of the unions to confront the basic structure of capitalism. Meanwhile, there are increasing demands for democratic accountability of the Labour Party's leadership to local parties (Coates). Those demands also offer a far more effective way of strengthening the power base of Labour councillors than such technocratic reforms as increased facilities for councillors—as well as tying them more directly to their working class base (Murgatroyd, pp. 25–36, Southampton ILP). One of the by-products of that could be a greater opportunity for community groups to intervene through local Labour Parties and win recognition for their interests, *before* they begin to grapple with the local council's bureaucracy. Industrial democracy within local government could also provide the mechanism for building a community/worker/political bond (Murgatroyd, pp. 19–25, Coventry CDP, p. 69, Somerton). Meanwhile, the pressure for MPs to be held accountable to the constituency Parties which select them could tie them more firmly to local roots. This, particularly in the light of the increasing tendency for MPs to act as case-work advocates, representing the interests of their constituents to the state bureaucracy (Morrell), could open up further opportunities for community groups to seize through their local Labour Parties: they could help to ensure that MPs genuinely acted as the arm of their communities rather than as prisoners of the system.

The Labour Party itself will of course have to break from the politics which has historically frustrated its socialist objectives. It needs to abandon its preoccupation with electoralism and adopt a campaigning perspective, mobilising outside the conventional political system, in the community and the workplace (Hain 1980). That would enable community groups to relate to the Party, thereby overcoming many of the obstacles which they presently face. The precise manner in which they do relate will depend on particular local circumstances: it need not be a uniform or mechanistic link but, preferably, a flexible one.

If this occurred, we could see both a renewal of the Labour Party and a rooting of socialism back in the people. For a legacy of the 'alternative politics' has been not simply to pose new forms of political action but to attempt a 'recovery of a libertarian socialist tradition' (Rowbotham, p. 47, Murgatroyd, pp. 53–4, Hain 1979) which has unfortunately tended to take second place to Leninist and parliamentary socialist strategies, both of which (albeit from markedly different standpoints) tend inevitably to centralised control. Under their direction, socialism has become too identified with top heavy decision-making, with bureaucracy and alienation. In short, socialism has become synonymous with statism. The alternative of a genuinely liberating form of socialism has been revived by the community politics and direct action of the 1960s and 1970s, emphasising self-organisation, decentralised decision-making, community control and workers' control under public ownership. And *that* could enable the promise of radical participation to be fulfilled.

APPENDICES

I

Forum Election Arrangements

The election was by postal ballot based on a Register of electors consisting of the names and addresses of people who qualified according to the following rules:

... a person must be 18 years or more and must have one or more of the following qualifications. He or she must:

(a)   live in Covent Garden as an owner/occupier or a leaseholder or as a tenant. 'Tenants' include families and lodgers of the actual tenant. Past tenants and owners including those who owned or leased premises or a business, so long as they wish to return and were in Covent Garden for at least one year after 1 January 1961 are also eligible. Additionally people who were tenants for at least 10 years before 1 January 1961 also qualify.

(b)   be an employee, owner, manager of a business or service (e.g. (i) shop, retail trade, wholesale establishment, (ii) office or professional practice, (iii) restaurant catering establishment, public house, hotel, (iv) theatre, studios, (v) craft or art workshop, (vi) hospital, social service or welfare organisation, educational institution, religious body, (vii) government department or nationalised corporation) and must work wholly or to a considerable extent in the area.

(c)   be the nominee of a corporation or association which owns or leases premises in the area.

(d)   be a student at a Covent Garden educational institution.

(e)   be a person whose office address may be outside Covent Garden but who spends a large part of his work time in the area (e.g. a postman).

Each candidate's nomination needed to be signed by five electors who also needed to belong to the same sub-group for which the candidate was standing. The sub-groups were as follows:

(i) *Resident tenants*—(including registered former resident tenants):—
   (a) Council tenants
   (b) Housing Trust tenants
   (c) All other tenants
(ii) *Businesses*—(includes: owners, managers, and employees):—
   (a) Shops, retail traders and wholesalers
   (b) Offices and professional practices
   (c) Restaurants, caterers, public houses and hotels
(iii) *Services*—(includes: owners, managers and employees):—
   (a) Theatres
   (b) Crafts, workshops and arts
   (c) Hospitals, welfare and social services, educational institutions and religious bodies
(iv) *Owners*—(residential or business):— Freeholders, ground lessees and leaseholders whose present lease had an original term certain of seven years or more.

Two staff were engaged by the Working Party to work fulltime on the election, concentrating on registering voters by direct contact with those eligible. At its meeting on 22nd February 1974, the GLC Covent Garden Development Committee agreed to provide funds not exceeding £1500 to conduct the election, including wages for the two staff employed.

II

Communications: Paper by
D.L. Blackhurst (10th October 1974)

1. At the 'round-table conference' on 26 September I was asked by the Chairman of the Forum to put forward some ideas and proposals for improving methods of communication between the Forum and the GLC. As an introduction to the detailed suggestions made at the end of this paper, I think it necessary to make some comments on three aspects of the problem which the Chairman referred to as a 'breakdown of communications'.

2. *The 'us and them' attitude.* Some members of the Forum talk and write about 'participation' but some of the same members (not all) persist in regarding the GLC, the Development Committee and the officers as fundamentally hostile—a body which has preconceived (and sinister) intentions to make changes in Covent Garden against the wishes and interests of the community. There can be no 'participation' between two groups of people when one regards the other as an enemy who cannot be trusted.

3. 'Participation' means sharing, in particular sharing the responsibility for decisions by making a contribution to the process of choice between alternative policies and courses of action. It does not and cannot mean a complete transfer of responsibility from the GLC to the Forum, by which the GLC would immediately and automatically carry out anything the Forum proposed.

4. This attitude of making 'demands' and resenting any delay in satisfying them is based on regarding the Forum as just another pressure group—like developers, small traders and businesses, tenants' associations, or even the Community Association. Pressure groups do *not* 'participate'; they are 'consulted'. It is the proper function of a pressure group to make 'demands' on behalf of its members and to support these demands by every kind of argument and agitation, without regard to the merits of rival 'demands' by other pressure groups representing different

special interests. This leaves the responsible public authority to judge between the claims of the rival pressure groups and to make a final decision which will please some and disappoint others.

5.   If 'participation' is to have any real meaning, it calls for a body which will contribute to the process of judging between pressure groups and their demands—a body which will use its local knowledge and its opportunity to listen to and question the spokesmen for special interests to help the GLC find a solution which is genuinely the best possible, taking account of all the facts and opinions. Without such a body there is always a danger that the GLC's decisions will be either 'remote' (i.e. not sufficiently responsive to special local circumstances), or, on the other hand, too much influenced by which-ever of the pressure groups is best organised to make a loud and persistent noise.

6.   I hope the Forum will come to play this role—testing the arguments put forward by individual pressure groups and passing on the 'demands' with its support only when it has satisfied itself that they are realistic and are in the best interests of Covent Garden as a whole. If the Forum does behave in this way it will gain real influence over decisions by the GLC, but it will also come to be regarded—by disappointed pressure groups—as part of 'the Establishment'. This is an inevitable consequence of real participation.

7.   *The size and complexity of the GLC organisation* is a second element in the problem of communication. This is the source of persistent complaints about 'passing the buck', delay, and the frustration of not being able to talk direct (usually at short notice) to someone who can really get something done.

8.   No amount of complaint and protest can alter this. We have to accept as a fact of life that the GLC is one of the largest local authorities in the world and that even Camden and Westminster are very large and complex. They are necessarily organised on a basis of specialisation to make the best use of 'experts' in professional matters which are relevant to all parts of the GLC's area. The main consequence of this is that elected members (who take final decisions) and very senior officers (who take final responsibility for advice given to members) know a great deal about broad policies and general principles but do not—

without notice—know the details of individual projects or problems. On the other hand, more junior officers, who do know the details, do not have the authority or the wide range of knowledge of policy to enable them to give definite answers about what the GLC will do.

9.   Covent Garden is unusually well placed in this respect. There is one Committee which deals only with Covent Garden and which has the right to *advise* other Committees on matters affecting Covent Garden even when the CGDC does not have the power of executive decision. There is also a very accessible full-time Team, wholly occupied with Covent Garden, who have very extensive knowledge of details.

10.   Nevertheless, any plan for improved communications must take account of these two facts:—

    a)   There is no single authoritative officer, member or Committee which can take a quick final decision about what is to be done in Covent Garden. Some degree of consultation or of passing a report for action to another committee or authority will be normal.

    b)   Members and senior officers will only very rarely be able to deal satisfactorily with points raised at short notice.

11.   *There are two levels of communication*, which require rather different methods. The first level is the gathering of *information* and its presentation to the Forum or its 'committees' so that the Forum can reach a considered decision on what it believes should be done. The second level is the conveyance of the Forum's views (and the reasons for them) to the appropriate level, members or officers, of the GLC or Camden/Westminster or elsewhere.

Suggestions for 'Communication'

1.   The first step is to make a clear distinction between the two levels of communication. For the purpose of *getting information* the normal channel should be the Team at King Street. They will know whether they have or can get what is asked for; if officers of other departments or of the Borough Councils need to be brought in, either the Team will make the contact or they will advise the Forum representative who to approach. It is time-wasting for the Forum to make direct requests to members for detailed information which the members can obtain only by themselves asking the Team!

2. For the purpose of conveying formal views, opinions and decisions of the Forum (or its Committee) to the GLC the normal channel should be the Director-General, whose duty it is to see that any such representations by the Forum are put to the Chairman of the Committee concerned and (subject to the Chairman's powers to take urgent action on behalf of the Committee) to the Committee itself. There is however no objection to copies of such letters being sent to a Chairman or member, or to the letter being addressed to the Chairman with a copy to the Director-General. The quickest possible attention to any letter is achieved only when the Director-General's department is dealing with it—our responsibility is to see that it receives prompt attention by *all* departments and/or Committees who may be concerned.

3. The second step in improving communications is to establish very precisely 'who speaks for the Forum'. Individual members of the Forum have no more (and no less) right to ask for information or express views to members/officers of the Council than any other member of the public: they can use the Information Centre (plus Mrs. Williams) or can speak or write to the Chairman or a member or officer just as anyone else can, but they will receive no special privileges. On the other hand, the Chairman, Vice-Chairman, Hon. Secretary or the Hon. Treasurer will be treated as acting for the Forum (and so for the Covent Garden 'community' as a whole) and what they have to say will receive greater attention and carry greater weight. Similar special attention *can* be given to anyone the Forum specially authorises to act as its spokesman on particular matters. For example, a formally-appointed Chairman or Secretary of the Planning Filter Committee would be treated as an officer of the Forum on all matters concerning planning applications, but an ordinary member of the Filter Committee would not.

4. Apart from correspondence and formal communication we have to consider face-to-face meetings. Again, there are several levels.

    (a) Properly authorised officers of the Forum or small groups authorised to represent the Forum can and should meet appropriate members of the Team (plus other GLC/ Borough Council officers as the Team think necessary) informally for quite wide ranging discussion. All that is needed is reasonable notice and an appointment and a general indication of the matters to be discussed. On the other hand, neither the Team nor other GLC officers can spare time for frequent unorganised talks with individual Forum members.

(b)   Appropriate GLC officers will continue to attend meetings of the Forum and its Committees to the extent the Forum wishes. They will, on request and within reason, prepare and circulate in advance information papers as a basis for discussion at such meetings, but they will *not* take the initiative in producing papers for the Forum because this could be interpreted as reducing the Forum's independence.

(c)   If meetings involving members of the GLC (any of its Committees) are to be useful, they must be arranged to deal with specific topics and the meetings must be restricted to what is on the prepared agenda. Members cannot be expected to give useful, definite answers on questions when they have had no warning and no opportunity to inquire into the full facts.

Recommendations

(a)   Decisions of the Forum calling for urgent action or consideration by the Development Committee (or other Committee) should be sent in writing by the Hon. Secretary to the Director-General, or by some other properly authorised officer of the Forum.

(b)   Wherever possible a decision conveyed under (a) should be accompanied by a statement of what investigation the Forum had undertaken and the reasons for its decision and an indication whether the Forum was unanimous or divided. A copy of the relevant Minutes (e.g. the Minutes of the Policy Working Group's discussions of Traffic and Transport Management) under cover of a brief note drawing attention to the items calling for attention would suffice in most cases.

(c)   The Hon. Secretary shall be responsible for asking the Team (or other GLC officers concerned) to take action on matters which were informally agreed at a Forum meeting. GLC officers shall not be left to 'interpret' the discussion or act on Minutes unless they have specifically undertaken at the meeting to do so and it is so recorded in the Minutes.

(d)   Unless formally authorised to do so, individual members of the Forum shall not make requests to the GLC or convey views to the GLC which purport to be 'for the Forum'.

(e)   Meetings between representatives of the Forum and officers of the GLC shall be pre-arranged, with due notice, to deal with topics of which notice has been given.

(f)   Meetings between the Forum and members of the GLC and/or the two Borough Councils shall be arranged to consider a limited number of specific topics, so that the appropriate members can be specially asked to attend and can be 'briefed' with relevant facts. Discussion at the meeting to be confined to these topics except that, with the consent of both the GLC and Forum members present, additional topics can be raised after the agenda items have been dealt with.

(g)   The Forum should consider whether it wishes to ask for special rights for one or more Forum spokesmen to attend *and take part in* meetings of the Development Committee and, if so, whether generally or on specific occasions.

SOURCES
and
BIBLIOGRAPHY

GENERAL

Alinsky, S., *Rules for Radicals* (New York, Vintage, 1972).

Almond, G. and Powell, G.B., *Comparative Politics: a developmental approach* (Boston, Little, Brown & Co., 1966).

Altshuler, A., *Community Control* (New York, Bobbs-Merrill, 1970).

Ambrose, P. and Colenutt, B., *The Property Machine* (Harmondsworth, Penguin, 1975).

Angell Ward Neighbourhood Council, *Report: October 1971–May 1973.*

Anson, B., *A Tale from the Top of my Head* (issued by the author, London, December 1972).

Arnold-Baker, C., *The New Law and Practice of Parish Administration* (Longcross Press, 1970).

Arnstein, S.R., 'A ladder of citizen participation in the USA', *Journal of the Town Planning Institute*, vol. 57, No. 4 (April 1971), pp. 176–82.

Arnstein, S.R. (as told to), 'Maximum Feasible Manipulation', *Public Administration Review* (July/August 1972), pp. 377–90.

Aronson, R., 'The Movement and its Critics', *Studies on the Left*, vol. 6, No. 1 (January–February 1966), pp. 3–19.

Aronson, R. and Cowley, J., 'The New Left in the United States', in *The Socialist Register 1967* (Merlin Press, 1967), pp. 73–90.

Bachrach, P., *The Theory of Democratic Elitism* (University of London Press, 1969).

Bachrach, P., and Baratz, M.S., *Power and Poverty* (Oxford University Press, 1970).

Baine, S., *Community Action and Local Government*, Occasional Papers on Social Administration No. 59 (Bell, 1975).

Barber, J.D., *The Lawmakers* (Yale University Press, 1965).

Barker, A., *Strategy and Style in Local Community Relations* (Runnymede Trust, 1975).

Barr, A., *Student Community Action* (Bedford Square Press, 1972).

Barratt Brown, M., *From Labourism to Socialism* (Nottingham, Spokesman Books, 1972).

Beer, S.H., *Modern British Politics* (Faber, 1965).

Bell, C., and Newby, H., 'Community, Communion, Class and Community Action: the Social Sources of the New Urban Politics', in D. Herbert and R. Johnson (eds.), *Social Areas in Cities: Vol II Spatial Perspectives on Problems and Policies* (Chichester, Wiley, 1976), pp. 189–207.

Bell, D. and Held, V., 'The Community Revolution', *The Public Interest*, No. 16 (Summer 1969), pp. 142–79.

Bell, J. and Paton, J., *Glasgow: Its Municipal Administration* (Glasgow, Jones Maclehose, 1896).

Benello, C.G. and Roussopolous D. (eds.), *The Case for Participatory Democracy* (New York, Viking Press, 1972).

Benewick, R., 'British Pressure Group Politics: the NCCL', *Annals of the American Academy of Political and Social Science*, vol. 413 (May 1974), pp. 145–57.

Benewick, R. and Smith, Trevor (eds.), *Direct Action and Democratic Politics* (Allen & Unwin, 1973).

Benington, J., *Local Government Becomes Big Business* (Coventry, C.D.P., September 1975).

Benn, A.W., *The New Politics* (Fabian Tract 402, 1970).

Benveniste, G., *The Politics of Expertise* (Croom Helm, 1972).

Benyon, H., *Working for Ford* (Harmondsworth, Penguin, 1973).

Benyon, H. and Wainwright, H., *The Workers' Report on Vickers* (Pluto, 1979).

Beresford, S. and P., *A Say in the Future* (Battersea Community Action, August 1978).

Birch, A.H., *Representation* (Pall Mall, 1971).

Blackhurst, D.L., 'Electing a Covent Garden Forum', *Greater London Intelligence Quarterly*, No. 35 (June 1976), pp. 5–8.

Blair, T., *The International Urban Crisis* (Paladin, 1974).

Blondel, J., *Political Parties: a genuine case for discontent?* (Wildwood House, 1978).

Boddington, S., *Neighbourhood Councils and Modern Technology* (Nottingham, Spokesman Pamphlet No. 28, 1972).

Bottomore, T.B., *Critics of Society* (Allen & Unwin 1969).

Bourges, H. (ed.), *The Student Revolt* (Panther, 1968).

Breed, W., *The Self-Guiding Society* (New York, Free Press, 1971).

Broadbent, T.A., *Planning and profit in the urban economy* (Methuen, 1977).

Bryant, R., 'Community Action', *The British Journal of Social Work*, vol. 2, No. 2 (1972), pp. 205–15.

Bryant, R., 'Linking Community and Industrial Action', *Community Development Journal*, vol. 9, No. 1 (1974), pp. 28–32.

Buckman, P., *The Limits of Protest* (Panther, 1970).

Bull, D. (ed.), *Family Poverty* (Duckworth, 1971).

Bulpitt, J.G., 'Participation and Local Government: territorial democracy', in Geraint Parry (ed.), *Participation in Politics* (Manchester University Press, 1972), pp. 281–302.

Calouste Gulbenkian Foundation, *Community Work and Social Change* (Longman, 1968).

Calouste Gulbenkian Foundation, *Current Issues in Community Work* (Routledge & Kegan Paul, 1973).

Carter, April, *Direct Action and Liberal Democracy* (Routledge & Kegan Paul, 1973).

Castells, M., *City, Class and Power* (Macmillan, 1977).

Castells, M., 'Towards a Political Urban Sociology', in Michael Harloe (ed.), *Captive Cities* (Wiley, 1977), pp. 61–78.

Castells, M., *The Urban Question* (Arnold, 1977).

Christensen, T., 'Covent Garden: A Struggle for Survival', *Political Quarterly*, vol. 50, No. 3 (July–September 1979), pp. 336–48.

Christensen, T., *Neighbourhood Survival* (Dorchester, Prism Press, 1979).

Christmas, L., 'Watching Watchdogs', *The Guardian*, 11th February 1976.

Clark, George, 'Neighbourhood Self-Management', in Peter Hain (ed.), *Community Politics* (John Calder, 1976), pp. 97–115.

Clarke, C., *et al*, *Planning for Community Councils* (Glasgow, University of Strathclyde, 1975).

Clarke, T., 'Redundancy, worker resistance and the community', in Craig *et al*, *Jobs and Community Action* (Routledge 1979).

Cloward, R.A. and Piven, F.F., 'The Professional Bureaucracies: benefit systems as influence systems', in R. Kramer and H. Specht (eds.), *Readings in Community Organisation Practice* (Englewood Cliffs, Prentice-Hall, 1969a), pp. 359–72.

Cloward, R.A. and Piven, F.F., 'The Urban Crisis and the Consolidation of National Power', in Robert H. Conway (ed.), *Urban Riots* (New York, Vintage, 1969b), pp. 164–73.

Coates, K., *Democracy in the Labour Party* (Nottingham, Spokesman, 1977).

Coates, K. and Silburn, R., *Poverty: The Forgotten Englishman* (Harmondsworth, Penguin, 1970).

Cockburn, A. and Blackburn, R. (eds.) *Student Power* (Harmondsworth, Penguin, 1969).

Cockburn, C., *The Local State* (Pluto Press, 1977).

Cohen, A., 'Representativeness in Government—A Role for Social Planning Councils', *Journal of Sociology and Social Welfare*, vol. 1 Part 2 (Winter 1973/4), pp. 25–35.

Cohen, M. and Haley, D. (eds.), *The New Student Left* (Boston, Beacon Press, 1966).

Cohen, S.S., *Modern Capitalist Planning* (Weidenfeld & Nicolson, 1969).

Cohn-Bendit, G. and D., *Obsolete Communism: The Left Wing Alternative* (Harmondsworth, Penguin, 1969).

Coit, K., 'Local Action Not Citizen Participation', in W.K. Tabb and L. Sawers (eds.), *Marxism and the Metropolis* (New York, Oxford University Press, 1978), pp. 297–311.

Coit, S., *Neighbourhood Guilds* (Arno Press, 1974; first published, London 1891).

Cole, G.D.H., *The Future of Local Government* (Cassell & Co., 1921).

Cole, G.D.H., *Guild Socialism Re-stated* (Leonard Parsons, 1920).

Cole, G.D.H., *Local and Regional Government* (Cassell, 1947).

Cole, G.D.H., *Self-Government in Industry* (Bell, 1917).

Colenutt, B., 'Community action over local planning issues', in Craig, *et al*, *Jobs and Community Action* (Routledge, 1979), pp. 243–52.

Commission of the European Communities, *Employee participation and company structure*, Bulletin of the European Communities, Supplement 8/75 (1975).

Community Development Project, *Community Work or Class Politics* (CDP Political Economy Collective, July 1975).

Community Development Project, *The Costs of Industrial Change* (CDP Inter-Project Editorial Team, January 1977).

Community Development Project, *Gilding The Ghetto* (CDP Inter-Project Editorial Team, February 1977).

Community Development Project, 'Neighbourhood Democracy', Notes on a Discussion following the meeting of the CDP Consultative Council on 15th June 1973 (mimeo).

Community Development Project, *Profits Against Houses* (CDP Information and Intelligence Unit, 1976).

Cooley, M., 'Technology for community needs', in Craig *et al, Jobs and Community Action* (Routledge, 1979), pp. 281–94.

Corrigan, P., 'Community Work and Political Struggle: What are the Possibilities of working on the contradictions?', in Peter Leonard (ed.), *Sociology of Community Action* (Keele University, Sociological Review Monograph 21, 1975), pp. 93–111.

Counter Information Services, *The Recurrent Crisis of London* (CIS, 1973).

Cowley, J., *et al, Community or Class Struggle?* (Stage I, 1977).

Craig, G., Mayo, M. and Sharman, N. (eds.), *Jobs and Community Action* (Routledge & Kegan Paul, 1979).

Crenson, M.A., 'Nonissues in City Politics: The Case of Air Pollution', in Marvin Surkin and Alan Wolfe (eds.), *An End to Political Science* (New York, Basic Books, 1970), pp. 144–66.

Crick, B., 'Foreword', in William Hampton, *Democracy and Community* (Oxford University Press, 1970), pp. xiii–xxii.

Crosland, A., *The Future of Socialism* (Cape, 1956).

Cunningham, J.V., 'Citizen Participation in Public Affairs', in *Public Administration Review*, vol. 32 (October 1972), pp. 589–602.

Curno, P. (ed.), *Political Issues and Community Work* (Routledge, 1978).

Dahl, R.A., *A Preface to Democratic Theory* (University of Chicago Press, 1956).

Dahl, Robert, A., and Tufte, E.R., *Size and Democracy* (Stanford University Press, 1974).

Dahrendorf, R., *Class and Class Conflict in Industrial Society* (Stanford, 1959).

Damer, S. and Hague, C., 'Public Participation in Planning: a review', *Town Planning Review*, vol. 42 (July 1971), pp. 217–32.

Davies, J.G., *The Evangelistic Bureaucrat* (Tavistock, 1972).

Davis, A.F., *Spearheads for Reform* (New York, Oxford University Press, 1967).

Dearlove, J., 'The Control of Change and the Regulation of Community Action', in Jones, D. and Mayo, M., *Community Work One* (Routledge & Kegan Paul, 1974), pp. 22–43.

Dearlove, J., *The Politics of Policy in Local Government* (Cambridge University Press, 1973).

Dearlove, J., *The Reorganisation of British Local Government* (Cambridge University Press, 1979).

Demuth, C., *Government Initiatives on Urban Deprivation*, Briefing Paper (Runnymede Trust, 1977).

Dennis, N., 'The 'Popularity of the Neighbourhood Community Idea', in R.E. Pahl (ed.), *Readings in Urban Sociology* (Pergamon Press, 1968), pp. 74–92.

Dennis, N., *Public Participation and Planner's Blight* (Faber, 1972).

Dixey, Bob, *A Guide to Neighbourhood Councils* (Halstead, Association for Neighbourhood Councils, 1975).

Donajgrodzki, A.P. (ed.), *Social Control in Nineteenth Century Britain* (Croom Helm, 1977).

Donnison, D., 'Micro-Politics of the City', in Donnison, D. and Eversley, D. (eds.), *London: Urban Patterns, Problems and Policies* (Heinemann, 1973), pp. 383–404.

Dowse, R.E., and Hughes, J.A., *Political Sociology* (Wiley, 1972).

Dunleavy, P., 'Protest and Quiescence in Urban Politics: A Critique of Some Pluralist and Structuralist Myths', *Urban change and Conflict Conference: York University 1977* (Centre for Environmental Studies, 1977).

East London Claimants Union, 'East London Claimants Union and the concept of self-management', in D. Jones and M. Mayo (eds.), *Community Work One* (Routledge, 1974), pp. 79–89.

Eckstein, H., *Division and Cohesion in Democracy–a Study of Norway* (Princeton University Press, 1966).

Edelman, M., *The Symbolic Uses of Power* (Urbana, Ill., University of Illinois Press, 1964).

Edwards, B., 'Organising the unemployed in the 1920s', in Craig *et al, Jobs and Community Action, op cit*, pp. 27–32.

Edwards, J., and Batley, R., *The Politics of Positive Discrimination* (Tavistock, 1978).

Elkin, S.L., *Politics and Land Use Planning* (Cambridge University Press, 1974).

Erber, E. (ed.), *Urban Planning in Transition* (New York, Grossman, 1970).

Etzioni, A., *The Active Society* (Collier-Macmillan, 1968).

Etzioni, A., *Studies in Social Change* (New York, Holt, Rinehart & Winston, 1966).

Eversley, D., *The Planner in Society* (Faber, 1973).

Faludi, A. (ed.), *A Reader in Planning Theory* (Pergamon Press, 1973).

Ferris, J., *Participation in Urban Planning*, Occasional Papers in Social Administration 48 (Bell, 1972).

Field, Frank, 'Charitable Action', *New Society*, 31st January 1974, pp. 271–2.

Finer, S.E., 'Groups and Political Participation', in Parry, G., *Participation in Politics* (Manchester University Press, 1971), pp. 59–79.

Fromm, E., *The Sane Society* (Routledge & Kegan Paul, 1963 edition).

Frost, B., *The Tactics of Pressure* (Stainer & Bell, 1975).

Fruchter, N. and Kramer, R., 'An Approach to Community Organising Projects', *Studies on the Left*, vol. 6, No. 2 (1966), pp. 31–61.

Galbraith, J.K., *The Affluent Society* (Harmondsworth, Penguin, 1962).

Gamson, W.A., *Power and Discontent* (Homewood, Ill., The Dorsey Press, 1968).

Gavin, B. and O'Malley, J., 'What are our long-term political objectives?', in J. Cowley, *Community or Class Struggle?* (Stage 1, 1977), pp. 202–9.

Gitlin, T., 'Local Pluralism as Theory and Ideology', in Charles A. McCoy and John Playford (eds.), *Apolitical Politics* (New York, Thomas Crowell Co., 1967), pp. 124–45.

Gitlin, T., 'The Radical Potential of the Poor', in Massimo Teodori (ed.), *The New Left* (Cape, 1970), pp. 136–49.

Glass, R., 'Verbal Pollution', *New Society*, 29th September 1977, pp. 667–9.

Goodman, E., *The Impact of Size* (Acton Society Trust, 1969).

Goodman, R., *After the Planners* (Harmondsworth, Penguin, 1972).

Gorz, A., 'The reproduction of labour power: the model of consumption', in J. Cowley, *et al*, *Community or Class Struggle?* (Stage 1, 1977), pp. 22–39.

Gough, I., *The Political Economy of the Welfare State* (Macmillan, 1979).

Greaves, B., 'Communities and Power', in Peter Hain (ed.), *Community Politics* (John Calder, 1976), pp. 35–51.

Green, G., 'Politics, Local Government and the Community', *Local Government Studies*, No. 8 (June 1974), pp. 5–16.

Green, P., 'Decentralization, Community Control and Revolution: Reflections on Ocean-Brownsville', in Philip Green and Sanford Levinson (eds.), *Power and Community* (New York, Random House, 1970), pp. 247–75.

Green, P., 'Science, Government and the case of RAND: A Singular Pluralism', *World Politics*, vol. XX, No. 2 (January 1968), pp. 301–26.

Green, P. and Levinson, S. (eds.), *Power and Community* (New York, Random House, 1970).

Guthrie, R., 'The First Word', *Town and Country Planning*, vol. 37 (1969), pp. 396–9.

Gyford, J., *Local Politics in Britain* (Croom Helm, 1977).

Habermas, J., *Legitimation Crisis* (Heinemann, 1976).

Hain, P. (ed.), *Community Politics* (John Calder, 1976).

Hain, P., *Reviving the Labour Party*, (Nottingham, Spokesman, 1980).

Hain, P., *Radical Regeneration* (Quartet, 1975).

Hain, P., and Hebditch, S., *Radicals and Socialism* (Nottingham, Institute for Workers Control, 1978).

Hall, P., *Urban and Regional Planning* (Harmondsworth, Penguin, 1974).

Hampton, W., *Democracy and Community* (Oxford University Press, 1970).

Hampton, W., 'Popular Participation in Local Democracy', in Stephen Hatch (ed.), *Towards participation in local services* (Fabian Tract 419, 1973), pp. 46–52.

Hampton, W. and Chapman, J., 'Towards Neighbourhood Councils—I', *The Political Quarterly*, vol. 42, No. 3 (1971), pp. 247–54.

Hampton, W. and Chapman, J., 'Towards Neighbourhood Councils—II', *The Political Quarterly*, vol. 42, No. 4, pp. 414–22.

Harloe, M. (ed.), *Captive Cities* (Wiley, 1977).

Harloe, M., 'The New Urban Sociology', *New Society* (5th October, 1978), pp. 12–3.

Harrington, M., *The Other America* (Baltimore, Maryland, Penguin, 1962).

Harris, N., *Competition and the Corporate Society* (Methuen, 1972).

Harrison, P., 'Derry: from conflict to coexistence', *New Society*, 23rd January 1975, pp. 182–3.

Harrison, P., 'The Neighbourhood Council', *New Society*, 12th April 1973, pp. 73–5.

Harvey, D., 'Government Policies, Financial Institutions and Neighbourhood change in United States Cities', in Michael Harloe (ed.), *Captive Cities* (Wiley, 1977), pp. 123–39.

Harvey, D., *Social Justice and the City* (Edward Arnold, 1973).

Haug, M.R. and Sussman, M.B., 'Professional Autonomy and the revolt of the Client', *Social Problems*, vol. 17, No. 2 (1969), pp. 153–61.

Hawley, W., *et al* (eds.), *Theoretical Perspectives on Urban Politics* (Englewood Cliffs, Prentice-Hall, 1976).

Heineman, B.W., *The Politics of the Powerless* (Oxford University Press, 1972).

Heraud, B., *Sociology and Social Work, Problems and Perspectives* (Pergamon Press, 1970).

Herbert, D. and Johnson, R. (eds.), *Social Areas in Cities: Vol II Spatial Perspectives on Problems and Policies* (Chichester, Wiley, 1976).

Hill, Dilys M., *Democratic Theory and Local Government* (Allen & Unwin, 1974).

Hill, Dilys M., *Participating in Local Affairs* (Harmondsworth, Penguin, 1970).

Hill, M., *The State, Administration and the Individual* (Fontana, 1976).

Hill, M.J. and Issachroff, R.M., *Community Action and Race Relations* (Oxford University Press, 1971).

Hill, R.C., 'Fiscal Collapse and Political Struggle in Decaying Central Cities in the United States', in W.K. Tabb and L. Sawers (eds.), *Marxism and the Metropolis* (New York, Oxford University Press, 1978), pp. 213–40.

Hillery, G.A., 'Definitions of community: areas of agreement', *Rural Sociology*, vol. 20, No. 2 (1955), pp. 111–23.

Hillman, J., 'Tenant Cooperatives Idea', *The Guardian*, 16th January 1975.

Hindess, B., *The Decline of Working-Class Politics* (MacGibbon & Kee, 1971).

Hodgson, G., *Socialism and Parliamentary Democracy* (Nottingham, Spokesman, 1978).

Hoinville, G. and Jowell, R., 'Will the Real Public Please Stand Up?', *Journal for the Built Environment*, vol. 35, No. 3 (March 1972), pp. 159–61.

Holden, B., *The Nature of Democracy* (Nelson, 1974).

Holland, S., *The Socialist Challenge* (Quartet, 1975).

Hollis, P. (ed.), *Pressure from Without* (Edward Arnold, 1974).

The Hornsey Plan (Association for Neighbourhood Councils, August 1973).

Humble, S., 'Neighbourhood Councils and Race Relations', *New Community*, vol. VII, No. 1 (Winter 1978/9), pp. 85–91.

Humble, S. and Talbot, J., *A Community Forum for Coventry?* (Institute for Local Government Studies, University of Birmingham, April 1974).

Humble, S. and Talbot, J., *INC: Second Interim Report* (Institute of Local Government Studies, University of Birmingham, August 1976).

Humble, S. and Talbot, J., *Neighbourhood Councils in England: A Report to the Department of the Environment* (Institute of Local Government Studies, University of Birmingham, November 1977).

Humble, S. and Talbot, J., *A Survey of Neighbourhood Groups in England* (Institute of Local Government Studies, University of Birmingham, December 1976).

Ionescu, G., *Centripetal Politics* (Hart-Davis, MacGibbon, 1975).

Jackson, Ced, *Lambeth Interface* (published by the author, London SE24, 1975).

Jacob, S., 'Community Action in Glasgow Clearance Area: Consensus or Conflict?', in Peter Leonard (ed.), *The Sociology of Community Action* (University of Keele, Sociological Review Monograph 21, 1975), pp. 165–83.

Jacobs, P. and Landau, S., *The New Radicals* (New York, Random House, 1966).

Jay, A., *The Householder's Guide to Community Defence Against Bureaucratic Aggression* (Cape, 1972).

Jenkins, S., *Landlords to London* (Constable, 1975).

Jenkins, S., 'The Press as Politician in Local Planning', *The Political Quarterly*, vol. 44, No. 1 (January-March 1973), pp. 47–57.

Jones, A., *The New Inflation* (Harmondsworth, Penguin, 1973).

Jones, D. and Mayo, M. (eds.), *Community Work One* (Routledge & Kegan Paul, 1974).

Jones, D. and Mayo, M. (eds.), *Community Work Two* (Routledge & Kegan Paul, 1975).

Jordan, Bill, *Paupers: the making of the new claiming class* (Routledge & Kegan Paul, 1973).

Kalk, E., 'Participation or Manipulation', in *Citizen and the City in the Year 2000* (European Cultural Foundation, 1971).

Kariel, H., *The Decline of American Pluralism* (California, Stanford University Press, 1961).

Kariel, Henry S., *The Promise of Politics* (New Jersey, Prentice-Hall, 1966).

Katznelson, I., 'The Crisis of the Capitalist City: Urban Politics and Social Control', in W. Hawley, *et al* (eds.), *Theoretical Perspectives on Urban Politics* (Englewood Cliffs, Prentice-Hall, 1976), pp. 214–29.

Katznelson, I., 'Participation and Political Buffers in Urban America', *Race*, vol. XIV, No. 4 (April 1973), pp. 465–80.

Katznelson, I. and Kesselman, M., *The Politics of Power* (New York, Harcourt Brace Jovanovich, 1975).

Kay, A., 'Planning, participation and planners', in D. Jones and M. Mayo (eds.), *Community Work One* (Routledge, 1974), pp. 199–213.

Kay, A., Mayo, M. and Thompson, M., 'Inner London's Housing Crisis', in J. Cowley, *et al*, *Community or Class Struggle?* (Stage 1, 1977), pp. 128–68.

Keniston, K., *Young Radicals* (New York, Harcourt, 1968).

Kidron, M., *Western Capitalism Since the War* (Harmondsworth, Penguin, 1970).

Kimber, R. and Richardson, J.J. (eds.), *Campaigning for the Environment* (Routledge & Kegan Paul, 1974).

King, A., 'Overload: Problems of Governing in the 1970s', *Political Studies*, vol. XXIII, Nos. 2–3 (June-September 1975), pp. 284–96.

King, R. and Nugent, N. (eds.), *Respectable Rebels* (Hodder & Stoughton, 1979).

Klein, R. and Lewis, J., *The Politics of Consumer Representation: A study of Community Health Councils* (Centre for Studies in Social Policy, 1976).

Kohr, L., *The Breakdown of Nations* (Routledge & Kegan Paul, 1957).

Kornhauser, W., *The Politics of Mass Society* (Routledge & Kegan Paul, 1960).

Kotler, M., *Neighbourhood Government* (New York, Bobbs-Merrill, 1969).

Kramer, R. and Specht, H. (eds.) *Readings in Community Organisation Practice* (Englewood Cliffs, Prentice-Hall, 1969).

Lamarche, F., 'Property Development and the economic foundations of the urban question', in C.G. Pikvance (ed.), *Urban Sociology: Critical Essays* (Tavistock, 1976), pp. 85–118.

Lambert, J. *et al, Housing Policy and the State* (Macmillan, 1978).

Lapping, B. and Radice, G. (eds.), *More Power to the People* (Longmans, 1968).

Lasch, C., *The Agony of the American Left* (Deutsch, 1970).

Leat, D., 'Social Theory and the Historical Construction of Social Work Activity: the Role of Samuel Barnett', in Peter Leonard (ed.), *The Sociology of Community Action* (University of Keele, Sociological Review Monograph 21, 1975), pp. 21–37.

Lees, R., *Politics and Social Work* (Routledge & Kegan Paul, 1972).

Leighton, J., 'Fighting for better health services: the role of the Community Health Council', in G. Craig, M. Mayo and N. Sharman (eds.), *Jobs and Community Action* (Routledge, 1979), pp. 161–75.

Leonard, P. (ed.), *The Sociology of Community Action* (Sociological Review Monograph 21, University of Keele, 1975).

Liddell, H. and Bryant, R., 'A local view of community work', in Jones and Mayo, *Community Work One* (Routledge, 1974), pp. 90–100.

Lindsay, J.V., *The City* (Bodley Head, 1970).

Lipsky, M., 'Protest as a Political Resource', *American Political Science Review*, vol. LXII, No. 4 (1968), pp. 1114–58.

Lipsky, M., *Protest in City Politics* (Chicago, Rand McNally, 1970).

Loney, M., 'Criticism and containment', in Paul Curno (ed.), *Political Issues and Community Work* (Routledge, 1978), pp. 85–105.

Lowi, T., *The End of Liberalism* (New York, W.W. Norton, 1969).

Lowi, T., 'The Public Philosophy: Interest Group Liberalism', *American Political Science Review*, vol. LXI, No. 1 (1967), pp. 5–24.

Lucas, J.R., *Democracy and Participation* (Harmondsworth, Penguin, 1976).

Lynd, S., 'The New Radicals and Participatory Democracy', in Massimo Teodori (ed.), *The New Left* (Cape, 1972), pp. 228–33.

Mairowitz, D.A., *The Radical Soap Opera* (Wildwood House, 1974).

Malpass, P., *The Uses of Public Participation in the Creation and Maintenance of Consent* (Bristol Polytechnic, October 1977).

Mannheim, K., *Man and Society in an Age of Reconstruction* (Routledge & Kegan Paul, 1966 edition; originally published 1940).

Markusen, A.R., 'Class and Urban Social Expenditure: A Marxist Theory of Metropolitan Government', in William K. Tabb and Larry Sawers (eds.), *Marxism and the Metropolis* (New York, Oxford University Press, 1978), pp. 90–111.

Marris, P. and Rein, M., *Dilemmas of Social Reform* (Harmondsworth, Penguin, 1974).

Mason, T., 'Community Action and the Local Authority: A Study in the Incorporation of Protest', *Urban Change and Conflict Conference, York University, 1977* (Centre for Environmental Studies, 1977).

Mayo, M. (ed.), *Women in the Community* (Routledge, 1977).

Meadowcroft, M., *Liberals and the Popular Front* (Young Liberal Movement, 1975).

Megill, K., *The New Democratic Theory* (New York, Free Press, 1970).

Meynaud, J., *Technocracy* (Faber, 1968).

Milbrath, L.W., *Political Participation* (Chicago, Rand McNally & Co., 1965).

Miliband, M., *Parliamentary Socialism* (Merlin Press, 1972).

Miliband, R., *The State in Capitalist Society* (Weidenfeld & Nicolson, 1969).

Mill, J.S., *Essays on Politics and Culture* (New York, Anchor, 1963).

Mill, J.S., *Representative Government* (Everyman edition, 1910).

Miller, S.M., and Rein, M., 'Community participation: past and future', in Jones, D. and Mayo, M. (eds.), *Community Work Two* (Routledge & Kegan Paul, 1975), pp. 3–24.

Mitton, R. and Morrison, E., *A Community Project in Notting Dale* (Allen Lane, 1972).

Monahan, J., 'Up Against the Planners in Covent Garden', in Peter Hain (ed.), *Community Politics* (John Calder, 1976), pp. 175–92.

Moody, K., 'Can the Poor be Organised', in M. Cohen and D. Haley (eds.), *The New Student Left* (Boston, Beacon Press, 1966), pp. 147–53.

Moorhouse, B., Wilson, M., and Chamberlain, C., 'Rent Strikes–Direct Action and the Working Class', *The Socialist Register 1972* (Merlin Press, 1972), pp. 133–56.

Morrell, F., *From the Electors of Bristol* (Nottingham, Spokesman, 1977).

Morris, P., 'Race, community and marginality: Spiralynx', in Craig *et al, Jobs and Community Action* (Routledge, 1979), pp. 100–12.

Morton, J., 'Parish Pumps Revived', *New Society*, 29 January 1970, pp. 173–4.

Muchnik, D.M., *Urban Renewal in Liverpool*, Occasional Papers in Social Administration 33 (Bell, 1970).

Murgatroyd, S., Rees, B., Reynolds, D., *Taking Local Decisions* (Leeds, Independent Labour Publications, 1978).

Myrdal, G., *Beyond the Welfare State* (Duckworth, 1960).

McConnell, G., *Private Power and American Democracy* (New York, Vintage, 1970).

McKay, D.H. and Cox, A.W., *The Politics of Urban Change* (Croom Helm, 1979).

National Community Development Project, *Inter-Project Report* (CDP, 1974).

Nettl, J.P., *Political Mobilization* (Faber, 1967).

Newfield, J., *A Prophetic Minority* (Anthony Blond, 1967).

O'Connor, J., *The Fiscal Crisis of the State* (New York, St. Martin's Press, 1973).

O'Malley, Jan, *The Politics of Community Action* (Nottingham, Spokesman Books, 1977).

Ono, S., 'The Limits of Bourgeois Pluralism', *Studies on the Left*, vol. 5, No. 3 (Summer 1965), pp. 46–72.

The Open Group, *Social Reform in the Centrifugal Society* (New Society Publications, 1970).

Pahl, R.E., 'Managers, Technical Experts and the State: Forms of Mediation, Manipulation and Dominance in Urban and Regional Development', in Michael Harloe (ed.), *Captive Cities* (Wiley, 1977), pp. 49–60.

Pahl, R.E. (ed.), *Readings in Urban Sociology* (Pergamon Press, 1968).

Pahl, R.E. and Winkler, J.J., 'The Economic Elite: Theory and Practice', in P. Stansworth and A. Giddens (eds.), *Elites and Power in British Society* (Cambridge University Press, 1974), pp. 102–122.

Parenti, M., 'Power and Pluralism: A view from the Bottom', in Marvin Surkin and Alan Wolfe (eds.), *An End to Political Science* (New York, Basic Books, 1970), pp. 111–43.

Parry, Geraint, *Participation in Politics* (Manchester University Press, 1972).

'The Participation Swindle: Skeffington Betrayed', *Community Action* (February 1972), pp. 21–3.

Pateman, C., *Participation and Democratic Theory* (Cambridge University Press, 1970).

Pembroke, S., *CDA No 114 (Covent Garden). Summary of Objections made at the Local Public Inquiry (July—September 1972)*, published by the author (London WC2E 9AR, February 1973).

Philo, J., *Patterns of Community Development* (Liverpool University Thesis, 1972).

Pikvance, C.G., 'From "Social Base" to "Social Force": Some Analytical Issues in the Study of Urban Protest', in Michael Harloe (ed.), *Captive Cities* (Wiley, 1977), pp. 175–86.

Pikvance, C.G., 'On the study of urban social movements', in Pikvance (ed.), *Urban Sociology: Critical Essays* (Tavistock, 1976), pp. 198–218.

Pikvance, C.G. (ed.), *Urban Sociology: Critical Essays* (Tavistock, 1976).

Pinkerton, A., *Community Councils* (Glasgow, The Planning Exchange, March 1974).

Pitt, J., *Gentrification in Islington* (Barnsbury Peoples Forum, 1977).

Piven, F.F., 'Social Planning or Politics', in Ernest Erber (ed.), *Urban Planning in Transition* (New York, Grossman, 1970), pp. 45–51.

Piven, F.F. and Cloward, R.A., *Poor People's Movements: why they succeed, how they fail* (New York, Pantheon, 1977).

Piven, F.F. and Cloward, R.A., *Regulating the Poor* (New York, Pantheon, 1971).

Playford, J., 'The Myth of Pluralism', in F.G. Castles, *et al* (eds.), *Decisions, organisations and society* (Harmondsworth, Penguin, 1971), pp. 364–75.

Pranger, R.J., *The Eclipse of Citizenship* (New York, Holt, Rinehart & Winston, 1968).

Prophet, J., 'A Case for Parish Councils in Scotland', *Public Administration*, vol. 49 (Winter 1971), pp. 457–62.

Pruger, R. and Specht, H., 'Assessing Theoretical Models of Community Organisation Practice: Alinsky as a Case in Point', *The Social Service Review*, vol. 43, No. 2 (June 1969), pp. 123–35.

Rabinovitz, F.F., 'Politics, Personality and Planning', in Andreas Faludi, *A Reader in Planning Theory* (Pergamon Press, 1973), pp. 265–76.

Radford, Jim, 'The Community Movement', in Peter Hain (ed.), *Community Politics* (John Calder, 1976), pp. 65–76.

Read, P., *The Urban Aid Programme: the role of local authorities* (MA Thesis, University of Sussex, 1974).

Redcliffe-Maud Lord and Wood, B., *English Local Government Reformed* (Oxford University Press, 1974).

Rees, A., 'Democracy in local government', in Brian Lapping and Giles Radice (eds.), *More Power to the People* (Longmans, 1968), pp. 119–42.

Rees, I.B., *Government by Community* (Charles Knight, 1971).

Rein, M., 'Decentralisation and Citizen Participation in the Social Services', *Public Administration Review,* vol. 32 (October 1972), pp. 687–700.

Rein, M., 'Social Planning: the Search for Legitimacy', *Journal of the American Institute of Planners*, vol. XXXV, No. 4 (1969), pp. 233–44.

Repo, M., 'The fallacy of "community control" ', in J. Cowley, *et al, Community or Class Struggle?* (Stage 1, 1977), pp. 47–64.

Report of the Wolfenden Committee, *The Future of Voluntary Organisations* (Croom Helm, 1977).

Rex, J., 'The Sociology of a Zone of Transition', in R.E. Pahl, (ed.), *Readings in Urban Sociology* (Pergamon Press, 1968), pp. 224–31.

Rex, J. and Moore, R., *Race, Community and Conflict* (Oxford University Press, 1967).

Richards, P.G., *The Reformed Local Government System* (Allen & Unwin, 1973).

Richies, G., 'Settlements as agencies for social change', in D. Jones and M. Mayo (eds.), *Community Work Two* (Routledge, 1975), pp. 142–9.

Ridley, F.F. and Banks, J.A., *Community Councils in Liverpool* (Social Science Research Council, HR 827, 1972).

Rivers, P., *Politics by Pressure* (Harrap, 1974).

Rokkan, S., *Citizens Elections Parties* (Oslo, Universitets-forlaget, 1970).

Rose, G., *Local Councils in Metropolitan Areas* (Fabian Research Series 296, 1971).

Rose, H., 'Bread and Justice: The National Welfare Rights Organisation', in Peter Leonard (ed.), *The Sociology of Community Action*, Sociological Review Monograph 21 (University of Keele, 1975), pp. 113–41.

Rose, H. and Hanmer, J., 'Community Participation and Social Change', in

Jones, D. and Mayo, M., *Community Work Two* (Routledge & Kegan Paul, 1975), pp. 25–45.

Rowbotham, S., Segal, L. and Wainwright, H., *Beyond the Fragments* (Merlin Press, 1979).

Rowe, A., 'Avoiding the straitjacket', *Municipal and Public Services Journal*, vol. 83, No. 28 (11th July 1975a), pp. 920–2.

Rowe, A., *Democracy Renewed* (Sheldon Press, 1975b).

Salmon, H., *The Hillfields Community Association: A Case Study* (Coventry, CDP Occasional Paper No. 3, October 1972).

Sartori, G., *Democratic Theory*, (New York, Frederick Praeger, 1965).

Saunders, P., 'They Make the Rules: Political Routines and the Generation of Political Bias', *Policy and Politics*, vol. 4, No. 1 (September 1975), pp. 31–58.

Saunders, P., *Urban Politics: A Sociological Interpretation* (Hutchinson, 1979).

Schattschneider, E.E., *The Semisovereign People* (New York, Holt, Rinehart & Winston, 1960).

Schmandt, H.J., 'Municipal Decentralization: An Overview', *Public Administration Review*, vol. 32, special issue (October 1972), pp. 571–88.

Schumacher, E.F., *Small is Beautiful* (Abacus, 1974).

Scottish Council of Social Service, *Topic 2: Community Councils*, (Edinburgh, SCSS, 1974).

Shonfield, A., *Modern Capitalism* (Oxford University Press, 1965).

Silburn, R., 'The Potential and limitations of community action', in David Bull (ed.), *Family Poverty* (Duckworth, 1971), pp. 134–44.

Sills, P., 'Voluntary Initiative and Statutory Reaction: A study in the Political Control of Social Reform', *Community Development Journal,* vol. II, No. 2 (1976), pp. 120–5.

Smith, C.S., and Anderson, B., 'Political Participation Through Community Action', in Geraint Parry (ed.), *Participation in Politics* (Manchester University Press, 1972), pp. 303–18.

Smith, J., 'Hard lines and soft options: a criticism of some left attitudes to community work', in Paul Curno (ed.), *Political Issues and Community Work* (1978), pp. 17–35.

Smith, T., *Anti-Politics* (Charles Knight, 1972).

Smith, T., 'Politics, Economics and Political Economy', *Government and Opposition*, vol. 8, No. 3 (Summer 1973), pp. 263–79.

Smith, T., *The Politics of the Corporate Economy* (Martin Robertson, 1979).

Smith, T., 'Protest and Democracy', in Robert Benewick and Trevor Smith (eds.), *Direct Action and Democratic Politics* (Allen & Unwin, 1973), pp. 305–14.

Somerton, M., *Industrial Democracy in Local Government* (Nottingham, Institute for Workers Control, 1978).

Southampton ILP, *Red or Expert?* (Southampton ILP, 1978).

Stolz, M.F. (ed.), *Politics of the New Left* (New York, Glencoe Press, 1971).

Tabb, W.K. and Sawers, L. (eds.), *Marxism and the Metropolis* (New York, Oxford University Press, 1978).

Teodori, M. (ed.), *The New Left* (Cape, 1970).

Thomas, D.N., *Organising for Social Change* (Allen & Unwin, 1976).

Thomas, P., *Taming the concrete jungle* (Sydney, New South Wales branch of the Australian Building Construction Employees nd Builders Laborers Federation, 1973).

Thompson, D.F., *The Democratic Citizen* (Cambridge University Press, 1970).

Tilley, J., 'Local Government Councillors and Community Work', *Community Development Journal*, vol. 10, No. 2 (April 1975), pp. 89–94.

Toynbee, Polly, 'Consumer Council', *The Guardian*, 5th December 1977.

Trades Union Congress, *Industrial Democracy* (TUC, 1974).

Verba, S., *Small Groups and Political Behaviour* (Princeton University Press, 1961).

Verba, S., and Pie, N.H., *Participation in America* (Harper & Row, 1972).

Wainwright, H., in Rowbotham, Segal and Wainwright, *Beyond the Fragments* (Merlin Press, 1979).

Walker, J.L., 'A Critique of the Elitist Theory of Democracy', *American Political Science Review*, vol. LX, No. 2 (1966), pp. 285–95.

Walzer, M., 'Politics in the Welfare State', *Dissent*, vol. 15 (January–February 1968), pp. 26–40.

Ward, C., *Tenants Take Over* (Architectural Press, 1974).

Ward, M., *et al, Prosperity or Slump? The Future of Wandsworth's Economy* (London Borough of Wandsworth, October 1976).

Ward, S., 'The ethics of planning', *Journal of the Royal Town Planning Institute*, vol. 58, No. 8 (1972), pp. 364–5.

Webb, S. and B., *English Local Government Volume 1: The Parish and the County* (Frank Cass, 1963; first published, 1906).

Weil, S., *Oppression and Liberty* (Routledge & Kegan Paul, 1958).

Weissman, H.H., *Community Councils and Community Control* (University of Pittsburgh Press, 1970).

White, K. and Clarke, R., 'Community Councils: Conflict Ahead', *Focus*, No. 29 (Edinburgh, June 1974), pp. 2–4.

Williams, G., 'Participation at Neighbourhood Level in Britain', *Community Development Journal*, vol. 7, No. 3 (1972), pp. 165–8.

Wilson, D., 'Social Class and Community Councils', *Focus*, No. 40 (Edinburgh, June 1975), pp. 14–5.

Wilson, D., 'Sociological Perspectives: Community Councils in Scotland—II', *Social Work Today*, vol. 6, No. 6 (12th June 1975), pp. 165–7.

Wilson, Des, *Minority Report* (Quartet, 1973).

Wolfe, A., 'Conditions of Community: The Case of Old Westbury College', in Philip Green and S. Levinson (eds.), *Power and Community* (New York, Random House, 1970), pp. 195–222.

Wolin, S., 'Political Theory as a Vocation', *American Political Science Review*, vol. LX111, No. 4 (1969), pp. 1062–82.

Woolley, T. 'The politics of intervention', in J. Cowley, *Community or Class Struggle?* (Stage 1, 1977), pp. 210–21.

Worksett, R., 'Conservation and Public Participation', *The Planner*, vol. 61, No. 7 (July/August 1975), pp. 268–9.

Wright, A.W., 'What Sort of Crisis?', *Political Quarterly*, vol. 48, No. 3 (July–September 1977), pp. 260–9.

Yates, D., *Neighbourhood Democracy* (D.C. Heath & Co. 1973).

Young, K., 'Values in Urban Politics: The Case of "Localism"', paper for the *European Consortium for Political Research* (London, 1975).

Young, M., 'Parish Councils for Cities', *New Society*, 29 January 1970, pp. 178–9.

Young, T., *Central Initiatives at the Local Level: the National Community Development Project* (MA Thesis, Sussex University, 1974).

Young, T., 'The Industrial Connection', in Peter Hain (ed.), *Community Politics* (John Calder, 1976), pp. 116–34.

Government Publications

Committee on Local Authority and Allied Personal Social Services, *Report,* Cmnd. 3703 (HMSO, 1968).

Committee on the Management of Local Government, *Report* (HMSO, 1967).

Committee on Public Participation in Planning, *People and Planning* (HMSO, 1969).

Department of the Environment (1), Circular 121/77 (12 December 1977).

Department of the Environment (2), *Local Government in England*, Cmnd.4584 (HMSO, February 1971).

Department of the Environment (3), *50 Million Volunteers: A Report on the Role of Voluntary Organisations and Youth in the Environment* (HMSO, February 1972).

Department of the Environment (4), *Neighbourhood Councils in England*, Consultation Paper, 30th July 1974.

Department of the Environment (5), *The New Local Authorities: Management and Structure* (HMSO, 1972).

Department of the Environment (6), *Policy for the Inner Cities*, Cmnd. 6845 (HMSO, 1977).

Department of the Environment (7), *Press Notice*, No. 402, 5th June 1974.

Department of the Environment (8), Town and Country Planning Act 1971 Part II, *Development Plan Proposals: Publicity and Public Participation*, Circular 52/72 (HMSO, 1972).

Department of the Environment (9), *A Voice for Your Neighbourhood* (HMSO, 1977).

Department of Prices and Consumer Protection, *National Consumer Agency,* Cmnd. 5726 (HMSO, 1974).

Department of Trade and Industry, *Report of the Committee of Inquiry on Industrial Democracy,* Cmnd. 6706 (HMSO, 1977).

Hansard Parliamentary Debates, Vol. X, 14th March–10th April 1893, clmns 679–722.

Home Office, *Immigration from the Commonwealth,* Cmnd. 2739 (HMSO, 1965).

Ministry of Housing and Local Government, *Housing Act 1969: Area Improvement,* Circular 65/69 (HMSO, 1969).

Ministry of Housing and Local Government, *The Needs of New Communities* (HMSO, 1967).

Ministry of Housing and Local Government, *Old Houses into New Homes,* Cmnd. 3602 (HMSO, 1968).

Planning Advisory Group, *The Future of Development Plans* (HMSO, 1965).

Royal Commission on Local Government in England, vol. I, *Report,* Cmnd. 4040; vol. II, *Memorandum of Dissent by Derek Senior,* Cmnd. 4040—I; vol. III, *Research Appendices,* Cmnd. 4040–II (HMSO, June 1969).

Royal Commission on Local Government in England, Written Evidence of the National Association of Parish Councils (HMSO, 1967), pp. 162–200.

Royal Commission on Local Government in Scotland, *Report,* Cmnd. 4150 (HMSO, September 1969).

Scottish Development Department, *Community Councils* (HMSO, 1974).

Scottish Office, *Reform of Local Government in Scotland,* Cmnd. 4583 (HMSO, 1971).

Welsh Office, *Community Councils,* Circular 285/73 (HMSO, December 1973).

Welsh Office, *Local Government in Wales,* Cmnd. 3340 (HMSO, 1967).

Welsh Office, *The Reform of Local Government in Wales,* Consultative Document (HMSO, 1971).

INDEX

activist theory, 19–20, 44–7, 173,
  190
Angell Ward Neighbourhood
  Council, 41–2, 45
Anson, B., 82, 89, 90, 93, 144–5
Arnstein, S., 21–3, 30, 41, 45, 54,
  78, 106, 167
Association for Neighbourhood
  Councils, 24, 25–9, 30, 33, 36,
  40, 69, 71, 75
Avebury, Lord, 25

Bains Report, 67
Barnsbury Forum, 43
Beer, S., 51, 52
Benn, T., 17
Blackhurst, D., 99, 100, 102, 103,
  107, 108, 109, 110–1, 112, 113,
  125, 137–9, 144–5, 150, 151,
  171–3, 179, 182–3, 208–13
building workers, Australia, 196–7
Bullock Report, 58–9

Calouste Gulbenkian Foundation, 49
Castells, M., 174–5
chartism, 74
City Poverty Committee, 37, 100
claimants unions, 19, 198
Clark, George, 15, 27, 100
class, role of in participation, 23, 35,
  39–44, 46, 50–1, 53, 64, 67, 94,
  149, 159–62, 173–4, 176, 179,
  184, 185–8, 190, 191
Cockburn, C., 17, 46, 104, 170,
  177–8, 179, 193, 194
Cole, G.D.H., 17, 64
Community Action, 35, 38, 42
community control, 19, 20, 94, 203
Community Development Projects,
  55–6
Community Health Councils, 57
community, notion of, 29, 86
conflict model of change, 20, 41–2,
  94–5, 137
consensus model of change, 20, 35–6,
  39, 40, 41–2, 44, 74, 94, 114,
  137, 140, 141, 147, 159–62,
  185–9

Conservative Party, 26, 75, 98, 103,
  167
Consumer Council, 57
co-option, 52, 53, 181
corporate planning, 66–7, 178, 179,
  180
councillors, role of in participation,
  125, 134, 180, 182, 183, 202
counter institutions, 20
Covent Garden,
  Camden Council, 83, 125, 209
  community, 82–3, 86–8, 95–6,
    102, 184
  Community Association (CGCA),
    88–97, 98, 101–1, 102, 103,
    108, 109, 122, 123, 125, 132,
    136, 139, 141, 142–4, 148,
    149, 151, 152, 153–8, 161–2,
    165, 167, 171, 180, 181, 183,
    184, 186, 187
  Conservative Party, 98, 103, 167
  developers, influence of, 84–6,
    109, 115, 117–8, 143, 163–5,
    167, 180
  feasibility studies, 152–7, 162,
    165–6
  gentrification of, 146, 165, 174
  Interim Working Party, 100–5,
    107, 108, 110, 112, 118, 147
  Jubilee Market Building, 136
  Labour Party, 97, 103
  market, 82, 83, 88
  middle class activists, 112, 113,
    116–7, 127, 140, 149, 151,
    159–62, 185–8
  Odhams site, 133–4
  planners, 85, 118, 120, 153, 157,
    162, 165, 166, 167, 181, 184
  political parties, role of, 98, 103
  Public Inquiry, 84, 92–3, 94, 96
  radical activists, 91, 94, 97, 119,
    146, 152, 153, 154, 155, 160,
    161, 181
  Seven Dials Development, 132–3,
    134
  Westminster Council, 83, 148–9,
    209
  women, role of, 116, 149, 161,
    194